OUTRAGE

Arnaldur Indridason worked for many years as a journalist and critic before he began writing novels. His crime novels featuring Erlendur, Elínborg and Sigurdur Óli are consistent best-sellers across Europe. The series has won numerous awards, including the Nordic Glass Key (both for *Jar City* and *Silence of the Grave*) and the CWA Gold Dagger (for *Silence of the Grave*). His most recent novel is *Black Skies*.

ARNALDUR INDRIDASON

Outrage

TRANSLATED FROM THE ICELANDIC BY
Anna Yates

VINTAGE BOOKS
London

Published by Vintage 2012

First published with the title *Myrká* in 2008 by Forlagið, Reykjavík

First published in Great Britain in 2011 by
Harvill Secker

Vintage
Random House, 20 Vauxhall Bridge Road,
London SW1V 2SA

www.vintage-books.co.uk

Addresses for companies within The Random House Group Limited
can be found at: www.randomhouse.co.uk/offices.htm

The Random House Group Limited Reg. No. 954009

A CIP catalogue record for this book
is available from the British Library

This translation has been published with the
financial assistance of NORLA

The Random House Group Limited supports The Forest Stewardship
Council (FSC®), the leading international forest certification organisation.
Our books carrying the FSC label are printed on FSC® certified paper.
FSC is the only forest certification scheme endorsed by the leading
environmental organisations, including Greenpeace.
Our paper procurement policy can be found at
www.randomhouse.co.uk/environment

Typeset in Minion by Palimpsest Book Production Limited,
Falkirk, Stirlingshire

Printed in Great Britain by
Clays Ltd, St Ives plc

OUTRAGE

1

He dressed himself in black jeans, a white shirt and a comfortable jacket, put on a pair of smart shoes he had had for three years, and considered the venues in the city centre that one of the women had mentioned.

He mixed himself two stiff drinks, which he drank as he watched TV and waited until it was time to go into town. He didn't want to set off too early – someone might notice him hanging around in a half-empty bar and he wanted to avoid that. The most important thing was to melt into the crowd, to go unnoticed, to be like everyone else. He mustn't be memorable in any way, must not stand out. In the unlikely event that anyone asked him about his movements that evening, he would say he had been at home all night, watching TV. If everything went according to plan, no one, anywhere, would remember his presence.

When the time was right he drained his glass and left. He was slightly tipsy. He walked from his home near the city centre through the autumn darkness towards the bar. The town was already buzzing with weekend revellers. Queues were forming at the most popular venues, bouncers were flexing their muscles and people were wheedling for admission. Music could be heard in the street, and food smells from restaurants mingled with the alcoholic fumes seeping from the bars. Some people were drunker than others. He despised them.

He had only a short wait before he made it inside. It wasn't one of the most fashionable places, but it was crammed all the same. That was fine. He had already been on the lookout for girls or young women on his way through town: preferably not much over thirty, preferably not stone-cold sober. It was all right if they'd had a bit to drink but he didn't want them too drunk.

He kept a low profile. He patted his jacket pocket once more, to be sure he had it. He had touched the pocket lightly several times on the way, knowing that he must be one of those neurotic types who were forever checking whether they'd locked the door, forgotten their keys, whether the coffee maker was definitely switched off or a hotplate had been left on. He was obsessive like that – he recalled reading about it in some magazine. Another article had been about a different compulsion of his: washing his hands twenty times a day.

Most people were drinking half-litres of beer, so he ordered the same. The bartender hardly glanced at him, and he took care to pay cash. He found it easy to blend in. Most of the customers were about his age, out with friends or colleagues. The drinkers raised their voices to be heard over the heavy rap beat of the music and the din was deafening. He took a leisurely look around, observing groups of women sitting and standing together. Other women were with boyfriends or husbands, but there was no one who appeared to be alone. He left without finishing his drink.

At the third place he spotted a woman he recognised – he thought she was probably about thirty and she seemed to be on her own. She sat at a table in the smoking area, surrounded by other smokers, but she was clearly not with them. He observed her from a distance as she sipped a margarita and smoked two cigarettes. The bar was packed, but no one who approached her seemed to know her.

Two men spoke to her but she shook her head and they left. A third man loomed over her, apparently unwilling to take no for an answer.

She was a brunette with a pretty face, a bit heavyset but nicely dressed in a skirt and a short-sleeved T-shirt and with a beautiful shawl around her shoulders. Across the T-shirt the words *San Francisco* were stencilled, with a little flower growing up out of the letter *F*.

She managed to shake off her persistent suitor, who made an angry remark and left.

He gave her time to settle down before he approached her. 'Have you been there?' he asked. The brunette looked up. She couldn't place him.

'To San Francisco?' he added, pointing at the shirt.

She looked down at her breasts.

'Oh, this?' she asked.

'It's a delightful city,' he said. 'You should go sometime.'

She looked at him, debating whether to tell him to push off like she'd told the others. Then she seemed to remember meeting him before.

'There's so much going on there,' he said. 'In Frisco. A lot to see.'

She smiled.

'Fancy meeting you here,' she said.

'Yes, nice to see you. Are you here alone?'

'Alone? Yes.'

'So, what about Frisco? You must go.'

'I know, I've . . .'

Her words were drowned out by the noise. He passed his hand over his jacket pocket and leaned over her.

'The airfare's not cheap,' he said. 'But I mean . . . I went there once, it was great. A delightful city.'

He used certain words deliberately. She was looking up at him, and he imagined her counting on the fingers of one hand how many young men she had met in her life who would use a word like *delightful*.

'I know. I've been.'

'Oh. Well, then. May I join you?'

She hesitated for a moment, then moved over to make room for him.

Nobody took any notice of them in the bar, nor when they left a little over an hour later and headed back to his place, taking deserted side streets. By then the drug was working. He had offered her another margarita, and as he'd returned from the bar with her third drink he'd slid his hand into his jacket pocket to palm the pill and slipped it into her glass. They were getting along fine, and he was sure she would give him no trouble.

The Criminal Investigation Department received the notification two days later. Elínborg was on duty and she called out the team. When she arrived at the scene traffic police had already closed off the road, in the Thingholt district, and the forensics officers were just pulling up.

She saw a representative of the Regional Medical Officer get out of his car. At the start of a case only forensics team members were permitted to enter the flat, to carry out their investigations. They 'froze' the scene, as they put it.

Elínborg made the necessary arrangements as she waited patiently for the forensics team to give her the go-ahead. Journalists and other media reporters were gathering, and she observed them at work. They were pushy – some were even rude to the police who were keeping them away from the crime scene. One or two of the TV reporters looked familiar: a vacuous quiz-show host who had recently transferred to the news, and the presenter of a political chat show. She had no idea why he should be down here with the news teams. Elínborg recalled her early days with the CID, when she'd been one of only a handful of women detectives: back then the reporters had been much more polite, and far fewer. She preferred the press journalists. Print-media people were less rushed, less overbearing and less self-important than the TV reporters toting their video cameras. Some of them could even write.

Neighbours stood at their windows or had stepped out into their doorways, arms crossed in the autumn chill, puzzlement on their faces; they had no idea what had happened. Police officers had started questioning them: had they noticed anything unusual on the street, or specifically at the house, anyone coming or going? Did they know the resident? Had they been inside?

Elínborg had once rented a flat in Thingholt, long before it had become fashionable. She had liked living in this historic area on the hillside above the old town centre. The houses, which varied in age, encapsulated a century of the history of building and architecture in the city: some had been humble labourers' cottages, others had been grand villas built by wealthy entrepreneurs. Rich and poor, masters and workers, had always lived there in harmony side by side until the district had started to attract young home-buyers with no interest in settling in the sprawling new suburbs that were stretching into the upland heaths, and who preferred to make their homes close to the heart of the city. The artistic and fashionable classes moved into the old timber-framed houses, and the splendid mansions were bought up by the super-wealthy and nouveau riche. They wore their downtown postcode like a badge of honour: *101 Reykjavík.*

The head of forensics appeared at the corner of the house and called to Elínborg. He reminded her to be careful, and not to touch anything.

'It's nasty,' he said.

'Oh?'

'Like an abattoir.'

The entrance to the ground-floor flat was at the rear,

facing the garden, and was not visible from the road; a paved path led round to the back of the house. As she entered the flat Elínborg saw the body of a young man lying on the living-room floor. His trousers were around his ankles and he was wearing nothing but a blood-soaked T-shirt with the words *San Francisco* stencilled on it. A little flower was growing up out of the letter *F*.

2

On her way home Elínborg stopped to buy food. She usually took her time shopping and avoided the no-frills supermarkets, finding that they offered a limited range and quality consistent with the bargain prices. But this time she was in a hurry. Both boys had rung to check that she would be cooking dinner as she had promised and she'd confirmed that she would, only she'd be a bit on the late side. She did her best to have a proper family dinner every day – if only for fifteen minutes while the kids wolfed down their food.

And she knew that if she didn't cook then the boys would go and buy expensive fast food, wasting what little money they had earned during the summer holidays – or would get their dad to do so. Her husband Teddi, a motor mechanic, was a hopeless cook; he could prepare a sort of porridge, or fry an egg, but that was about it. But he was good at clearing and washing up, and did his bit around the house.

Elínborg looked around for something quick. At the cold counter she saw some minced fish which looked as if it would do, then she grabbed a bag of rice, some onions, a few other things she needed, and within ten minutes was back in the car.

About an hour later they sat down at the kitchen table. The older boy grumbled about the fish-balls, complaining that they'd had fish the day before. He would not eat onion and carefully left it at the side of his plate. The younger boy, like his father, ate whatever was put in front of him. The youngest of the children, Theodóra, had rung to ask if she could have dinner at her friend's house. They were doing their homework together.

'Isn't there anything but soy sauce?' asked the older boy, Valthór. He was sixteen and had just started high school. He knew exactly what his ambitions were and had opted to complete his secondary education at the Commercial College. Elínborg thought he had a girlfriend, although he gave no hint. He never said anything about himself, but no detective work by his mother had been necessary: when she'd been putting his jeans into the washing machine a packet of condoms had fallen out of the pocket. She did not mention it to him: it was the way of the world, but she was glad he was taking precautions. She had not managed to gain his trust and their relationship could be tense; the boy was fiercely independent and sometimes truculent. It was a character trait that Elínborg disliked, and she did not know where he got it from. Teddi handled him better – father and son shared an interest in cars.

'No,' said Elínborg, pouring the dregs of a bottle of white wine into her glass. 'I couldn't be bothered to make a sauce.'

She looked at her son and considered yet again whether she ought to confront him about her discovery. But she felt too tired to cope with an argument. She was sure he would say that she was interfering.

'You said you'd cook steak this evening,' Valthór reminded her.

'Who was the dead body you found?' asked the younger boy, Aron. He had been watching the TV news and had caught sight of his mother outside the house in Thingholt.

'A man of about thirty,' Elínborg replied.

'Was he killed?' asked Valthór.

'Yes,' answered Elínborg.

'It said on the news that they didn't know yet whether

11

it was murder,' commented Aron. 'They said *suspected* murder.'

'The man was murdered,' said Elínborg.

'Who was he?' asked Teddi.

'No one we know.'

'How was he killed?' asked Valthór.

Elínborg looked at him. 'You know you can't ask me that.'

Valthór shrugged.

'Was it drugs?' asked Teddi. 'Was that why—?'

'Will you all please stop talking about it?' pleaded Elínborg. 'We don't know anything yet.'

They knew that they must not press her. Elínborg felt it was inappropriate to discuss her job. The men of the family had always been fascinated by police work, and when she was involved in a major case they could not resist asking her for the details. They even came up with suggestions of their own, but if the investigation dragged on they generally lost interest and left her alone. They watched a lot of American crime drama on TV, and when the boys were smaller they had been excited and impressed that their mum was a detective like the heroes and heroines of the TV shows. But they had soon realised that the stories on screen were a world away from what she told them about her job – and what they saw for themselves. The TV detectives were glamorous, wise-cracking, insightful sharpshooters who traded repartee with plausible villains, engaged in white-knuckle car chases and, with never a hair out of place, talked psychopaths into surrender. In every episode horrifying murders were committed – two, three or four – and in the end the perpetrator was always caught and received his or her just deserts.

The boys were well aware that Elínborg did a lot of overtime. As she said, her basic salary was low so she needed to increase her earnings. She had never been in a car chase, she told them, and she carried no pistol, let alone an automatic rifle like an American cop: the Icelandic police were unarmed. The villains were mostly unfortunates and losers, as Sigurdur Óli called them: the usual suspects. Burglary and car theft made up the majority of cases. Assault. Drugs were the province of the Drug Squad, while serious crimes such as rape landed regularly on Elínborg's desk. Murder was rare, but the numbers varied each year: some years went by without a single case, while in others there might be up to four. Recently the police had observed a dangerous trend: crime was becoming more organised, more people were carrying weapons, and violence was becoming more extreme.

Elínborg generally came home from work exhausted, made dinner, then spent a little time developing new recipes – cookery was her hobby. Or she simply lay down on the sofa and fell asleep watching TV.

Now and then the boys would look up from their cool crime dramas to glance at their mother. The Icelandic police did not impress them.

Elínborg's daughter was quite unlike her brothers; from early childhood Theodóra had shown herself to be unusually gifted, and this had led to problems at school. Elínborg was reluctant to move her up a year as she wanted her to develop socially in step with her contemporaries, but the schoolwork was far too easy for her. She needed constant stimulation: she played handball, took piano lessons, and was a Girl Guide. She did not watch much television and had no particular interest in films or video games; she was a bookworm who read from morning to night. When Theodóra had been younger Elínborg and Teddi were kept busy borrowing books for her from the library, and as soon as she was old enough she got her own library card. She was now eleven years old. A few days earlier she had tried to summarise for her mother the main points of *A Brief History of Time*.

When Elínborg thought the children were out of earshot she would sometimes talk to Teddi about her work colleagues. They knew that one was a man named Erlendur, who was something of an enigma to them: sometimes Elínborg spoke as if she did not like working with him, while at other times it sounded as if she could not do without him. The youngsters had more than once heard their mother wonder aloud how such a failure of a father, such an irascible loner, could be such an insightful detective. She admired his work but she did not necessarily like him. Another person she sometimes discussed in whispers with Teddi was Sigurdur Óli: a bit of a weirdo, so far as the kids could tell. Their mother sometimes groaned when his name came up.

Elínborg was dozing off when she heard a sound. They were all in bed except Valthór, who was still on the computer; she did not know whether he was working on a school assignment, or just chatting or blogging. He would not sleep until the middle of the night. Valthór had his own internal clock: he did not go to bed until the early hours and would lie in until evening, given the chance. This worried Elínborg but she saw little point in discussing it. She had tried many times, but he was obstinate and dogmatic, insisting on his rights.

The Thingholt victim was on Elínborg's mind all evening. Even if she had wanted to, she could not have described the horrifying scene to her boys: the man's throat had been cut, and the chairs and tables in the living room had been drenched in blood. The pathologist had not yet made his report.

The police reckoned that the killing had been premeditated. The perpetrator must have come to the victim's home with the intention of attacking him. There was little sign of a struggle and the actual wound appeared to be a confident slash straight across the throat, at precisely the right point to inflict maximum damage. Smaller cuts on the neck indicated that the blade had been held at the victim's throat for some time. It looked as if the assault had been sudden and unexpected: there was no damage to the outside door, which might suggest that the victim had let his killer in, while another possibility was that someone who had entered the flat with the man, or had been his guest, had launched the brutal attack without warning. Nothing seemed to have been stolen and there was no sign that the flat had been ransacked.

It was unlikely that the victim had been killed by burglars but he might conceivably have disturbed them before any damage had been done, leading them to panic and attack him.

The body was almost completely drained of blood, much of which had pooled and dried on the floor of the flat. That meant that the man's heart had continued to beat for a little while after the attack.

After seeing all that gore Elínborg simply could not have cooked a bloody steak, however much her elder son moaned about the dinner menu.

3

The name of the murdered man in Thingholt was Runólfur. He had worked for a telecoms company, had no criminal record, and had never come to the attention of the police. He had moved to Reykjavík from his home village more than ten years ago, and he lived alone. His elderly mother, who was still living in the same village, said he had not been in touch recently. A police officer and the local clergyman went to her home to notify her of her son's death. Runólfur was an only child, and it transpired that his father had died in an accident some years before: he had collided with a lorry on the upland road over the Holtavörðuheidi moor.

Runólfur's landlord spoke well of him. He always paid his rent on time; he was neat and tidy; there was never any noise from his flat; he went out to work every morning. The landlord could not praise him highly enough.

'All that blood,' he said, with a resentful look at Elínborg. 'I'll have to get a cleaning company in. I'll probably have to replace the flooring. Who would do a thing like that? It won't be easy to find new tenants.'

'So you've never heard anything from the flat?' Elinborg asked.

'Not a whisper,' replied the landlord. He had a protruding belly, a week's growth of white whiskers, a balding head, sagging shoulders and stubby arms. He lived above Runólfur. He said he had rented out the downstairs flat for years, and Runólfur had been his tenant for the past two years or so. He had discovered the body when he brought down some bills which had been mistakenly delivered to his flat; he pushed them through the letter box, but as he passed the living-room window he had seen the bare feet of someone who was lying on the floor in a pool of blood. He had felt the best thing was to ring the police at once.

'Were you home on Saturday evening?' asked Elínborg. She pictured the inquisitive landlord peering into the flat. It couldn't have been easy to see in. The curtains were drawn, with only a narrow gap between them.

Preliminary investigations indicated that the murder had been committed either on the Saturday evening or during the night. It seemed more likely that someone had been in the flat with Runólfur before the attack occurred than that anyone had forced entry. The odds were on a woman. It looked as if Runólfur had had sex shortly before he died, as a condom had been found on the bedroom floor. The T-shirt he was wearing when he was discovered probably did not belong to him but to a woman. It was far too small for him, and in addition dark hairs were found on it, matching hairs collected from Runólfur's sofa. There was a hair on his jacket, possibly from the same person, and in his bed, in a bedroom off the living room, there were pubic hairs. He might have invited a woman to stay the night.

It would have been easy to leave the house through the garden and climb over into an adjacent garden behind a three-storey concrete house in the next street. Nobody had been seen in the garden two days ago.

'I'm at home most days,' said the landlord.

'You say Runólfur went out that evening?'

'Yes, I saw him walk off down the street. It must have been about eleven. I didn't see him after that.'

'You didn't notice when he came home?'

'No. I was probably asleep by then.'

'So you don't know if anyone came back with him?'

'No.'

'Runólfur didn't live with a woman, did he?'

'No, nor with a man,' the landlord replied, with an enigmatic smile.

'Not at any time while he was your tenant?'

'No.'

'But do you know if he had girlfriends who stayed over?' The landlord scratched his head. It was shortly past lunch-time; he had just finished eating horsemeat sausage, and now he was sitting calmly on a sofa opposite Elínborg. She had spotted the leftovers on a plate in the kitchen; a rancid smell hung in the air and she hoped the odour would not taint her coat, a recent sale bargain. She had no desire to stay here any longer than necessary.

'Not particularly,' he said finally. 'I don't think I ever saw him with a woman. Not as far as I remember.'

'You didn't know him all that well?'

'No. I soon realised he wanted to be left alone. So . . . No, I didn't have much to do with him.'

Elínborg stood up. She saw Sigurdur Óli at the door of the house across the road, talking to the neighbours. Other police officers were taking statements from local residents.

'When can I hose down the flat?' asked the landlord.

'Soon,' answered Elínborg. 'We'll let you know.'

Runólfur's body had been removed the previous evening, but when Elínborg arrived with Sigurdur Óli, the morning after the discovery of the body, forensics officers were still at work in the flat. The evidence was that this was the home of a neat young man, who had wanted to make a pleasant, comfortable base for himself.

Elínborg had the impression that the fittings had been carefully selected. They included porcelain wall-plaques – not a common sight in a young person's home – a beautiful rug on the parquet floor, a sofa and a matching easy chair. The bathroom was small but tasteful. In the bedroom was a double bed. The kitchen, adjoining the living room, was spotless. There were no books and no family photographs, only a huge flatscreen TV and three framed posters of superheroes: Spider-Man, Superman and Batman. High-quality collectable superhero figures were displayed on a table.

'Where were you lot when it happened?' asked Elínborg, glancing from one poster to the next.

'Kinda cool,' commented Sigurdur Óli as he gazed at the cartoon heroes.

'It's just a load of old tat, isn't it?' said Elínborg.

Sigurdur Óli bent down to inspect the state-of-the-art sound system. Next to it lay a mobile phone and an iPod.

'A *nano*,' said Sigurdur Óli. 'He's got all the latest stuff.'

'The ultra-thin one?' asked Elínborg. 'My younger boy says they're too girly. I don't know what that's supposed to mean. I've never laid eyes on one.'

'You don't say,' commented Sigurdur Óli, and blew his nose. He was feeling rather under the weather after a bout of flu.

'Anything wrong with that?' asked Elínborg as she opened the refrigerator.

The contents were sparse: the owner's culinary skills appeared to have been limited. A banana, a pepper, cheese, jam, peanut butter, eggs. An open carton of skimmed milk.

'Didn't he have a computer?' Sigurdur Óli asked one of the two forensics officers who were processing the scene.

'We took it down to the station,' he said. 'We still haven't found anything to explain the bloodbath. Have you heard about the Róhypnol?'

The forensics officer looked at each of them. He was thirtyish, unshaven and unkempt: *slovenly* was the word Elínborg was looking for. Sigurdur Óli, himself always immaculately turned out, had commented disparagingly to her that the grunge look was practically de rigueur today.

'Rohypnol?' asked Elínborg, with a shake of her head.

'There are some pills in his jacket pocket, and quite a lot more on the table in the living room,' said the officer, who was wearing a white overall and latex gloves.

'The date-rape drug?'

'Yes. They've just called us with the findings. We're

supposed to investigate with that in mind. He had some in his jacket pocket, as I said, which could mean that—'

'He used it on Saturday evening,' interjected Elínborg. 'The landlord saw him leave. So he had it in his pocket when he went out on the town?'

'Looks like it, assuming he was wearing this jacket. All his other clothes were neatly put away. The jacket and shirt are on this chair, the underpants and socks in the bedroom. He was lying here in the living room with his trousers around his ankles, but he wasn't wearing any underwear. It looks as if he might have put the trousers on to leave the bedroom, maybe to get a glass of water. There's a glass by the sink.'

'So he took Rohypnol with him for a night out?' Elínborg wondered aloud.

'It looks as if he had sex just before he died,' said the forensics officer. 'We think the condom is his, and there were physical signs, so to speak. The autopsy will clarify the details.'

'A date-rape drug,' said Elínborg, recalling a recent case she had handled. A driver in the suburban town of Kópavogur had spotted a half-naked woman of twenty-six vomiting by the roadside and had come to her aid. She could give no account of where she had been and had no recollection of where she had spent the night. She asked the man to drive her home. In view of the state she was in he wanted to take her to hospital, but she insisted there was no need. The woman had no idea what she had been doing in Kópavogur. As soon as she got home she fell asleep and slept for twelve hours, but when she woke up she ached all over. She had a stinging pain in the genital area and her knees were reddened and sore, but her mind was a blank. She had never before blacked out from drinking and, despite her amnesia, she was convinced that she had not been drinking heavily. She took a long shower, washing thoroughly. Late that evening a friend rang to ask what had become of her; they had gone out with another woman, and she had become separated from them. Her friend had seen her leave with a man she did not recognise.

'Wow,' said the woman. 'I don't remember that at all. I don't remember anything.'

'Who was he?' asked her friend.

'No idea.'

As they chatted the woman gradually recalled meeting a man at the club. He had bought her a drink. She did not know him and had only a hazy recollection of his appearance, but he had seemed friendly. She had hardly finished her drink when another appeared on the table. She went to the loo, and when she returned the man suggested that they should move on. That was the last thing she remembered from that evening.

'Where did you go with him?' asked her friend.

'I don't know. I just . . .'

'You didn't know him?'

'No.'

'Do you think he might have put something in your drink?'

'In my drink?'

'Since you don't remember anything. There are . . .' Her friend hesitated.

'What?'

'Rapists who do that.'

Shortly after that the young woman went to the rape-trauma centre at the National Hospital. By the time the case landed on Elínborg's desk the woman was convinced that she had been raped. A medical examination revealed that she had had sexual intercourse during the night, but there was no sign of any drug in her blood. This was not surprising because the most commonly used date-rape drug, Rohypnol, disappears within a few hours.

Elínborg showed her the gallery of mugshots of convicted rapists but she did not recognise anyone. She took the woman back to the club where she had met the man but the staff did not remember her, nor the man she was supposed to have met there. Elínborg knew that cases of drug-facilitated rape were difficult to prove. In general no trace of the drug was found in samples of blood or urine, as it had been eliminated from the body by the time the victim was examined, but there were other indications such as amnesia, semen in the vagina, and physical trauma. Elínborg informed the woman that she might have been drugged before the rape. It was possible that the man had slipped her some gamma-hydroxybutric acid or GHB, which works the same way as Rohypnol. Colourless and odourless, it can be administered in powder or liquid form; GHB targets the central nervous system, reducing the victim to a helpless state and sometimes leaving them with no recollection whatsoever of events.

'Which makes it all the more difficult for us to prosecute the bastards,' Elínborg told the young woman. 'Rohypnol works for three to six hours, then vanishes completely from the body. You only need a few milligrams to induce a trance state, and if it's taken with alcohol the effects are intensified. Side effects include hallucinations, depression, dizziness. Even seizures.'

Elínborg looked around the flat in Thingholt and thought about the attack on Runólfur, and the hatred that had evidently motivated it.

'Did he have a car, this Runólfur?' she asked the forensics officers.

'Yes, it was parked outside,' one of them replied. 'We've taken it in to process it.'

'I want to give you a DNA sample from a woman who was assaulted recently. I need to find out if he could have been her assailant – whether he drove her out to Kópavogur and chucked her out.'

'No problem,' said the forensics officer. 'And there's another thing.'

'What?'

'Everything in the flat belongs to a man – clothes, shoes, coats . . .'

'Yes?'

'Except that bundle over there,' said the forensics officer, pointing at something rolled up in a plastic evidence bag.

'What is it?'

'Looks like a shawl,' he replied, picking up the bag. 'We found it in a heap under the bed. It certainly seems to corroborate the idea that he had a woman here.'

He opened the bag and held it up to Elínborg's face.

'It's got an unusual smell,' he said. 'A bit of cigarette smoke, her perfume, and then there's something . . . sort of spicy.'

Elínborg sniffed.

'We haven't identified it yet,' the officer observed.

Elínborg took a deep breath. The woollen shawl was purple. She smelt the odour of cigarettes and perfume, and he was right – there was another familiar pungent fragrance.

'Do you recognise it?' Sigurdur Óli asked in astonishment.

She nodded. 'It's my favourite,' she said.

'What do you mean, favourite?' asked the forensics officer.

'Your favourite spice?' asked Sigurdur Óli.

'Yes,' Elínborg replied. 'But it's not one spice. It's a masala, a mixture of spices. Indian. It's like . . . it reminds me of tandoori.'

4

The neighbours were on the whole eager to help. The police conducted systematic interviews with everyone living within a certain radius of the crime scene, whether or not they believed they had anything to contribute. The police would determine what was important and what was irrelevant. In the lower Thingholt district, most of the inhabitants said they had been asleep that night and so had noticed nothing out of the ordinary. None of them knew the victim. Nobody had observed anyone near the house or seen anything unusual in the days before the crime. Residents nearby were interviewed first, then the area of enquiry was gradually widened. Elínborg spoke to the investigating officers to review what had been revealed, and paused when she saw the statement of one woman who lived at the periphery of the area under investigation. Although the information provided seemed meagre, she decided to call on the woman herself.

'I don't know if it's worth it,' said the policeman who had questioned her.

'Oh?'

'She's a bit odd.'

'Odd? How?'

'She kept going on about electromagnetic waves. She said they gave her a constant headache.'

'Electromagnetic waves?'

'She said she's measured them, using some rods she has. The waves come mainly from her walls.'

'Oh, really?'

'I don't know if you'll get anything useful out of her.'

The woman lived on the upper floor of a two-storey building in the street up the hill from Runólfur's home but some distance away, so whatever she thought she had seen might well be irrelevant. Yet Elínborg was curious. And since the police had little to go on as yet, she reckoned that she might as well check the woman out and see if she remembered anything more.

Petrína was in her late sixties. She opened the door to

Elínborg, wearing a dressing gown and worn felt slippers. Her hair was a mess, her face pale and wrinkled, her eyes bloodshot. In one hand she held a cigarette. As she welcomed Elínborg in she said she was pleased that someone was taking an interest at last.

'It's about time,' she said. 'I'll show you. They're massive waves, I tell you.'

Petrína vanished into the flat, leaving Elínborg to follow her. Elínborg found herself in a stifling cigarette fug; all the curtains were drawn and the rooms were dark. She managed to work out that it would be possible to see down into the street from the living-room window. The woman had gone into her bedroom, and now called out to her. Elínborg went through the living room, past the kitchen and into the bedroom where she saw Petrína beneath a solitary light bulb that hung unadorned from the ceiling. A bed and bedside table stood in the centre of the room.

'I'd like to tear the walls down,' said Petrína. 'I can't afford to have all the electrical wiring insulated. I must just be especially sensitive. Look here.'

Elínborg gazed in astonishment at the two longer walls of the room, which were covered from floor to ceiling in aluminium cooking foil.

'It gives me such a headache,' said Petrína.

'Did you do all this yourself?' asked Elínborg.

31

'Me? Myself? Of course I did. The foil helps, but I don't think it's enough. You'll have to take a look.' Petrína picked up two metal rods and held them loosely in her hands with the ends towards Elínborg, who stood motionless in the doorway. Then the rods turned gradually until they pointed at one of the walls.

'It's the electrical wiring,' said Petrína.

'Oh?' said Elínborg.

'You can see that the foil helps. Come on.'

She shoved past Elínborg, her wild hair sticking out and the metal rods in her hands, looking like a caricature of a mad scientist. She went into the living room and switched on the TV. The test card appeared.

'Roll up your sleeve,' Petrína told Elínborg, who did so without a word. 'Hold your arm near the screen, but don't touch it.'

Elínborg brought her arm close to the screen. The hairs on her forearm bristled, and she felt the magnetic field. She had often noticed the effect at home if she stood close to the TV.

'That's what the walls of my room were like,' said Petrína. 'Just like that. They made my hair stand on end. It was like sleeping up against a television screen all night. Alterations were made to the flat, you see – they installed wooden partition walls, plywood, all full of electrical wiring.'

As she rolled down her sleeve Elínborg asked cautiously: 'Who do you think I am?'

'You?' asked Petrína. 'Aren't you from the power company? They were going to send someone. Isn't it you?'

'No, I'm afraid not,' said Elínborg. 'I'm not from the power company.'

'You were going to take readings here,' said Petrína. 'You were supposed to come today. I can't go on like this.'

'I'm from the police,' said Elínborg. 'A serious crime was committed in the next street, and I believe you saw someone outside here, in front of the building.'

'But I spoke to a policeman this morning,' said Petrína. 'Why have you come back? And where's the man from the power company?'

'I don't know, but I can ring them if you like.'

'He should have been here ages ago.'

'Perhaps he'll come later today. May I ask what you saw?'

'What I saw? What am I supposed to have seen?'

'According to your statement this morning, you saw a man in the street on Saturday night. Is that right?'

'I've tried and tried to get them to come here and look inside the walls, but they don't listen to a word I say.'

'Do you always keep the curtains closed?'

'Of course I do,' said Petrína, absently scratching her head.

33

Elínborg's eyes had grown accustomed to the gloom of Petrína's home and now she could see the shabby flat more clearly, with its ragged furniture, framed pictures on the walls and family photographs on tables. On one table were photographs of young people and children, presumably young descendants or relatives of Petrína. The ashtrays were all overflowing with cigarette stubs, and Elínborg noticed scorch marks here and there on the pale carpet.

Petrína stuck the cigarette she had just finished into the pile in one of the ashtrays. Looking at a burn in the carpet, Elínborg thought that the old lady probably dropped a smouldering stub on the floor from time to time. She wondered if she should contact Social Services; Petrína could be a danger to herself and others.

'If you always have the curtains drawn, how can you see down into the street?' asked Elínborg.

'I open them, of course,' said Petrína, looking at Elínborg as if there were something odd about her. 'What did you say you were doing here?'

'I'm from the police,' Elínborg reiterated patiently. 'I'd like to ask you about a man you said you saw outside the house last Saturday night. Do you remember that?'

'I don't sleep much – because of the waves, you see. So I wander around, and wait for them. See my eyes? See them?' Petrína craned her head forward to show Elínborg her bloodshot eyes. 'It's the waves. That's what they do

34

to my eyes. Those bloody waves. And I have a headache all the time.'

'Don't you think that might be the cigarettes?' Elínborg asked politely.

'So I sat by the window here, and waited for them,' said Petrína, ignoring Elínborg's comment. 'I sat and waited all night, and all day Sunday, and I'm still waiting.'

'For?'

'For the men from the power company! I thought that was who you were.'

'So you sat here at the window, watching the street. Did you think they would come at night?'

'How should I know when they'll come? And then I saw that man I told you about this morning. I thought maybe he was from them, but he walked straight past. I thought of shouting out to him.'

'Had you ever seen him around here before?'

'No, never.'

'Could you tell me a bit more about him?'

'There's nothing to tell. Why are you asking about him?'

'A crime was committed near here, and I may have to trace him.'

'You can't,' asserted Petrína.

'Why not?'

'You don't know who he is,' observed Petrína, amazed that Elínborg could be so dense.

'No, and that's why I'm asking you to help me. You said this morning he was wearing a dark jacket and a cap. Was it a leather jacket?'

'I've no idea. But he had a hat on. A knitted woolly hat.'

'Did you notice his trousers?'

'Nothing special. They were those ones for running, with the legs torn up to the knee. There was nothing special about them.'

'Was he driving a car?'

'No. I didn't see a car.'

'Was he alone?'

'Yes, he was alone. I only saw him for a moment because he moved fast, despite being lame.'

'Lame?' asked Elínborg. She did not recall hearing anything about this from the officer who had interviewed Petrína.

'Yes, lame. Poor man. He had an aerial thing around his leg.'

'Did he seem to be in a hurry?'

'Oh, yes, but everybody hurries past here. It's the waves. He wouldn't want to let the waves get into his leg.'

'What kind of aerial was it?'

'I don't know.'

'Did he limp heavily?'

'Yes.'

36

'And he didn't want the waves in his leg? What do you mean?'

'That was why he limped. The waves were massive. Really massive waves in his leg.'

'Could you feel the waves?'

Petrína nodded. 'Who did you say you were?' she asked. 'Aren't you from the power company? Do you know what I think it is? Do you want to know? It's all because of this uranium. Massive uranium, that comes down with the rain.'

Elínborg smiled. She should have listened to the policeman who had said it probably wasn't worth talking to this witness again. She thanked Petrína, and promised to telephone the power company to remind them about the electromagnetic waves which were making her life so difficult – though she doubted whether they would be the right people to help the poor lady with her headaches.

There were no other witnesses to speak of. One middle-aged man came forward, who had been walking through Thingholt that Saturday night to his home on Njardargata. Though in the throes of a severe hangover, he wanted to state, while it was still fresh in his memory, that on the way home he had seen a woman sitting alone in a parked car. She was in the passenger seat, and it seemed to him that she had been trying to avoid attracting attention. He

37

had no further explanation to offer. He gave them the name of the street where he had seen the car, which was some distance from the crime scene, but could give no proper description of the woman who he thought was probably about sixty and had been wearing a coat. He had no more to tell them. He remembered nothing about the car: neither its colour nor its make. He did not know much about cars, he explained.

5

The flight was short, and the humming of the propellers was soothing. Elínborg sat in a window seat as she invariably did on domestic flights. She enjoyed seeing something of the country but this afternoon the weather was cloudy and she caught only glimpses of mountain or valley, or a river meandering across the snowy landscape. As she grew older, she was becoming increasingly afraid of air travel, although she could not explain her phobia. In the past she had never seen a flight as any more risky than a drive. But over the years she had developed a fear of flying which she attributed to having children and acquiring responsibilities in life. Generally she found it easier to cope with a short domestic flight than an international journey, although there were exceptions to the rule. She remembered one hazardous midwinter flight in stormy weather, swooping between the mountains and down into the narrow fjord of Ísafjördur: she had felt as if she were in a horror film that would culminate in a terrifying crash. She thought her time had come and clenched her eyes shut, praying until the undercarriage wheels touched down safely on the icy runway. Complete strangers had hugged each other in relief. On long international flights Elínborg took care to choose an aisle seat and tried not to worry about exactly how the heavy aircraft managed to take to the air and stay aloft, laden with passengers and their luggage.

The local police met her at the little airport and drove to the village where Runólfur's mother lived. A dusting of snow highlighted the rich autumnal hues of the vegetation. Elínborg sat silently in the police car's back seat, unable to focus on the beautiful natural scenery around her. She was thinking about her son Valthór. A month ago she had discovered by chance that he was blogging on the Internet, and now she had a guilty conscience about the boy. She did not know what to do.

Elínborg had been picking up clothes from the floor of his room when she saw on the computer screen that he had been writing about himself and his family. She jumped when she heard him approach and when they met in the doorway she pretended nothing was wrong. But she had made a mental note of the Internet thread, and after a slight tussle with her conscience she had keyed it into the family computer in the TV den. It felt like reading her son's private correspondence, until she realised that the content of the blog was open to be read by anyone. When she saw how freely he wrote about himself she broke out into a cold sweat. He had never mentioned to her or to Teddi anything that she read in the blog, or said anything about it at home at all. There were links to other blogs. Elínborg looked through some of them, and saw that Valthór's candid style was far from unusual. People had no inhibitions about writing about themselves, their family, their deeds, desires, emotions, opinions – anything that came into their minds as they sat at the computer, and with no self-censorship. Anything and everything went up. Elínborg had never taken any particular interest in blogs, except in the context of her work, and she had not imagined that her own children might be involved.

Since first coming across Valthór's blog, Elínborg had stealthily accessed the site from time to time, read about the music her son listened to, films he had seen, and what he was doing with his friends, about school and what he thought of it and of individual teachers. Everything that

Elínborg and he never talked about. He reported her own remarks on a sensitive issue under debate in society; he wrote about his gifted sister and how difficult it was to cater for her – because all the special-needs teaching was directed at the needs of dunces, Valthór stated, quoting his mother.

When she read her own words repeated on the Internet for all to see, Elínborg was furious: the boy had no right to go gossiping about her opinions. Valthór occasionally quoted his father too, but that was mostly on the subject of cars in which they shared an interest. The boy also posted some of his father's very politically incorrect jokes.

'What's wrong with him?' Elínborg sighed.

But what really caught her attention was another aspect of his shameless behaviour: the blog indicated unmistakably that Valthór was something of a ladies' man. It was clearly no coincidence that Elínborg had found a condom in his trouser pocket. He was forever mentioning girls he knew and writing about his social life with them: dances, trips to the cinema, none of which Elínborg knew anything about. Under the heading *Say what you think*, readers were invited to post their responses. It seemed to Elínborg that two, if not three, of her son's girlfriends were competing for his affections.

As the car sped through the glorious autumn woodland, under her breath Elínborg cursed the very idea of Valthór and his blog.

'Pardon?' said the policeman who was driving. The other sat in the front passenger seat, apparently asleep. They had given her some information about Runólfur's mother and the village, but otherwise had not spoken.

'Nothing. Sorry, I've got a bit of a cold,' said Elínborg, digging a tissue out of her bag. 'Do you have a police station in the village?'

'No, we don't have the funding. It all costs money. But nothing ever happens there. Nothing that matters, anyway.'

'Is it much further?'

'Half an hour,' answered the policeman. They did not speak for the rest of the journey.

Runólfur's mother, Kristjana, lived in a fairly small modern townhouse and was expecting the police. She met Elínborg at the door. Looking tired and withdrawn, she left the door open and went back inside without speaking. Elínborg stepped inside and closed the door on her local colleagues. She wanted to speak to the woman in private.

It was late afternoon. The weather forecast was for snow showers, but bright rays of sunshine broke briefly through the thick cloud cover, illuminating the room before vanishing again. It grew dark suddenly. Kristjana had taken a seat facing the television. Elínborg sat on the sofa.

'I don't want to hear any details,' said Kristjana. 'The

vicar told me some of it, but I've stopped watching the news. I heard something about a brutal attack with a knife. I don't want to know any more.'

'I'm sorry for your loss,' said Elínborg.

'Thank you.'

'It must have been a terrible shock.'

'I don't know what to say about how I feel,' said Kristjana. 'It was incomprehensible when my husband died, but this . . . this is . . .'

'Is there someone who could come and be with you?' Elínborg asked when Kristjana stopped in mid-sentence.

'We had him rather late,' said Kristjana, as if she had not heard. 'I was nearly forty. My husband, Baldur, was four years older than me. We weren't young when we met. I'd been living with someone for a few years. Baldur had lost his wife. Neither of us had children. So Runólfur was . . . We didn't have any more.'

'I know the local police asked you about this when they informed you of Runólfur's death, but I want to ask you again: do you know of anyone who might have had a grudge against him?'

'No. I told them, I can't imagine that. I simply can't conceive how someone would want to do such a thing. I think Runólfur was a chance victim, like in a car crash. That's how Baldur went. They told me he probably fell

44

asleep at the wheel – that poor man driving the lorry said he thought he had seen Baldur nodding off. I didn't feel sorry for myself, although I was left alone. Self-pity's no use.'

Kristjana fell silent. There was a box of tissues on the table. She took one and wound it in her fingers. 'You shouldn't be feeling sorry for yourself all the time,' she repeated.

Elínborg watched the wrinkled hands twisting the tissue, the hair in a ponytail, the bright eyes. She knew that Kristjana was seventy and had lived in this remote community all her life. The policemen who had driven Elínborg had told her that Kristjana was well known in the village for never having been to Reykjavík. She said there was nothing to take her there – even though her son had been in the city for more than a decade. Enquiries had revealed that he rarely visited his mother. Scarcely ever, in fact. Over recent decades many people had left the area, as Kristjana's son had done, and Elínborg's impression was that the woman had been abandoned, marooned in a vanished era. Her world had remained unchanged while Iceland had undergone a transformation. In that sense Kristjana reminded Elínborg of Erlendur, who could never shake off his past, nor wished to; his mindset and manners were old-fashioned, and he clung fast to values which, without anyone particularly noticing or caring, were rapidly disappearing. How could she tell this woman that her son had carried a date-rape drug in his pocket?

'When did you last hear from him?' asked Elínborg.

Kristjana hesitated, as if this simple question required careful thought. 'Probably a bit over a year ago,' she said.

'Over a year?' Elínborg repeated.

'He didn't have much contact with me,' Kristjana said.

'Yes, but hadn't you heard from him for over a year?'

'No.'

'When did you last see him?'

'He last came here three years ago. Didn't stay long, probably about an hour. He didn't speak to anyone but me. He said he was passing through, in a hurry. I don't know where he was going. I didn't ask.'

'Were you estranged?'

'No, not as such, but he didn't feel any need to be in touch,' said Kristjana.

'But what about you? Didn't you ring him?'

'He was always changing his phone number, so eventually I gave up trying. And, since he wasn't interested, I didn't want to impose. I left him alone.'

Neither woman spoke for a while.

'Do you know who did it?' Kristjana finally asked.

'We have no idea,' Elínborg replied. 'The investigation's in its early stages, so . . .'

'It could take a long time?'

'Possibly. So you didn't know much about his private life – friends, women in his life, or . . .'

'No, I didn't know anything about that. Did he live with a woman? The last I knew, he didn't. That was one of the things I talked to him about, whether he was going to settle down, start a family and that. He didn't give me much of an answer. He probably thought I was nagging.'

'We believe he lived alone,' said Elínborg. 'His landlord had that impression. Did he have any friends here in the village?'

'They've all moved away. The young people all leave, that's nothing new. They're talking about closing down the school, bussing the children over to the next fjord every day. This place has had the kiss of death. Maybe I should have left, too, gone to your wonderful Reykjavík. I've never been, and I never shall. People didn't travel much in the old days, and somehow I never had reason to go to the capital. I don't care, though. There's never been anything for me there. Nothing. Did you grow up there?'

'Yes,' said Elínborg. 'I like the city, and I quite understand those who want to move and settle there. So, your son: was he not in contact with anyone here in the village?'

'No,' answered Kristjana firmly. 'Not so far as I know.'

'Did he ever get into trouble here? Anything illegal? Did he make any enemies?'

'Here? No. Absolutely not. I don't know much about him after he left here. As I said, I wasn't aware of his circumstances, so I can't answer questions like that. I'm sorry I can't help. It's just the way he was.' She gazed at Elínborg. 'You can't tell what will become of your children. Do you have kids of your own?'

Elínborg nodded.

'What do you know about what they're up to?' said Kristjana. Elínborg thought of Valthór. 'How do you know what they may do?' Kristjana asked. 'I realise it's not an acceptable thing to say, but I didn't know my son well: I didn't know what he did from day to day, or what he was thinking. In many ways he was a stranger to me, and a mystery. I'm sure I'm not alone in that. Your children go away, and they gradually become strangers to you, except . . .' Kristjana had shredded her tissue into tiny pieces. 'You just have to grit your teeth,' she said. 'I soon learned that when I was young. Not to be sorry for myself. So now I'll just grit my teeth, as usual.'

Elínborg's mind went to the Rohypnol. If it was found in the pocket of a young man who had gone out for the evening and brought a woman home, the inference was fairly obvious.

'When Runólfur lived here,' Elínborg asked cautiously, 'was he involved with any women?'

'I've no idea,' Kristjana answered. 'Why are you asking about that? Women? I don't know about any women!'

'Well, could you tell me if there's anyone in the village who knew him, who I could speak to?' Elínborg asked calmly.

'Answer me! Why are you asking about women?'

'We know nothing about him. But . . .'

'Yes?'

'It's possible that his conduct was unusual,' said Elínborg. 'With women.'

'His conduct? Unusual?'

'Maybe even involving drugs.'

'What do you mean? What drugs?'

'They're sometimes called date-rape drugs,' Elínborg replied.

Kristjana was staring at her.

'It's also possible that he was only selling the drugs, but we aren't excluding the other possibility. We could be wrong. At this point we haven't got much to go on. We don't know why he had the drugs in his pocket when he was found dead.'

'A date-rape drug?'

'It's called Rohypnol. It's a sedative, which puts you to sleep and causes memory loss. We felt you should know. It's the kind of detail that the media may get hold of.'

Suddenly the storm battered against the wall of the

house. A blizzard masked the view from the windows, and the room grew darker still.

For a long time Kristjana sat without uttering a word. 'I can't imagine why he would carry such a thing,' she said at last.

'No, of course not.'

'As if I hadn't heard enough.'

'I understand that this must be hard for you.'

'Now I hardly know which is worse.'

'I'm sorry?'

Kristjana gazed out of the window into the snowstorm. 'That he was murdered, or that he was a rapist.'

'We don't know that for sure,' said Elínborg.

Kristjana met her gaze. 'No, you lot never know anything.'

6

Elínborg had to stay the night. She settled into her spacious room in a small guest house on a hill just outside the village, and rang Sigurdur Óli to tell him about her interview with Kristjana – not that it had yielded much. She rang home and spoke to Teddi, who had picked up a takeaway, and to Theodóra who was eager to tell her mother about a planned trip with the Girl Guides to Úlfljótsvatn lake in a fortnight's time. They had a long talk. The boys were out at the cinema. Elínborg reflected that she would probably be able to read all about it on the Internet before long.

Not far from the guest house was a restaurant that also

served as a pub, sports bar, video-rental shop and, apparently, a laundrette. As she entered, she saw a man handing his dirty washing over the bar, commenting that it would be good to have it back on Thursday. The menu included the usuals: sandwiches, burger and chips with pink cocktail-sauce, roast lamb, deep-fried fish. Elínborg opted for the fish. Two of the tables were occupied. At one of them three men were drinking beer and watching football on a flat-screen TV; at the other an elderly couple, outsiders like her, were eating the fried fish.

She was missing Theodóra, not having seen her for two days. Elínborg smiled to herself as she thought of her daughter. She would sometimes make surprising pronouncements about life. Her speech was rather formal and a little bit old-fashioned, and Elínborg worried that Theodóra might be teased at school. But apparently there was no cause for concern. 'Why's he so lugubrious?' she had asked about a miserable newsreader on TV. 'That's rather droll,' she would say when she read something funny in the paper. Elínborg assumed that she must have picked up such words from her extensive reading.

The fish was not bad, and the freshly baked bread served with it was delicious. Elínborg left the chips, which she had never particularly liked. When she had finished her fish she asked if the restaurant served espresso. The bartender, a woman of uncertain age who also cooked, baked, rented out videos and took in washing, conjured up a cup of good espresso in no time. The door opened, and someone came in to look at the videos.

The shawl that had been found in Runólfur's flat was a puzzle. It did not necessarily mean that a woman had been there at the time of the killing – or that his assailant had been a woman. The shawl could have been lying on the floor where it was found, under the bed, for several days. Yet the inescapable conclusion was that Runólfur might have used the date-rape drug that evening, that he could have brought a woman home with him – a woman who'd accompanied him willingly or otherwise – and that something had happened which had prompted the violent attack. Perhaps the effects of the drug had worn off and when the woman had regained consciousness she had seized the nearest weapon, whether for self-defence or revenge.

The murder weapon, a knife, had not been found in the flat and the murderer had left no trace, except for his or her evident hatred and rage against the dead man. If Runólfur had raped the woman who owned the shawl, and had then been attacked and killed by her, how did that help the police? Where had the shawl been bought? Officers would try to identify the shop that had sold it, but it did not look new and that line of enquiry might yield no result. The woman had worn perfume that lingered in the shawl.

The fragrance had not yet been identified but it was only a matter of time before it was, and enquiries would then be made at stores where it was sold. The shawl also smelt of smoke, which might only indicate that the owner had worn it in bars where people were smoking, or alternatively that she was a smoker herself. Runólfur was in his early thirties, and it was possible that he had met a woman of similar age. Dark hairs had been found on the shawl and in Runólfur's flat. They were not dyed. So the woman was a brunette. She must wear her hair short, as the hairs found were not long.

Perhaps she worked at a restaurant that served tandoori dishes. Elínborg knew something about tandoori cookery, and had even included some tandoori dishes in the cookery book that she had published. She had read up on tandoori cuisine and felt pretty well-informed about it. She owned two different clay tandoori pots. In India they would traditionally be heated in a pit filled with burning charcoal so that the meat was cooked evenly from all sides at a high temperature. Elínborg had occasionally buried a tandoori pot in her back garden in the authentic manner, but usually she put it in the oven or heated it over charcoal on an old barbecue. The crucial factor was the marinade, for which Elínborg used a combination of spices, blending them to taste with plain yoghurt. For a red colour she added ground annatto seed; for yellow, saffron. She generally experimented with a mixture of cayenne pepper, coriander, ginger and garlic, or with a garam masala that she made herself by using roasted or ground cardamom, cumin, cinnamon, garlic and black pepper, with a little nutmeg. She had also been trying out variations using Icelandic herbs such as wild thyme, angelica root, dandelion leaves and lovage. She would rub the marinade into the meat – chicken or pork – and leave it for several hours before it went into the tandoori pot. Sometimes a little of the marinade would splash on to the hot coals, bringing out more strongly the tangy tandoori fragrance that Elínborg had smelt on the shawl. She wondered if the woman they were looking for might have a job in Indian cookery. Or perhaps, like Elínborg, she was simply interested in Indian food, or even specifically in tandoori dishes. She too might have a tandoori pot in her kitchen, along with all the spices that made the dish so mouth-watering.

The elderly couple had finished their meal and gone, and the three football fans left as soon as the match ended. Elínborg sat for some time on her own, then went to the bar to pay. She thanked the bartender for a good meal. They spoke briefly about the bread, which Elínborg had enjoyed. The woman asked what brought her to the village and Elínborg told her.

'He was at primary school here with my son,' said the

bartender. She was plump and dressed in a sleeveless black top, with sturdy upper arms and a heavy bosom under a voluminous apron. She said she had seen the news on TV. Runólfur was the talk of the village.

'Did you know him at all?' Elínborg enquired, looking out the window. It had started to snow again.

'Everyone knows everyone around here. Runólfur was quite an ordinary lad. A bit rebellious, perhaps. He left as soon as he could – like most of the youngsters. I never had much to do with him. I know Kristjana was rather rough on him – she could lash out if he misbehaved. She's hard as nails. She used to work in the local fish factory until it closed down.'

'Are any of his friends still living here?'

The woman folded her hefty arms and thought. 'They've all moved away, so far as I know,' she said. 'The population's half what it was ten years ago.'

'I see,' said Elínborg. 'Well, thank you.'

She was on her way out when she saw a shelf of video-tapes and DVDs in a niche by the door. Elínborg did not go in for films much, but she watched sometimes if the males of the family rented something interesting. But crime films had no appeal, and romances left her cold. She preferred comedy. Theodóra had similar tastes, and occasionally the two of them would rent a comedy while Teddi and the boys were glued to some thriller.

Elínborg glanced over the shelf, and recognised one or two films she had already seen. A girl of about twenty was making her choice. She looked over at Elínborg and said hello. 'Are you the policewoman from Reykjavík?' she asked.

Elínborg realised that news of her presence had spread through the whole village.

'Yes,' she replied.

'There's one person here in the village who knew him,' the girl said.

'*Him?* You mean . . . ?'

'Runólfur. His name's Valdimar. He runs the garage.'

'And who are you?'

'I was just taking a look at the films,' replied the girl. Then she slipped past Elínborg and out the door.

Elínborg walked the streets in the heavy snow until she found a small motor workshop at the northern end of the village. Above the half-open sliding door of an old garage building a weak light shone on a weather-beaten sign on which the name of the business was illegible. It looked to Elínborg as if it had been peppered with shotgun pellets. She went through the reception area and into the workshop, where a man of about thirty was working behind a large tractor. He was wearing a tatty baseball cap and overalls that had once been dark blue but were now blackened with dirt. Elínborg introduced herself, and explained that she was from the police. The man twisted an oily rag in his hands as he returned Elínborg's greeting, uncertain whether he should offer her his greasy hand. He was tall and lanky, awkward-looking. He said his name was Valdimar.

'I heard you were here,' he said. 'Because of Runólfur.'

'I hope I'm not disturbing you,' said Elínborg, with a glance at her watch. It was past ten o'clock.

'No, you're not,' Valdimar assured her. 'I'm just working on the tractor. I've got nothing else on. Did you want to talk to me about Runólfur?'

'I gather you were friends when he lived here. Did you stay in touch?'

'No, not really – not after he left. I visited him once when I went to Reykjavík.'

'You don't know anyone who might have had reason to hate him?'

'No, not at all – but, as I say, we weren't in touch. I haven't been to Reykjavík in donkey's years. I read that his throat was cut.'

'That's right.'

'Do you know why?'

'No. We don't know much yet. I came here to speak to his mother. What was Runólfur like as a boy?'

Valdimar put down his oily rag, opened a thermos of

piping hot coffee and poured himself a cup. He glanced over at Elínborg as if to offer her one, but she shook her head.

'Everyone knows everyone else around here, of course,' he said. 'He was older than me so we didn't play together much as boys. He wasn't as wild as some of us who were raised here in the village, maybe because he had a strict upbringing.'

'But were you friends?'

'No, not really, though we knew each other quite well. He left when he was very young. Things change. Not least in a little community like this.'

'Did he go away to high school, or . . . ?'

'No, he just moved to Reykjavík to work. He always wanted to go there. He talked about going as soon as he got the chance. Or even travelling, abroad. He wasn't about to waste his life in this backwater. He called it a hole. I've never thought of it that way – I've always been OK here.'

'Was he interested in action comics, thriller films, do you know?'

'Why do you ask?'

'Because we found indications of it at his home,' answered Elínborg, without describing the posters and collectable figures in Runólfur's flat in any more detail.

'I don't know. I don't remember anything like that.'

'I've been told his mother was a harsh parent. You mentioned a strict upbringing.'

'She had a rather short fuse,' said Valdimar, sipping his coffee carefully. He took a biscuit from his pocket and dunked it in the cup. 'She had her own approach to parenting. I never saw her hit him, but he said she did. He only spoke of it once, so far as I know. He was embarrassed – I think he was ashamed. They were never close.'

'What about his father?'

'The old man was a bit of a wimp. Never said a word.'

'He died in an accident, didn't he?'

'That was just a few years ago, after Runólfur had moved to Reykjavík.'

'So have you any idea why Runólfur was murdered?'

'No, I've no idea at all. It's tragic, quite tragic, that things like that happen.'

'Did you know anything about women in his life?'

'Women?'

'Yes.'

'In Reykjavík?'

'Yes. Or in general.'

'I knew nothing about that. Is this to do with women?'

'No,' said Elínborg. 'Or, at least, we don't know. We don't know what happened.'

Valdimar put down his coffee cup and took a spanner from a toolbox.

60

He worked calmly, his movements unhurried. He searched for a bolt in another box, feeling around with a finger until he found one that was the right size.

Elínborg looked at the tractor. There was apparently no pressure of work at this garage, yet here Valdimar was, working late into the evening.

'My husband's a mechanic,' volunteered Elínborg without thinking. She was not in the habit of telling strangers anything about herself, but it was warm in the garage and the man was friendly. He came across as reliable and likeable. Outside, the storm was rising. She knew no one in this place and she felt a long way from her husband and children.

'Oh?' replied Valdimar. 'So I suppose his hands are always black?'

'I won't allow it,' said Elínborg, with a smile. 'He must have been one of the first mechanics in Iceland, or maybe in the world, who started wearing gloves for work.'

Valdimar looked down at his own filthy hands. Elínborg saw old scars on their backs and on his fingers which she recognised, after her years with Teddi, as being the result of struggling with engine parts. Teddi had not always been careful: sometimes he got carried away, or his tools were faulty.

'A woman's touch,' Valdimar said.

'And I get a special hand-cleaning cream for him, which

61

works wonders,' added Elínborg. 'Didn't you ever want to move away, like the others?'

She saw that Valdimar was trying not to smile.

'I can't think what that's got to do with anything,' he said.

'No, it was just a thought,' said Elínborg, a little embarrassed. The man had that effect upon her; he seemed frank and at peace with himself.

'I've always lived here, and never wanted to leave,' he said. 'I'm not one for change. I've been to Reykjavík a few times and I didn't like what I saw. All that chasing after empty things – conspicuous consumption, bigger houses, more expensive cars. They hardly even speak proper Icelandic any more. They hang around in junk-food joints, getting fatter and fatter. I don't think it's the Icelandic way. We're all drowning in bad foreign habits.'

'I have a friend who thinks rather like you.'

'Good for him.'

'And of course you have family here,' added Elínborg.

'I'm not a family man,' Valdimar said, disappearing under the tractor. 'I never have been, and I can't imagine I ever will be now.'

'You never know,' Elínborg ventured.

The man looked up from beneath the tractor. 'Was there anything else?' he asked.

Elínborg smiled and shook her head, apologised for disturbing him and then set off, back out into the storm.

When she reached the guest house she met the woman who had served her at the restaurant. She was still wearing her apron, with a name badge on it: *Lauga*. She was on her way out, and it occurred to Elínborg that perhaps she was involved in the guest-house operation too. That's multitasking for you, she thought.

'I heard that you talked to Valdi,' said Lauga, holding the door open for Elínborg. 'Did you get anything out of it?'

'Not a lot,' answered Elínborg, surprised again at the speed with which news spread round here.

'No, he's not much of a talker, but he's a good lad.'

'He seems to work hard. He was still working when I left.'

'There's not much else to do,' observed Lauga. 'He likes it, always has. Was it the tractor?'

'Yes, he was working on a tractor.'

'I should think he's been fiddling around with it for ten years now. I've never seen such care and attention as he lavishes on that tractor. It's like his pet. They gave him a nickname – Valdi *Ferguson*.'

'Well,' said Elínborg. 'I have to get back to town early in the morning, so . . .'

'Sorry. I wasn't meaning to keep you up all night.'

Elínborg smiled and looked out at the forlorn village that was gradually disappearing in the blizzard. 'I don't suppose you have much crime here?'

Lauga was closing the door. 'No, that's for sure,' she replied with a smile. 'Nothing ever happens here.'

But for a niggling question at the back of her mind Elínborg would have dropped off as soon as her head touched the pillow; it might mean anything, or nothing. It was the girl she had bumped into at the video rack: she had spoken in whispers, as if she had not wanted anyone to overhear their conversation.

7

Elínborg landed in Reykjavík around midday. Accompanied by a counsellor from the rape-trauma centre, she went straight to the home of the young woman who had been found at the roadside in Kópavogur.

The counsellor, Sólrún, was about forty. Elínborg had worked with her before. On the way, they discussed the increasing incidence of rape reported to the police. The number of offences varied: one year, twenty-five; another, forty-three. Elínborg was familiar with the statistics: she knew that around seventy per cent of rapes took place in the home, and in about fifty per cent of cases the victim knew the rapist. Rape by strangers was on the increase, although cases were still relatively rare. Such assaults might not necessarily be reported to the police; often, more than one man was involved. And each year the police dealt with six to eight cases in which the use of a date-rape drug was suspected.

'Did you speak to her?' asked Elínborg.

'Yes, she's expecting us,' answered Sólrún. 'She's still in a bad way. She's moved back in with her parents and doesn't really want to see or talk to anyone. She's cut herself off. She sees a psychologist twice a week, and I put her in touch with a psychiatrist too. It's going to take her a long time to get over it.'

'And it can't help that the justice system treats these victims with such contempt,' Elínborg said. 'Eighteen months on average for a rape conviction? It's a disgrace.'

The young woman's mother met them at the door and showed them into the living room. Her husband was not at home but was expected before long.

She went to let her daughter know that the visitors had arrived, and a brief argument ensued. So far as Elínborg could make out, the daughter was protesting that she didn't want this – she didn't want to speak to the police any more, she wanted to be left alone.

Elínborg and Sólrún stood up when the mother and daughter entered the room. The young woman, Unnur, had met both women before and recognised them, but she made no reply when they said hello.

'I'm so sorry we're imposing,' said Sólrún. 'This won't take long. And you can stop whenever you want.' They sat down, and Elínborg took care not to waste any time with small talk. Although Unnur tried to conceal it, Elínborg could see that she was uncomfortable as she sat by her mother's side. She was striving to put on a brave face. Elínborg had learned to recognise the long-term consequences of major physical assault, and she knew what mental scars it left. To her mind, rape was the worst form of physical assault, almost equivalent to murder.

From her pocket she took a photograph of Runólfur, copied from his driving licence. 'Do you recognise this man?' she asked, passing it to Unnur.

She gave it a brief glance. 'No,' she replied. 'I've seen his picture on the news, but I don't know him.' She returned the photo to Elínborg. 'Do you think that's him? The man who raped me?' Unnur asked.

'We don't know,' answered Elínborg. 'We do know he was carrying a date-rape drug when he went out on the evening he was murdered. That information hasn't been made public and you mustn't tell anyone. But I wanted you to hear the truth. Now you see why we were anxious to meet with you.'

'I don't know if I could identify him, even if he were standing right here in front of me,' said Unnur. 'I don't remember anything. Nothing. I vaguely remember the man I was last speaking to, at the bar. I don't know who he was, but it wasn't that Runólfur.'

'Would you be willing to come to his flat with us, and look around? In case it jogs your memory?'

'I . . . no, I . . . I haven't really been out anywhere since it happened,' said Unnur.

'She doesn't want to leave the house,' said her mother. 'Maybe you could show her some pictures.'

Elínborg nodded. 'It would be very helpful if you felt up to coming with us,' she said. 'And he had a car – we'd be grateful if you would look at it.'

'I'll think about it,' said Unnur.

'The most noticeable feature of his home is that there are big posters of Hollywood action heroes on the living-room walls. Superheroes, like Superman and Batman. Does that . . . ?'

'It's all a blank.'

'And another thing,' added Elínborg, producing the shawl, wrapped in a plastic evidence bag. 'We found this at the scene of the crime. I'd like to know if you recognise it. I'm afraid I can't take it out of the bag, but it's all right to open it.'

She handed it to the young woman.

'I don't wear shawls,' Unnur said. 'I've only ever owned one, and this isn't it. Did you find it at his place?'

'Yes,' replied Elínborg. 'That's another thing that hasn't been released to the media.'

Unnur was beginning to see where the questions were leading. 'Was there a woman with him when he . . . when he was attacked?'

'It's possible,' Elínborg said. 'We know at least that he was involved in some way with women who came to his home.'

'Had he drugged her, or was he planning to?'

'We don't know.'

Silence reigned.

'Do you think it was me?' Unnur asked eventually.

Her mother stared at her. Elínborg shook her head. 'Absolutely not,' she replied. 'You mustn't think that. I've already told you more than you're supposed to know, and you mustn't misinterpret it.'

'You think I attacked him.'

'No,' Elínborg said firmly.

'I couldn't, even if I wanted to. I'm not that kind of person,' said Unnur.

'What sort of questions are these?' asked her mother. 'Are you accusing my daughter of attacking that man? She doesn't even leave the house. She was with us all weekend!'

'We know. You're reading far too much into what we've said,' Elínborg said.

She hesitated. Mother and daughter watched her. 'But we do need a sample of your hair,' she said at last. 'Sólrún can take the sample. We want to establish whether you were in his flat the evening you were assaulted. Whether he might have been the one who drugged you and took you home to rape you.'

'I've done nothing wrong,' Unnur objected.

'No, of course you haven't,' agreed Sólrún. 'The police just want to rule out the possibility that you were in his flat.'

'And what if I *was* there?'

Elínborg felt the horror behind the young woman's words. She could barely imagine how she must feel, knowing nothing of the night when she was raped. 'That would give us more information about what happened to you in the hours before you were found in Kópavogur,' she pointed out. 'I know this is hard, but we're all looking for answers here.'

'I'm not even sure that I want to know,' Unnur said. 'I'm trying to pretend to myself that it never happened – that it wasn't me, but some other girl.'

'We've talked about this,' said Sólrún. 'You shouldn't repress it. It will only take much longer for you to understand that you're not at fault at all. You didn't do anything that led to the assault. You have no reason to blame yourself. You were brutalised. There's no need to hide away. You don't need to withdraw from society, or feel unclean. You aren't, and you never can be.'

'I'm . . . just scared,' said Unnur.

'Of course,' said Elínborg. 'That's entirely understandable. I've sat with women like you. I always tell them it's a question of how they feel about the offender. Just think what status you accord those animals by shutting yourself up here. It's not right that they can imprison you. You must show them you're able to fight back against the harm they want to inflict on you.'

Unnur gazed at Elínborg. 'But it's so horrible to know . . . you can never again . . . something's been taken away from me, and I can never, never get it back, and my life can never be as it was.'

'But that's how it is,' said Sólrún. 'For all of us. We can never get things back. That's why we look to the future.'

'It happened,' said Elínborg reassuringly. 'Don't dwell on it. If you do, then the bastards win. Don't let them get away with it.'

Unnur passed the shawl back to her. 'She smokes. I don't smoke. And there's another smell, a perfume – not mine – and then there's something spicy . . .'

'It's tandoori,' interjected Elínborg.

'Do you think she's the one that attacked him?'

'That's a possibility.'

71

'Good for her,' said Unnur through clenched teeth. 'Good for her, killing him! Good for her, killing that pig!'

Elínborg glanced at Sólrún. She thought the young woman seemed to be on the road to recovery already.

When Elínborg got home, late that evening, the boys were in the middle of a blazing row. Aron, the middle child who somehow always felt left out, had had the audacity to go on Valthór's computer. His older brother was yelling at him, in such a rage that Elínborg had to shout at him to make him shut up. Theodóra was listening to her iPod as she did her homework at the dining table, and was ignoring her bickering brothers. Teddi lay on the sofa watching TV. He had picked up fried chicken pieces on the way home, and the containers were scattered around the kitchen, along with cold chips and empty sauce tubs.

'Why don't you clear up this mess?' Elínborg called out to Teddi.

'Leave it,' he answered. 'I'll do it later. I just want to finish watching this programme . . .'

Elínborg did not have the energy for an argument. She sat down next to Theodóra. A few days earlier they had met Theodóra's teacher to talk about additional study material for her. The teacher was keen to find her something more challenging. They had discussed the possibility that Theodóra might take the last three years of compulsory schooling in a single year, if she wished, and enter high school early.

'It said on the news that you'd found a date-rape drug on that man,' said Theodóra, removing her earphones.

'How on earth do they get this information?' sighed Elínborg.

'Was he a scoundrel?' asked Theodóra.

'Maybe,' answered Elínborg. 'Please don't ask me about these things.'

'They said you were looking for a woman who was with him that night.'

'It's possible that someone who was there with him attacked him. Now be quiet,' retorted Elínborg amicably. 'What did you have to eat at school?'

'Rye-bread soup. It was horrible.'

'You're too fussy about your food.'

'I eat *your* bread soup.'

'Of course you do. It's a work of genius.'

Elínborg had told Theodóra that she too had been a fussy eater as a child. She was brought up eating old-fashioned Icelandic food, in old-fashioned Icelandic circumstances. When she described it to her daughter, it was like telling her about life in the Middle Ages. Elínborg's mother had been a housewife who shopped and then cooked lunch every day. Her father, who had worked in the offices of a fishing company, would come home, eat

73

his meal, then lie down on the sofa to listen to the midday news, which went out at 12.20 p.m. precisely – for the convenience of workers like him. The chimes of the news theme usually rang out just as he swallowed his last bite and put his feet up.

At lunchtime Elínborg's mother served boiled fish with bread and butter, or made a meat loaf served with mashed or more often boiled potatoes, an invariable accompaniment to every meal.

As for the evening meal, the weekly menus generally followed a strict daily sequence. Elínborg's mother did all the cooking. On Saturdays they had saltfish, presoaked in a tub in the kitchen – the same tub in which her husband bathed his aching feet. To this day, Elínborg could hardly stomach saltfish. On Sunday there was a roast leg or rack of lamb, with brown gravy made with the meat broth, and caramelised potatoes. To ring the changes they sometimes had lamb chops. The roast was always served with pickled red cabbage and tinned peas. Salted mutton with boiled swedes or horsemeat sausage with a white sauce might crop up on any day, but these were rarities. Mondays always meant fish, unless there were enough leftovers from the Sunday roast, in which case the fish was moved over to Tuesday. It was usually fried in breadcrumbs and served with melted margarine and mayonnaise. Wednesday was air-cured fish, which Elínborg regarded as all but inedible. After it had been boiled for so long that all the windows misted up, an abundance of melted suet was not enough to make the cured fish any more palatable. Wednesday could also be cod roe and liver, which was marginally preferable. Elínborg found the membrane of the roe off-putting, and she never touched the liver. On Thursdays her mother sometimes threw caution to the winds: one memorable Thursday, Elínborg first tasted spaghetti, boiled to within an inch of its life. She found it completely tasteless, but a little more palatable with tomato ketchup. On Friday, fried lamb or pork cutlets in breadcrumbs were accompanied by melted margarine, as with the fried fish.

Week followed week, adding up to months and years of Elínborg's childhood, with hardly a variation. A ready-made meal was bought perhaps once every two years or so: her father would bring home open sandwiches of smoked lamb on malted bread, or prawns and mayonnaise on white.

Elínborg was nineteen when the first piece of grilled chicken entered her home, in a carton with 'French fries'. That was another unforgettable day. She did not particularly like either foodstuff and her parents never repeated the experiment. She enjoyed reading about food in books, and often all she remembered from children's stories and novels were the descriptions of meals and cooking:

unfamiliar foreign delicacies, unavailable in Iceland in those days, such as 'marmalade', 'bacon' and 'ginger beer'. She recalled reading one day about 'melted cheese'. It took her some time to understand what it meant. She had never heard of cheese being eaten in any other way than straight from the fridge, sliced on to bread.

Elínborg was picky about certain foods and was a constant source of disappointment to her mother, who was a firm believer in the virtues of boiling: she believed that food was inedible unless reduced to a mush, and she would boil slices of haddock for twenty-five to thirty minutes. Elínborg was always terrified of choking on a fish bone at the kitchen table. She did not like the fatty breadcrumb coating of the cutlets, found the meat bland and flavourless, and the caramelised potatoes were disgusting. Lamb's liver in onion sauce, served on Tuesdays except when her mother plumped for hearts and kidneys, she simply could not get down. Nor did she think heart or kidney could be considered proper food. Her culinary blacklist was endless.

It came as no surprise to Elínborg when her father suffered a heart attack in his early sixties. He survived, and her parents were still living in the same place, Elínborg's childhood home. Both were now retired, but remained alert and self-sufficient. Her mother still boiled her air-cured fish until the windows misted over.

When it had become clear that Elínborg's fussiness

about food was incurable, and as she grew old enough to find her way around the kitchen, her parents allowed her to start cooking for herself, using whatever her mother had bought. She would take some of the haddock or cutlets, or the fish loaf served on Thursdays after the pasta experiment came to an end, and prepare something that she really wanted to eat. And she developed an interest in cookery: she always asked for cookbooks for Christmas and birthday presents, subscribed to recipe clubs, and read cookery columns in the papers. Yet she did not necessarily want to be a chef; she just wanted to prepare food that was not inedible.

By the time Elínborg left home she had had some impact on the family's eating habits, while other aspects of their life had changed of their own accord. Her father, for instance, no longer came home to eat lunch and lie down to listen to the news. Her mother went out to work and came home exhausted in the evening, relieved that Elínborg was willing to cook. She worked in a grocery shop where she was run off her feet all day long, and every evening she soaked in a hot bath, her feet red and sore. But she was more cheerful than before, as she had always been a sociable person.

Elínborg graduated from high school, left home and rented a small basement flat. During the summer vacations she worked as a police officer, having secured the job through an uncle. She decided to study geology at university. In her teens she had enjoyed travelling around the country with friends, one of whom, who was keen on geology, urged Elínborg to enrol with her. Although she was initially fascinated by the subject Elínborg knew before she graduated that a career in geology was not for her.

She watched Theodóra at her homework and wondered what her daughter would do when she grew up. She was interested in science – physics and chemistry – and talked about doing it at university. She also wanted to study abroad.

'Do you have a blog, Theodóra?' asked Elínborg.

'No.'

'Perhaps you're too young.'

'No, I think it's silly. I think it's ridiculous to go talking about everything I do and say and think. It's nobody's business but mine. I have no interest in putting it on the net.'

'It's surprising how far people go.'

Theodóra looked up. 'Have you been reading Valthór's blog?'

'I didn't even know he blogged. I only found out by chance.'

'He writes total nonsense,' said Theodóra. 'I've told him I don't want him mentioning me.'

'And?'

'He says I'm an idiot.'

'Do you know these girls he writes about at all?'

'No. He never tells me anything. He tells everyone everything about himself, but he never tells me anything. I gave up trying to talk to him ages ago.'

'Do you think I should let him know I've been reading his blog?'

'Get him to stop writing about us, at least. He writes about you too, you know. And Dad. I meant to say, but I didn't want to be a telltale.'

'How does it work . . . if I read his blog, am I snooping?'

'Are you going to talk to him?'

'I don't know.'

'Then maybe you are snooping. I'd been reading it for months before I lost my temper over something he'd written about us, and told him. He wrote that I was a lame swot. I don't know why he puts it on the net if we're not allowed to read it without being accused of spying on him.'

'Months, you say? How long has he been doing it?'

'Over a year.'

Elínborg did not feel that she was spying on her son by reading a public blog. She did not want to interfere, because she felt he must take responsibility himself, but she was concerned that he was writing too openly about his family and friends.

'He never tells me anything,' she said. 'Maybe I should talk to him. Or your dad could.'

'Let him be.'

'Of course, he's almost a grown man, he's at college . . . I feel I've lost touch with him. We used to be able to talk but now we hardly ever do. All I can do these days is read his blog.'

'Valthór has already moved out – up here,' said Theodóra, tapping at her forehead with a finger. Then she went back to her homework.

'Did he have any friends?' asked Theodóra after a little while, without taking her eyes off her books.

'He? Valthór?'

'The man who was killed.'

'I assume so.'

'Have you spoken to them?'

'No, not me. Other people are tracing them. Why do you ask?' Her daughter sometimes spoke in riddles.

'What did he do?'

'He was a telecoms engineer.'

Theodóra looked at her pensively. 'They meet people.'

'Yes, they go to people's homes.'

'They go to people's homes,' Theodóra repeated, and returned to her easy maths assignment.

Elínborg's mobile rang from the pocket of her coat in the hall closet. It was her work phone. She went into the hall to answer it.

'We've just had the preliminary autopsy results for Runólfur,' said Sigurdur Óli without so much as a hello.

'Yes?' said Elínborg. She was annoyed by people who did not identify themselves on the phone, even if they were close colleagues. She glanced at her watch. 'Couldn't this have waited until tomorrow?' she asked.

'Do you want to know what they found or don't you?'

'Sigurdur . . .'

'They found Rohypnol,' said Sigurdur Óli.

'Yes, I know. I was there with you when they told us.'

'No, I mean they found Rohypnol *in* Runólfur. Inside him. There was a load of it in his mouth and throat.'

'What are you talking about?'

'He was up to his eyeballs in the stuff himself!'

8

The manager of the Customer Support Division at the phone company met Elínborg and Sigurdur Óli after lunch. Sigurdur Óli was distracted – he was working on another demanding case and had only half his mind on the Thingholt murder. In addition, his relationship with Bergthóra was not improving. He had moved out and their attempts to resolve their differences had failed. She had invited him over one evening recently but they had finished up quarrelling. He did not tell Elínborg. He wanted to keep his personal life private. They had hardly spoken on the way to the phone company except for Elínborg asking if he had heard anything from Erlendur since he left for the East Fjords.

'Nothing,' said Sigurdur Óli.

Elínborg had gone to bed late and had not managed to get to sleep until the middle of the night. Her mind had been racing with thoughts of Runólfur and the date-rape drug. She had not yet spoken to Valthór about his blog. He had been out of the house when she intended to tell him to stop writing about his family on the net.

Teddi snored quietly next to her. She never remembered him having any trouble sleeping, or having a restless night – no doubt a sign that he was at peace with himself and with the world. He did not complain, and was not much of a talker. He did not take the initiative, preferring to live in peace and quiet. His job was not particularly stressful and he never brought it home with him. Sometimes, when Elínborg felt oppressed by her work, she considered whether she should have stuck to geology and imagined what she might be doing now if she had not joined the police. She might be a teacher; she had taught a few courses at the Police Training College and she enjoyed the role of instructor. She might have pursued postgraduate studies and become a scientist, researching glacial floods and earthquakes. Sometimes, when she observed the work of the police forensics officers, she thought that it might have suited her. She was not especially unhappy in her work, but from time to time she was overcome by the degradation and horrors she

83

had to witness. She could not fathom how human beings could behave like savage beasts.

'What is it exactly that a telecoms engineer does?' Elínborg asked the manager. 'What does the job involve?'

'Well, it can involve various things,' the manager – Lárus – said. 'They're responsible for the telephone system, and they handle maintenance and installation. I checked up on Runólfur in our records. He'd been with us for several years – joined us straight from technical college. An excellent worker. The company was very happy with him.'

'Was he liked?'

'Yes, so far as I know. I didn't have much direct contact with him but I'm told he was sober, punctual and pleasant. Nobody here understands this. We can't grasp what really happened.'

'No,' Elínborg replied. 'Do they go to people's houses, these engineers?'

'Runólfur did. He handled Internet connections, broadband, in-house phone systems, digital tuners, fibre optics. We offer an outstanding service. People have no idea about computers and technology. Someone who had been stamping on his mouse all day rang recently. He thought it was a foot pedal.'

'Can you give us a list of customers that Runólfur visited in recent months?' asked Elínborg. 'He covered the Reykjavík area, didn't he?'

'You'll need a warrant. I'm sure we've got a list, but I should think it's confidential, so . . .'

'No problem,' said Elínborg. 'You'll have one by close of business today.'

'Are you going to interview everyone he visited?'

'If necessary,' said Elínborg. 'Do you know of any friends of Runólfur we could speak to? Either here at the company, or anyone at all?'

'I don't, but I'll ask around.'

On the weekend when he was murdered Runólfur had not been picked up by any CCTV camera in the downtown area where his landlord assumed he had gone on the last evening of his life. There were eight cameras monitoring the busiest locations in the city centre. Perhaps it meant nothing: there were many other routes to and from his home. Perhaps Runólfur knew where the cameras were and had deliberately avoided them. Taxi drivers were questioned: had they seen him, or even picked him up? But this yielded no result. The same applied to the drivers of night buses in the area. Runólfur's credit- and debit-card transactions were checked, but he seemed to use the cards only for grocery shopping and instalment payments on his computer and iPod, and regular outgoings like phone, heating, electricity and TV bills.

The police had been provided with data that tracked

Runólfur's mobile-phone signal so they could tell whether he had moved from one transmission zone to another on the night in question. Even if he had not used his phone his movements could still be tracked, but as a telecoms engineer he must have known that his position still could not be pinpointed since the whole of the downtown area was covered by a single transmitter with a radius of three kilometres. Had Runólfur wanted to go farther afield without his movements being traceable he might have left his mobile at home: it turned out that the phone had not left the downtown area that night.

A hair sample from the young woman who had been found in distress in Kópavogur was sent abroad for DNA analysis, so that it could be compared with samples from Runólfur's home and car. It would take some time to establish whether she had been his victim a few weeks before he was killed. But she was not a suspect and had a reliable alibi. The T-shirt that Runólfur had been wearing when he'd died and the shawl found in his flat were also sent for analysis, to reveal whether both had belonged to the same woman. Nothing had been found on his computer that would help the police to determine who had been with him on the night of the murder. In fact the computer contained very little history of Internet usage at all. It appeared that he had been intending to buy a second-hand car since websites selling used cars were listed prominently on the day of his death, along with Icelandic and foreign sports sites, and subjects relevant to his job. All his e-mails related to his work.

'He didn't use e-mail as most of us tend to,' said the forensics officer. 'And it looks to me as if that's deliberate.'

'What do you mean, deliberate?'

'He leaves no trail,' he explained.

Elínborg was standing in the doorway of an office at police headquarters. The space was so tiny and constricted that she could not actually enter the room. The officer, who was both tall and proportionately broad, seemed almost to be trapped in his miniature office, unable to move.

'But is there anything unusual about that? Some people write whatever comes into their heads, while others are more cautious. After all, how do we know who will read our e-mails?'

'You can get access to anything, and steal it,' he observed. 'As we've seen in practice – suddenly people's private affairs appear on the front pages of the papers. Speaking for myself, I would never put anything important in an e-mail. But I have a feeling that this man is rather more than just cautious – he seems to be almost obsessive. It's as if he did his utmost not to leave anything personal whatsoever on the hard drive. There are no links, other than those relating to his work. No chat rooms. No documents. No personal thoughts. No calendar. Nothing. We know he was interested in films and football. That's all we got.'

'Nothing about girlfriends?'

'Nope.'

'Because he wanted it that way?'

'Yes.'

'Because he had something to hide?'

'That could be one reason,' the forensics man replied, reaching for his own computer. 'He seems to have made a habit of deleting the day's web-page history before turning off his computer at night.'

'Not surprising, perhaps, since he was carrying roofies.'

'No, perhaps not.'

'So no one knows what he was up to online?'

'I'm going to see if I can dig anything up. Not everything necessarily goes when the delete button is pressed. His Internet service provider may be able to help us. Actually, it looks as if it's hosted abroad, so it may take for ever to find out,' he sighed, shifting in his chair, which creaked in response.

The post-mortem revealed that Runólfur had been in excellent health, with no physical ailments. He was short, slim and well-proportioned. There were no scars or blemishes on his body and his organs had functioned normally.

'In short, a healthy young man,' said the pathologist as he finished his recital.

He was standing opposite Elínborg, across from Rúnólfur's body, in the city mortuary. The autopsy had been completed and the body had been transferred to a lateral cold chamber. The pathologist had pulled out the drawer and now Elínborg looked down at the corpse.

'It wasn't an easy death,' the pathologist went on. 'He sustained a number of cuts before he was killed. There are several small cuts on the neck, near to the main wound, and a bruise to the throat, as if someone had held him fast. There's no indication that he made any real attempt to defend himself.

'It's not particularly complicated, but interesting in its way. It's been done cleanly. The throat has been slit with a razor-sharp blade, almost as sharp as a surgical scalpel. The actual cut was one continuous stroke with absolutely no hesitation marks. It's rather like an expert surgical incision. I would think that his assailant overpowered him and held him helpless for a time – that's the inference of the small cuts – before slitting his throat and dropping him to the floor. He survived for a little while. Not long, but perhaps up to a minute. You didn't find any signs of a struggle, did you?'

'No.'

'He had intercourse shortly before he died, as you no doubt know. As to whether the sex was non-consensual, I couldn't say. There's no indication that it was. Except the fact that's he's dead, of course.'

'No marks on the body? No scratches, no bites?'

'No, but then you wouldn't expect any if the woman concerned was sedated.'

The team investigating the case had repeatedly discussed the condition in which Runólfur's body had been found in his home, and what clues it might provide. He'd been wearing a T-shirt which was far too small for him and probably belonged to a woman. With the exception of the shawl, no other female garments were found in his flat. They deduced that the T-shirt had probably belonged to a woman who had accompanied him home: if a rape had taken place, Runólfur must have undressed the woman, then raped her, apparently getting some kick out of wearing her own shirt. It looked as if he had tried to create a romantic ambience: no electric lights had been on, except in the living room, and burnt-out tea-light candles were found in both the living room and the bedroom.

Some of the detectives were not convinced that there had even been a rape. They were reluctant to infer too much from the evidence found: although Runólfur had

Rohypnol in his home, that told them nothing of what had happened there, and no trace of the drug had been found in glasses, for instance. Perhaps he had sex with the woman, putting on her T-shirt during their love-making, and for some reason she picked up the knife and cut his throat. Other members of the team, Sigurdur Óli among them, were of the view that a third person must have intruded on the couple: Runólfur, flustered, had put on the T-shirt but had not managed to finish dressing before he was killed. It was possible that his companion had attacked him, but an alternative had also to be considered: that another person had committed the crime. Elínborg tended to favour that view, although she had no particular arguments to support her hunch. The murder weapon, a razor-sharp knife, might have belonged to the victim. Four kitchen knives were arranged on a magnetic strip on the wall. Perhaps there had originally been a set of five. The killer could have used the fifth, then taken it away when he or she left. It was not clear from the knives whether one was missing, and an exhaustive search of Thingholt and further afield had so far yielded no result.

And then there was the Rohypnol in Runólfur's mouth and throat. He could hardly have taken it of his own accord.

'Did you find a lot of Rohypnol in the body?' she asked.

'Yes – a good deal, really, which seems to have been forced down him.'

'But it hadn't reached the bloodstream?'

'We don't know yet,' replied the pathologist. 'Tox screening takes longer.'

Elínborg looked at him. 'Oh, yes, of course.'

'It would have taken about ten minutes to start working, and after that he wouldn't have been capable of defending himself in any way.'

'That's consistent with the fact that we found little sign of a struggle.'

'Absolutely. He wouldn't have been able to put up any resistance, however much he wanted to.'

'Just like his presumed victim.'

'He got a taste of his own medicine, if that's what you mean.'

'So someone forced him to swallow the stuff, then coolly slit his throat?'

The pathologist shrugged. 'That's your department.'

Elínborg looked down at the body. 'He looks pretty fit. Maybe he met women at a gym,' she said.

'That's possible, if he worked out.'

'And he went to people's homes and offices. He was a telecoms engineer.'

'He got around, then.'

'And there are all the clubs and bars.'

'Don't you think it's more likely that he picked women up at random, rather than targeting them specifically?'

The police officers had discussed this factor at length. Some felt that Runólfur's modus operandi was fairly straightforward: he met a woman at a bar and invited her home. Some liked the look of him and went with him. It remained unclear whether he drugged any of them since there were no witnesses. Other officers reckoned that he had definitely used drugs and worked in a systematic manner. He did not trust to luck in picking up a woman. He had some acquaintanceship with them, though perhaps only very slight.

'Maybe,' said Elínborg. 'Anyway, we have to find out how he met women. We haven't dismissed the possibility that a woman was with him when he was killed, and that she may be the killer.'

'The cut looks like that, at any rate,' said the pathologist. 'That was my first reaction when I saw it. My mind went to an old-fashioned straight razor, the kind where the blade folds into the handle. Do you know what I mean?'

'What did you say about the cut?'

The pathologist looked down at the body. 'It's smooth,' he said. 'When I saw it I thought to myself that it was . . . almost feminine.'

9

It was dark in the bar. A large window that faced on to the street had been broken and was now boarded up with plywood. The repair looked recent. Elínborg thought it was probably a temporary measure, but perhaps not. The pane of glass in the door had also been broken, but longer ago. It was covered with black-painted plywood that was scratched and graffitied. It did not look as if the proprietor intended to install new glass. Given up trying, thought Elínborg to herself.

The owner was crouched behind the bar. She was about to ask him about the window but then she lost interest. No doubt there had been a fight. Maybe someone had thrown a table through it. She did not want to know.

'Has Berti been in today?' Elínborg asked the proprietor, who was arranging bottles in a fridge. All she could see was the top of his head.

'Don't know anyone called Berti,' he replied without looking up from the beers. 'Fridbert,' Elínborg elaborated. 'I know he hangs out here.'

'A lot of people come in here,' the proprietor replied, standing up. He was a thin man of about fifty with a haggard face and a ragged moustache.

Elínborg looked around. She counted three customers. 'Always this busy, is it?' she asked.

'Why don't you get out?' he retorted, returning to his task.

Elínborg thanked him for his help. This was the second bar she had visited after she'd received a tip from the Drug Squad about where Rohypnol might be available. They were cooperating with the CID on the Thingholt case.

Elínborg knew that Rohypnol was a medication that was used to treat sleep disorders. Under strict Icelandic legislation it was obtainable only on prescription, from a doctor. Runólfur had not been registered with any GP but Elínborg was able to ascertain without much difficulty that he had been to two doctors since moving to Reykjavík. Three years had passed between the two occasions so Runólfur did not appear to have had any major health problems, just as the pathologist had said. Neither doctor would reveal any information about their consultations with Runólfur without a court order, but both were able to confirm that they had not prescribed Rohypnol. It was no surprise to Elínborg that she was unable to trace the Rohypnol concerned to a doctor. Runólfur could have bought the drug in another country, but he had not left Iceland in the past six years. So far as his colleagues remembered, his last trip abroad had been to Benidorm in Spain where he had spent three weeks. Airline manifests showed that he had not flown anywhere since then, so the likeliest explanation was that he had got hold of the drug in Iceland, on the black market.

Elínborg approached one of the bar's customers, a woman of indeterminate age who sat sucking in the smoke of her roll-up. The tiny stub burned her lip and she flicked it away. On the table stood a half-full glass of beer, and next to it an empty shot glass.

All at the taxpayer's expense, Sigurdur Óli would have growled.

'Seen Berti around, Solla?' Elínborg asked as she sat down.

The woman glanced up. She was wearing a grubby coat and a battered hat: she might well have been in her forties, or she could even have been getting on for eighty. 'What business is that of yours?' she replied hoarsely.

'I want to talk to him.'

'Why don't you talk to me instead?' retorted Solla.

'Maybe later,' Elínborg said. 'Right now I've got to get hold of Berti.'

'No one wants to talk to me,' Solla grumbled.

'Nonsense.'

'It isn't. Nobody does.'

'Have you seen Berti recently?' Elínborg asked again.

'No.'

Elínborg eyed the other two customers: a man and a woman she had not seen before, sitting with their glasses of beer, smoking. The man said something, then stood up and put a coin in the fruit machine in the corner. The woman stayed at the table, drinking.

'What do you want with Berti?' Solla enquired.

'It's in connection with a rape case,' replied Elínborg.

Solla turned her attention from her beer. 'Did he rape someone?'

'No, not him. I need some information from him.'

Solla took a gulp of her drink and watched the man playing the fruit machine. 'Fucking rapists,' she murmured.

Elínborg had come across Solla several times over the years. She no longer remembered the woman's full name, if she had ever known it. From a young age Solla had lived a pitiful life: she had fallen in with losers, incorrigible drinkers and junkies, lived on her own, been in residential care and in halfway homes, slept rough. She had had the occasional brush with the law, arising from some minor incident such as shoplifting or pinching clothes off washing lines, but she was quite harmless except when she was very drunk. Then she became touchy and aggressive, which tended to get her into trouble. She had been beaten up repeatedly, was a regular at the hospital casualty department, and had spent the odd night in police cells.

'I'm investigating an alleged rapist,' said Elínborg, wondering if *alleged* would mean anything to Solla.

'Hope you get the bastard,' Solla said.

'We've got him already. We want to find out who killed him,' Elínborg explained.

'He's dead? The case is solved, then, isn't it?'

'We want to know who did it.'

'Why? You going to give him a medal?'

'It was probably a woman who killed him.'

'Good for her!' exclaimed Solla.

'I hear Berti sometimes comes here . . .'

'He's an idiot,' Solla exclaimed. She lowered her voice. 'I don't use that bloody filth he sells.'

'I just need to talk to him. He hasn't been at home.'

According to the Drug Squad, Berti ran a nice line in getting hold of prescription medicines. He spun a story to various doctors around town and some of them would prescribe whatever he asked for, no questions asked. Berti sold on the drugs he got this way for a decent profit. Rohypnol was one such substance. There was no conclusive evidence that any of his clients were using it as a date-rape drug, any more than that they were taking it to treat sleep disorders. Rohypnol was also effective for the withdrawal symptoms experienced by cocaine addicts. In Runólfur's flat they had found no sign of any other drug use, which was taken to mean that he had used the Rohypnol for one purpose only – assuming that it had in fact belonged to the dead man.

Elínborg sat silently, watching Solla and thinking about prescription medications, coke, drug withdrawal and rape, and reflected on how sad and degraded human life could be.

'Do you know anything recent about Berti?' she asked. 'Any idea where I might be able to find him?'

'I've seen him with Binna Geirs,' Solla replied.

'Binna?'

'He's got a thing for that hag.'

'Thank you, Solla.'

'Yeah, thank me, right . . . will you buy me a beer? So he doesn't chuck me out,' she said, with a nod at the bar where the proprietor was frowning at them.

*   *   *

It emerged that Runólfur had worked out. A surveillance camera in the gym where he had been a member showed that he had been there on the day of his death, at around one p.m. on the Saturday. He left an hour and a half later. He was alone, and to judge from the footage had not spoken to anyone: no member of staff, and no woman who might have left with him. The staff did not specifically remember Runólfur that day but they were familiar with him as a regular and had no complaints about him.

One of the owners, a personal trainer, spoke well of Runólfur, who had transferred from another gym about two years ago. Elínborg gathered that this was one of the most popular gyms in the city. She saw a range of exercise equipment: treadmills, weight machines, exercise cycles and other machinery that she did not recognise. On the walls were giant flatscreens to entertain the clients as they went for the burn.

'He taught me, rather than me teaching him,' said the personal trainer, with a smile at Elínborg. They were standing in the main gym. 'He knew it all.'

'Did he come here regularly?' Elínborg asked. She was holding a gym membership card which they had found among Runólfur's possessions.

'Always three times a week, after work.'

'He seems to have been in good shape,' Elínborg said.

A muscular man of about thirty, the instructor radiated *joie de vivre* and exuberance. He was tanned a deep sun-lamp bronze, and his teeth shone bright as strobe lights.

'Runólfur was outstandingly fit,' he answered, looking Elínborg up and down. She felt he was appraising her fitness and she suspected that she knew what his verdict would be: a life sentence on the treadmill.

'Do you know why he changed gyms?' she asked. 'When he started here, two years ago?'

'No, I don't. I should think he just moved nearby. That's often the case.'

'Do you know where he used to work out before that?'

'I think he was at The Firm.'

'The Firm?'

'Someone mentioned it to me, someone who knew he used to go there. In this field people know each other a bit, at least by sight.'

'Did he make friends here, do you know?'

'Not really. He was generally on his own. He sometimes had a mate with him – I don't know the guy's name. A bit overweight, not at all fit. He didn't work out. Just sat in the café.'

'Did Runólfur ever talk to you about women when he was here?'

'Women? No.'

'So you don't know of any women he spoke to, or met here at the gym, or knew from anywhere else?'

The trainer took a moment to search his memory. 'No, I don't think so. He didn't talk much.'

'OK,' said Elínborg. 'Thank you.'

'You're welcome. I wish I could be more help, but I hardly knew him. What a terrible thing this is. Terrible.'

'Yes, it is,' said Elínborg. She said goodbye to the bronzed man who smiled cheerfully, instantly forgetting Runólfur's violent end.

Elínborg had reached the car park when a new idea occurred to her and she went back inside. She found the personal trainer leaning over a chunky woman of about sixty who lay prostrate in a gaudy tracksuit. Apparently stuck in one of the weight machines, she was explaining that she had strained a muscle.

'Excuse me,' said Elínborg.

The trainer looked up. Beads of sweat had formed on his forehead.

'Yes?'

'Did any women stop coming here after he joined?'

'Stop?'

'Did any woman suddenly cancel her membership? Without explanation? Someone who'd been a regular, and who left after Runólfur joined?'

'Please . . . ?' said the big woman, holding out her hand to the trainer with a pleading look.

'People are always cancelling memberships,' he said. 'I don't see . . .'

'I'm asking if you remember anything unusual. A woman who had always worked out here regularly, then suddenly stopped attending, perhaps.'

'I didn't notice anything,' answered the trainer. 'And I notice everything like that. I'm the owner, you know. Well, joint owner.'

'I suppose it's difficult to keep on top of exactly who signs up and who leaves. There are a lot of people, of course.'

'Ours is a very popular gym,' said the trainer.

'Yes, of course.'

'And no one stopped coming because of him,' the trainer said. 'Not that I'm aware of.'

'Look, would you mind . . .' The woman in the weight machine seemed to be quite helpless.

'OK,' said Elínborg. 'Thanks. Do you want me to give you a hand . . . ?'

The woman looked from one to the other.

'No, no. No problem,' answered the trainer. 'I've got it.'

As Elínborg left she heard the woman shriek, then snap angrily at the man of bronze.

* * *

The police had interviewed several acquaintances of Runólfur, including neighbours and work colleagues. All of them described him in glowing terms and none had anything critical to say. His death and the circumstances in which it had taken place were quite incomprehensible to them. One of Runólfur's colleagues knew he had a friend named Edvard; he did not work with them but Runólfur had occasionally mentioned him. Elínborg remembered that the name Edvard had appeared repeatedly in Runólfur's phone records. Edvard did not deny knowing the deceased when they tracked him down but he did not see how he could help the police with their enquiries. Nonetheless, Elínborg asked him to come down to the station.

Edvard had learned about the date-rape drug from the media. He found this detail perhaps even more astonishing than the violent death of his friend: he said it must be some misunderstanding about Runólfur having used a date-rape drug – he wasn't that kind of person. The twist that Rohypnol had also been found in Runólfur's body had not yet been released to the media.

'What kind of person would that be?' asked Elínborg as she offered Edvard a seat in her office.

'I don't know. But not him, that's for sure.'

Edvard gazed at her, wide-eyed, explaining that he had known Runólfur well. The two had become good friends soon after Runólfur had moved to Reykjavík. They had not been acquainted before. Edvard was a teacher, but had got to know Runólfur when they had worked together in construction during their summer vacations from college. They often went to the cinema, and both enjoyed English football. Both were single, and they had hit it off.

'And did you go out on the town together?' Elínborg asked.

'Now and then,' the man replied. He was in his early thirties, rather overweight, with a wispy beard, a jowly face, and thinning mousy hair.

'Did Runólfur have a way with women?'

'He was always very nice to them. I don't quite know what you're trying to get me to say, but I never saw him do anyone any harm. Neither a woman, nor anyone else.'

'And there wasn't anything in Runólfur's behaviour that might explain the Rohypnol we found in his pocket?'

'He was just a perfectly ordinary bloke,' said Edvard. 'Someone must have planted it on him.'

'Was he seeing a woman at the time he died?'

'Not so far as I know. Why? Has anyone been in touch with you?'

'Did you know about any women in his life?' asked Elínborg without answering his question. 'Someone he was seeing, or lived with?'

'I don't know of anyone he had a steady or long-term relationship with. He'd never lived with anyone.'

'When did you last see him?'

'I spoke to him before the weekend. We were thinking of meeting up. I asked if he had anything special planned but he said he was going to stay in.'

'And you phoned him on the Saturday?'

The police had examined Runólfur's phone records for several weeks before his death, both landline and mobile phones, and Elínborg had received the list earlier that day. Runólfur did not receive many phone calls. Most of them concerned his work, but there was a handful of numbers that the police intended to investigate further. Edvard's name cropped up more often than any other.

'I was going to suggest we watched the English football at the Sports Bar. We sometimes go – sometimes *went* there on Saturdays. He said there was something he had to do. He didn't say what.'

'Did he sound cheerful?'

'Just the same as usual,' Edvard replied.

'Did you ever go to the gym together?'

'I went with him now and then. I just had a coffee – I don't work out.'

'Did he ever mention his parents?' Elínborg went on.

'No. Never.'

'Anything about his childhood, the village where he grew up?'

'No.'

'What *did* you talk about?'

'Football . . . and all that. Films. The usual stuff. Nothing important.'

'Women?'

'Sometimes.'

'Did you know what he thought of women, in a general way?'

'Nothing unusual or abnormal. He didn't hate women – his attitude was quite ordinary. If he saw an attractive girl or something like that, he'd mention it. As we do. All of us.'

'He was interested in films?'

'Yes. American action movies.'

'Superheroes?'

'Yes.'

'Why?'

'He just enjoyed them. Me too. It was one of the things we had in common.'

'Do you have pictures of them on your walls?'

'No.'

'Don't they all live a double life?'

'Who?'

'Those superheroes.'

'I don't know what you're getting at.'

'Aren't they usually ordinary blokes who change into someone else? In a phone box, or whatever? I'm no expert.'

'Yes, I suppose so.'

'Did your friend live a double life?'

'I wouldn't know.'

10

Indian restaurants in Reykjavík were few and far between, and Elínborg was familiar with all of them. She did the rounds in the hope of tracing the owner of the shawl, which she took with her and showed to the restaurant workers. The pungent aroma had faded now and nobody said they had seen the shawl before. Elínborg could rule the restaurant staff out easily: they were few in number, and most worked in family businesses; they had no difficulty providing alibis for where they'd been at the time of the crime.

The restaurants had a number of regular customers; the police gathered information about them and investigated them, again without result. The same applied to the very few Indians who lived in Iceland. Within a short time the police were able to conclude that none of them was involved in the case.

Elínborg knew of only one place in Reykjavík that sold tandoori pots, along with other equipment – supplies, spices, oils and so on – for Indian cuisine. She shopped there herself and was acquainted with the owner, who was also the only employee. Jóhanna was about Elínborg's age, an Icelander who had once lived in India. She was a very frank woman, ready to tell anyone and everyone all about herself, so Elínborg knew that Jóhanna had travelled widely in the east when she'd been young, and that for her India was a promised land. She had spent two years there before returning to Iceland and opening a shop selling Asian imports.

'I don't sell a lot of tandoori pots,' said Jóhanna. 'One or two a year, I'd say. And some people don't want them for cooking, but as ornaments.'

She knew that Elínborg was a police officer; she was familiar with her interest in cookery and had commented favourably on Elínborg's cookbook. Elínborg had explained that she was looking for a young woman of around thirty, who might be interested in Indian cuisine. She said no more and did not mention the case in which the girl was involved, but Jóhanna was far too inquisitive and talkative to settle for such meagre information.

'What do you want with her?' Jóhanna asked.

'It concerns a drugs case,' Elínborg replied. She did not feel she was straying too far from the truth. 'I'm not necessarily thinking of tandoori pots as such, but the spices in general: the saffron, coriander, annatto, garam masala, nutmeg. Do you have a customer who buys them regularly – maybe someone with dark hair, maybe about thirty?'

'A drugs case?'

Elínborg smiled.

'So I won't get any more out of you?'

'It's just a routine enquiry,' answered Elínborg.

'It's not that murder in Thingholt, is it? Aren't you working on that case?'

'Does anyone come to mind?' asked Elínborg, avoiding Jóhanna's question.

'Business isn't all that good at the minute,' said Jóhanna. 'People can buy a lot of these supplies online, or in the better supermarkets. I don't have many good, dependable customers like you. Not that I'm complaining.'

Elínborg waited patiently. Jóhanna saw that she was not interested in hearing about the challenges of running a small business.

'I can't think of anyone in particular,' she said. 'All

sorts of people come here, as you know. Including women of about thirty. A lot of dark-haired ones.'

'This one might have been in a few times. She's probably interested in Asian cookery, Indian food, tandoori dishes. You might have talked to her about it.'

Jóhanna did not speak for a long time. Then she shook her head.

Elínborg took the shawl out of her bag and unfolded it on the counter. All the necessary tests had now been completed. 'Can you remember a young woman coming into the shop wearing this shawl?'

Jóhanna examined the shawl carefully. 'Isn't this cashmere?' she asked.

'Yes.'

'It's beautiful. It's an Indian design. Where was it made?' She looked for a laundry label, but found none. 'I don't recall ever seeing it before,' she said. 'I'm sorry.'

'That's all right,' answered Elínborg. 'Thank you.' She folded the shawl up and returned it to her bag.

'Are you looking for its owner?' asked Jóhanna.

Elínborg nodded.

'I can give you a few names,' said Jóhanna after a lot of thought. 'I . . . there are names on credit-card receipts, and so on.'

'That would be a great help,' said Elínborg.

'You mustn't say where you got the information,' said Jóhanna. 'I don't want anyone to know.'

'I understand.'

'I don't want my customers finding out that I've told the police about my dealings with them.'

'Of course. I'll take care of it. Don't worry.'

'Do you want to go back a long way?'

'Just start with the last six months, if you don't mind.'

Of the people Runólfur had met through his work, the majority described a polite and personable engineer who came and dealt with their problems with their telephone, broadband or TV. Whether he had visited them at home or at a place of work, they all spoke well of him. The list of his call-outs over the past two months was quite extensive. Runólfur had been sent on such house calls once or twice a day throughout that period; in some cases he had returned to the same place twice, or even three times. His reputation was excellent. People found him helpful and easy to talk to; he was efficient, made a good impression and was unfailingly courteous. When a job took an unusually long time he had sometimes accepted a cup of coffee. Elsewhere his visits had been much briefer; if there was no major repair, he just dashed in and out again.

Police questions about whether there had been anything odd in the engineer's conduct yielded no results – until Elínborg called on a single mother named Lóa in her second-floor flat in Kópavogur. In her early thirties, Lóa was divorced and had a twelve-year-old son. At the time of Runólfur's death she had been away for the weekend with three friends.

'Yes, I remember it clearly. I got broadband for Kiddi,' she said when Elínborg asked her if she remembered Runólfur's visit.

They sat down in the living room. The flat was small, a riot of clean laundry and dirty clothes, unwashed dishes, a CD player, a hi-fi, two video-game handsets, a large TV, free newspapers and junk mail. Lóa apologised for the mess. She said she worked a lot, and the boy couldn't be bothered to do anything around the place. 'He just sits at the computer all day long,' she said wearily. Elínborg nodded, thinking of Valthór.

Lóa was not particularly surprised that the police wanted to talk to her when she heard that the enquiry was connected with Runólfur's death. She had seen the news reports and remembered meeting Runólfur when he'd installed the broadband connection; she found it hard to believe that he had met such a violent end. 'How can you slit someone's throat?' she murmured.

Elínborg shrugged. She took to Lóa at once. There was

absolutely no pretence in her, and everything she said came straight from the heart. It was clear that she had been through trials and tribulations but she also gave an impression of resilience. She smiled charmingly, with her eyes as well as her lips: Elínborg found her both likeable and interesting.

'That poor man,' said Lóa.

'This Kiddi, is that . . . ?'

'My son. He'd been asking for broadband for a whole year – some wireless Internet thing. So I eventually agreed, and I don't regret it. It's such an improvement, having a fast connection. Kiddi said he could set it up himself but it all went wrong, so I rang up and they sent that man.'

'I see,' said Elínborg.

'So what's this got to do with me, anyway?' Lóa asked. 'Why are you asking me about him? Have I . . . ?'

'We're trying to get information from people who had any kind of contact with him,' answered Elínborg. 'We don't know much about Runólfur, or how he came to be killed. We have to try to get an idea of the events. He was from a small village and he didn't have many friends here in Reykjavík, other than colleagues at work. There's hardly anyone else.'

'But, I mean, I didn't know the guy at all. He just came and installed the broadband.'

'Yes, I know. What did you make of him?'

'He was fine. He came after five, when I'd got home from work, just like you. He just got on with it, connected us to the Internet. It didn't take long. Then he left.'

'And he came just that once?'

'No, actually he called back the following day, or the day after, because he'd left something behind – a screwdriver, I think. He wasn't in so much of a hurry that time.'

'So you chatted, did you, or . . . ?'

'A bit. He was very pleasant. Nice enough. He told me he went to a gym.'

'Do you work out too? Did he recognise you from there?'

'No, he didn't know me. I can't be bothered with gyms and I told him so. I bought a year's gym membership once. Highly optimistic. But I stopped going after a few weeks. He said he was never tempted to give up.'

'Did you get the impression he was coming on to you?' asked Elínborg. 'Did he say anything like that?'

'No, nothing like that. He was just pleasant.'

'That's what everybody says. That he was a good guy.' Elínborg smiled briefly, and thought to herself that this interview had given her nothing. She was about to go when Lóa took her by surprise.

'Then, later, I bumped into him in town,' she said.

'You did?'

'I was out for the evening and there he was, all at once. He started talking to me like we were old friends. He was very friendly, wanted to buy me a drink and all that. Really nice.'

'So you met by chance?'

'Absolutely.'

'Did he know you'd be there?'

'No, not at all. It was quite random.'

'And what happened?'

'Happened? Nothing did. We just chatted and . . . nothing.'

'Were you alone?'

'Yes.'

'No one was with you?'

'No.'

'When you were chatting here, did you tell him where you like to go for an evening out? What your favourite places were, or anything?'

Lóa thought back. 'We mentioned it, but only in passing. I never thought . . . Hang on, are you connecting this to . . . ?'

'I don't know,' said Elínborg.

'He was talking about nightlife. He said he lived downtown and he asked me what it was like here in the suburbs, in Kópavogur. So we talked a bit about that when he came back that time, for his screwdriver or whatever. So far as I remember, it was something like that.'

'And did you mention anywhere?'

Lóa thought again.

'There's one place I always go.'

'Which one?'

'Thorvaldsen.'

'Is that where you met him?'

'Yes.'

'By chance?'

'It *is* a bit odd, when you put it like that.'

'What's odd?'

'I had the feeling, somehow, that he'd been waiting for me. I don't quite know what it was but there was something fake about the way he was so pleased to see me, and surprised to meet me there, and all that. What a pleasant coincidence it was, and so on. He . . . I don't know. Anyway, nothing happened. All of a sudden he seemed to lose interest, and then he went off.'

'You say he offered you a drink?'

'Yes.'

'And you accepted?' asked Elínborg.

'No. Well, yes, but not an alcoholic one.'

'Yes? What?' Elínborg was trying not to push her but she failed abjectly.

'I've given up drinking,' said Lóa. 'I can't. Not a drop.'

'I understand.'

'My husband left me, you see, and everything was such a mess, and I thought they were going to take Kiddi away from me, but I managed to stop. I go to meetings, and everything. It's saved my life.'

'So Runólfur suddenly lost interest?' asked Elínborg.

'Yes.'

'Because you didn't want a drink?'

'Why do you say that?'

'He offered you a drink, but you didn't accept, because you don't drink, and he lost interest.'

'I had a ginger ale. He bought it for me.'

'It's not the same,' said Elínborg.

'The same as what?'

'Alcohol. When he was here, did you tell him you don't drink?'

'No, it was none of his business. What are you getting at?'

Elínborg said nothing.

'So will I never meet anyone ever again, because I don't drink?'

Elínborg smiled at her reasoning. 'It's possible that Runólfur was rather unusual in that respect,' she said. 'I can't say any more.'

'What do you mean?'

'Haven't you seen the news?'

'Sort of.'

'There have been reports that a particular drug was found in Runólfur's home. A date-rape drug.'

Lóa gazed at her. 'That he used?' she asked.

'Possibly.'

'Don't they put it into alcoholic drinks?'

'Yes. The alcohol intensifies the effect – it affects the memory as well. It's more likely to cause amnesia if it's taken with alcohol.'

Lóa started connecting the dots: the telecoms engineer who came twice to her home, whom she then ran into by chance at a bar in town; the reports of date-rape drugs slipped into women's drinks; the alcoholism with which she had battled for many years; the soft drinks she always ordered when she went out; how Runólfur suddenly lost interest; his violent death. All at once she saw herself in a bizarre, chilly, terrifying place. 'I don't believe it,' she sighed, looking at Elínborg in astonishment. 'Are you kidding me?'

Elínborg did not say a word.

'Was he planning to rape me?'

'I don't know,' answered Elínborg.

'Bloody hell!' exclaimed Lóa in a sudden fury. 'He didn't find the screwdriver when he came back here. He said he'd left one behind. Looked everywhere. Talked to me as if we were old friends. Maybe there was no screwdriver. Was he having me on?'

Elínborg shrugged.

'What a bastard!' said Lóa, staring at Elínborg. 'I would have killed him, that bloody shit. I would so have fucking killed him! What on earth is wrong with these men?'

'They're crazy,' said Elínborg.

Binna Geirs was short for a far more sonorous name: Brynhildur Geirhardsdóttir. Elínborg thought it suited her: she was tall and heavily built, almost like a trollwife from a book of fairy tales, with long hair cascading down her back like thickets of vegetation. She had a large-featured face with a red nose, a powerful jaw and neck, and long arms. Her legs were like tree trunks. Next to her Fridbert seemed almost elflike: small and puny, with a completely bald head, big protruding ears, and small eyes under furry brows.

Solla had been right; Berti, sometimes known as Shorty for obvious reasons, had moved in with Binna. They were living in a small wooden house – which Binna had inherited from her parents – on Njálsgata near the city centre. She had somehow contrived not to lose it through the many vicissitudes of her life. The once-elegant little house with its traditional corrugated-iron cladding was now dilapidated, with a leaky roof, draughty windows and creeping rust. Looking after her possessions was not one of Binna's talents.

Binna and Berti were both at home the second time Elínborg called round. The first time she had knocked at the door there had been no answer, and she had seen no sign of life when she peeked in at the window. On the second occasion the door was flung open and Brynhildur Geirhardsdóttir herself stood in the doorway, displeased at the interruption. She was wearing an old woollen sweater and faded jeans, and in one hand she held a wooden spoon.

'Hello, Binna,' said Elínborg. She was not sure whether Binna was in any state to recognise her. 'I'm looking for Berti.'

'Berti?' snapped Binna. 'What do you want with him?'

'I just need a word with him. Is he in?'

'He's asleep in there,' said Binna, gesturing towards the darkened interior. 'Has he done something wrong?'

Elínborg saw that Binna knew who she was. Like Solla, Binna was one of the many people that Elínborg had run into in the course of her work when Binna had fallen foul of the police. Being so big and strong she sometimes got into fights. She had a difficult personality and drink had a bad effect upon her, making her even more moody and aggressive. Binna had assaulted police officers more than once when the worse for wear, and had been taken in handcuffs down to the station to sleep it off. She had been involved with various men over the

122

years, and by one of them she had had a son, long ago. Elínborg was wary of Binna Geirs, although the two of them had never clashed. She had intended to take Sigurdur Óli along for moral support but had not been able to reach him.

'No, not so far as I know,' said Elínborg. 'Can I come in and talk to him?'

Binna glowered down at Elínborg as if to weigh her up, before opening the door wider and letting her in. A familiar odour filled Elínborg's nostrils: Binna was boiling air-cured haddock. It was early evening and daylight was fading. No lights were on in the house and only the faint glow from outside illuminated the interior. It was cold, too, as if the heating was off. Berti lay on a sofa, asleep. Binna tapped him with the wooden spoon and told him to wake up. Berti did not respond so she grabbed his legs and shoved them off the sofa, bringing him tumbling to the floor. He awoke with a start, jumped to his feet, then sat back down on the sofa.

'What's up?' he asked blearily.

'You've got a visitor, and the grub's nearly ready,' said Binna, and retreated into the kitchen.

Elínborg's eyes gradually grew accustomed to the dark. She saw patches of damp on the old wallpaper, ancient worn-out furniture, filthy rugs on bare boards.

'What the hell do you want?'

'I'd like to ask you a few questions,' Elínborg replied.

'Questions? Who are you?' asked Berti, peering at her in the dim light.

'My name is Elínborg. I'm from the police.'

'A copper?'

'I won't keep you long. We're trying to find out how a man who was murdered recently got his hands on a drug, Rohypnol. You may have seen something about it on the news.'

'What's that got to do with me?' retorted Berti in a hoarse, sleepy voice. He was struggling to understand what was happening.

'We know you sometimes sell prescription medications,' said Elínborg.

'Me? I don't sell them. I don't sell anything.'

'Come off it. You're on our list. You've done time for dealing drugs.'

Elínborg took a photo of Runólfur out of her pocket and passed it to Berti. 'Did you know Runólfur?'

Berti took the picture from her. He reached over to a table lamp and switched it on, then put on a pair of reading glasses. He took his time examining the photo of the dead man.

'Isn't this the photo that was in the papers?' he asked.

'It's the same picture,' answered Elínborg.

'I'd never seen this man before he was on the news,'

said Berti. He placed the photograph on the table between them. 'Why was he killed?'

'We're trying to find out. He was carrying Rohypnol, which hadn't been prescribed by a doctor. We think he bought it from someone like you. He might have used it to spike the drinks of women he met.'

Berti gave Elínborg a long look. She knew he was weighing up the pros and cons of agreeing to help her or of keeping his mouth firmly shut. A rattling of dishes was heard from the kitchen where Binna was hard at work. Berti had been inside for various offences – breaking and entering, forgery, drug dealing – but he was no career criminal. 'I don't sell to blokes like that,' he observed at last.

'Blokes like that?'

'Who use it for that.'

'What would you know about how they use it?'

'I just know. I don't sell to pervs. I don't sell to blokes like that. And I've never met that guy. I'm not lying. I've never sold anything to him. I know who I sell to, and who I don't.'

Binna appeared in the doorway and glowered at Berti, still clutching the wooden spoon. The odour of cured fish wafted with her out of the kitchen.

'Where else could he have got hold of it?' asked Elínborg.

'I don't know,' answered Berti.

'Who sells roofies?'

'There's no point asking me. I don't know anything about it. And even if I did, I wouldn't tell you.' A faint, gleeful smile flickered across Berti's features.

'Is this about that perv that got sliced up?' Binna asked Elínborg sharply.

'Yes.'

'The one with the date-rape drug?'

Elínborg nodded. 'We're trying to find out where he got it from.'

'Did you sell it to him?' Binna asked Berti, with a fierce glare.

He did not meet her gaze. 'No, I never sold him anything,' he replied. 'I just told her, I never saw that bloke.'

'There you are, then,' said Binna.

'Maybe he can tell me about someone else who might have got the roofies for him,' said Elínborg.

Binna watched her for a long time, deep in thought. 'He was a rapist, wasn't he, that perv?' she asked.

'He might have been,' said Elínborg. 'There are indications.'

'Come and eat your grub, Berti,' said Binna. 'Tell her what you know, then come and eat.'

Berti stood up. 'I can't tell her what I don't know,' he complained.

Binna had turned to go back into the kitchen, but she stopped in the doorway, spun on her heel and pointed the wooden spoon threateningly at Berti. 'Tell her!' she ordered him.

Berti grimaced at Elínborg.

Binna went into the kitchen, and shouted over her shoulder: 'Then come and have your fish!'

11

Elínborg looked at the alarm clock on the bedside table: 00.17.

She started to count backwards from 10,000 in her mind again: 9,999. 9,998. 9,997. 9,996 . . .

She strove to empty her mind until nothing was left but a meaningless series of numbers. It was her way of calming her thoughts and getting off to sleep.

Sometimes, when she could not sleep at night, her mind wandered back to a period of her life which as a rule she did her best to forget. It was to do with her first husband. Level-headed Elínborg, who never rushed into anything but gave careful consideration to every decision, large and small, had entered into a marriage which had turned out to be built on sand.

While studying geology she had met a fellow student named Bergsteinn from the West Fjords region. He took himself rather seriously. He was reserved but likeable, and they had got to know each other during a field trip. Then they had started seeing each other regularly. They rented a flat, lived on student loans – which were quite generous in those days – and two years later went to the registry office and were married. They held a big party for their families and friends. On that day Elínborg was sure that they would live together happily ever after. But it was not to be.

Elínborg had given up geology and joined the police force by the time their marriage started to collapse. Bergsteinn had completed his postgraduate studies, then worked for the State Drilling Authority, which searched out geothermal resources all over the country. In due time he became a manager. He was kept busy attending conferences, both in Iceland and abroad.

For some time Elínborg had felt that something was wrong: she was uneasy about Bergsteinn's long absences from home, his lack of interest in her and what she was doing, his attitude to the future and to having children, which had in fact changed abruptly. One day he shamefacedly admitted that he had met another woman at a conference in Norway: an Icelandic geothermologist, he specified. He had been seeing her ever since, for nearly six months, and he envisaged a future with her.

Elínborg was overcome with rage. She had no interest in hearing Bergsteinn's excuses and explanations, and least of all in fighting another woman for him. She told him to get out. She did not know what had made him turn away from her and look elsewhere, but suspected that it was something in his own character and nothing to do with her personally. At that point she did not care what he thought. She had been honest in the relationship, had respected him, loved him, and had believed it was mutual; the most painful part of the break-up was to know that she had been wrong. And to be rejected was a bitter experience, though she did not share that with anyone. In Elínborg's view, the failure of their marriage was entirely his fault; if he wanted a divorce, so be it. She was not going to try to win him back. Their divorce went through without any serious obstruction. Bergsteinn had destroyed their marriage, and he was gone. That was all there was to it.

Over insipid liver in brown onion gravy, Elínborg's mother confided that she had never really liked Bergsteinn, who she thought was a feeble idiot.

'Oh, come off it!' retorted Elínborg as she nibbled at the liver.

'He was always such a twerp,' said her mother.

Elínborg was well aware that her mother was trying to cheer her up, because she knew her daughter and realised that Elínborg was more deeply wounded than she would admit.

She grew more depressed and lonely than she had ever been, and was reluctant to talk about either Bergsteinn or the divorce. She resolved to grin and bear it, while underneath she was a seething mass of rage and helplessness and grief.

Her mother had a much higher opinion of Teddi, and was always commenting on what a solid, dependable man he was. 'He's so reliable, your Theodór,' she said.

Which he was. Elínborg had met Teddi at the annual police dinner, which he attended with a friend who had since left the force. Teddi was great fun, but Elínborg was not yet ready for a new relationship. Teddi, who like her was twenty-eight, was keener, and set out to win her over. He took her home from the police dance, rang two days later, then invited her to the cinema and dinner. She told him all about her failed marriage. For his part, he had never lived with anyone. She heard from Teddi's policeman friend that he had a sister who was enduring a long battle with cancer. The next time she saw him, she asked him cautiously about his sister, and he told her that she was the single mother of a son, that he and his nephew were close. His sister had been fighting the disease for years but the prognosis was not good. He had wanted to tell Elínborg about her, he said, but he had been hesitant as he did not know whether anything would come of their relationship.

Teddi's sister, it transpired, was very much in favour of her brother's new girlfriend, and was eager to meet Elínborg. He took her to visit one day, and the two women had a long talk while the uncle and nephew went on an expedition in search of ice cream. Teddi was caring and affectionate towards his sister; Elínborg was constantly discovering new aspects of his character.

Six months later she moved in with Teddi, who had a studio flat in the Háaleiti district and owned a garage in partnership with a friend. When Teddi's sister died of cancer the following year, the couple gained a foster-son. She had hardly known the boy's father, they had never lived together, and he had had nothing to do with his son. The boy, Birkir, was six years old; his mother had asked Teddi and Elínborg to take care of her little boy. They bought a larger flat and adopted Birkir, who missed his mother deeply. Elínborg embraced her new son unreservedly, doing all she could to ease his pain. She took time off work and made sure he settled in well at his new school. From the start, Elínborg's parents accepted the boy as their own grandchild.

Elínborg did not marry again; she and Teddi remained partners. Valthór was born, followed by Aron and finally Theodóra, all of whom worshipped Birkir, especially Valthór, who made him his role model from the first time he drew breath. When Birkir left home, Valthór blamed his mother for what happened, which made their relationship even more difficult.

Elínborg looked at the alarm clock. 03.08.

In four short hours she would have to get up, and she knew that her lack of sleep would make tomorrow a disaster.

Beside her Teddi slept peacefully. She envied him the calm disposition that had always been characteristic of him. She considered getting up and going into the kitchen to look at some recipes but found the effort too much, and started yet again to count down from 10,000.

9,999. 9,998. 9,997. 9,996 . . .

The Firm resembled the first gym that Elínborg had visited, but was considerably larger and in a better location. She arrived there, barely able to keep her eyes open after her sleepless night, on the Saturday morning one week after Runólfur's murder. People were pouring in: running, weightlifting, working up a sweat. Some brought their children, as The Firm offered a crèche, which was crammed. Elínborg was a little taken aback by the sight

– it seemed to be no more than a dumping ground in which a crowd of kids were watching cartoons on a gigantic flatscreen.

She sometimes worried about relationships between parents and their children: young children would spend all week in day care from early morning until five or so, and at the weekend some faced yet more hours in the crèche, while their parents were perspiring on the tread-mill. On a working day the children would probably go to bed at around nine p.m., having spent a total of two hours with their parents, most of which consisted of feeding them and getting them to bed. When their children were small Elínborg and Teddi had reduced their working hours in order to take better care of their family. They hadn't seen it as a sacrifice, but both a necessity and a pleasure.

Elínborg was shown in to meet the manager, who was busy taking delivery of two new flatscreens to be installed in the main gym. There was clearly a problem with the consignment since he was refusing delivery of one of the screens, and was on the phone venting his displeasure. Once he had hung up, he turned to Elínborg with a snarl and asked her what was the matter.

'Matter?' she asked. 'There's nothing the matter.'

'Oh,' replied the manager. 'Then what do you want?'

'I want to ask you about a man who used to come here

but stopped about two years ago. I'm from the police. You've probably heard about him on the news.'

'About who?'

'He lived in Thingholt.'

'The guy who was killed?' asked the manager.

Elínborg nodded. 'Do you remember him?'

'I remember him well. We didn't have so many clients back then and I used to know almost all of them. Now it's completely crazy. What about him? What's he got to do with us?'

A teenage girl appeared in the office doorway. 'One of the kids has thrown up everywhere,' she told the manager.

'So?'

'We can't find the parents.'

The manager gave Elínborg an apologetic smile. 'Talk to Silla,' he said to the girl. 'She'll sort it out.'

'Yeah, but I can't find her.'

'You can see I'm in a meeting here,' he said. 'Go and find Silla, dear.'

'The kid's sick as a dog,' whined the girl. 'This is just too much,' she grumbled as she left.

'I take it you're talking about Runólfur?' said the manager, who was wearing a blue tracksuit emblazoned with the logo of a fashionable and expensive sportswear label.

'Did you know him?'

'Only as a client. He worked out here all the time, pretty much from when we opened four years ago. He was one of our first members. Then he stopped coming here. He was a good guy. Kept himself fit.'

'Do you know why he left?'

'No idea. I never saw him again. Then I saw the report on the news – I could hardly believe it. Why are you asking us about him? Have we got something to do with his death?'

'No, not so far as I know. It's a routine enquiry. We know this was his gym.'

'Yes, I see.'

'Did anyone else stop coming here around the same time as him? Anyone who used to train here?'

The manager gave the matter some thought.

'I don't really remember . . .'

'A woman, maybe?'

'No, I don't think so.'

'Do you remember whether he was well liked, as a client?'

'Oh, yes, he was. Very well liked. Actually . . .'

'Yes?'

'You asked about women.'

'Yes.'

'There was one girl who worked for me, now you mention it,' said the manager. 'I'm not sure whether they both left at exactly the same time but it was certainly about then. Frída was her name. I don't remember the surname. Nice girl. A personal trainer. I can dig out the full name for you, if you like. They used to hang out together.'

'Were they a couple?'

'No, I don't think it went that far. But they got along well, and I think they may have gone out for drinks together, that kind of thing.'

The young woman stepped hesitantly into the flat that Runólfur had rented in Thingholt, and looked apprehensively around her. Elínborg was immediately behind her. Both Unnur's parents were there, as was the psychiatrist who had been treating her. Elínborg had been forced to take a firm line with Unnur to persuade her to agree to look at the flat. Her mother had finally sided with Elínborg and had urged her daughter to do what she could to help the police.

Nothing had been altered since Runólfur's body had been removed. The crime scene had been left untouched, and Unnur hesitated when she saw the blackened dried blood on the floor.

'I don't want to go in,' she begged.

'I know, Unnur,' replied Elínborg reassuringly. 'It will only take a minute, and then you can go home.'

Unnur stepped cautiously through the hall and into the living room, where she averted her gaze from the blood-stains. She looked at the superhero posters, the sofa, the coffee table and TV. She glanced up at the ceiling. It was late evening. 'I don't think I've ever been here,' she murmured to herself. She inched her way from the living room into the kitchen, with Elínborg at her heels. They had already examined Runólfur's car, which had been impounded by the police. It rang no bells for Unnur.

It was also possible that she did not want to remember.

They reached the bedroom doorway, and Unnur looked down at the double bed – the quilt lay on the floor and at the head were two pillows. As in the living room, the floor was parquet. The bed was flanked by small bedside tables. Elínborg presumed that this was for symmetry, as Runólfur would not need two just for himself. On each was a small reading lamp, testament to the owner's good taste, like everything else in the flat; Elínborg had noticed on her first visit that Runólfur's home had a certain style and charm. On either side of the bed was a small rug. Clothes hung in the wardrobe, while his shirts were neatly folded and his underwear and socks arranged in drawers in an orderly fashion. Runólfur's home revealed that he had his life completely under control and took pleasure in nice things.

'I've never been here,' said Unnur. Elínborg sensed her

relief. Unnur stood motionless in the bedroom doorway, as if she did not dare enter.

'Are you sure?' she asked.

'Nothing's familiar,' said Unnur. 'I don't remember this place at all.'

'We've got plenty of time.'

'No, I don't remember ever being here. Not here, nor anywhere else in this flat. Can we go now? I can't help you. I'm sorry. I feel uncomfortable in this place. Can we leave?'

Unnur's mother gave Elínborg a pleading look.

'Of course,' said Elínborg. 'Thank you for being willing to do this.'

'Was she in here?' Unnur took one step into the bedroom.

'We think he was with a woman the night he was killed,' said Elínborg. 'He had sex shortly before the attack.'

'Poor girl,' said Unnur. 'I suppose he brought her here against her will?'

'That's a possibility.'

'But if he drugged her, how could she have killed him?'

'We don't know. We haven't worked out what happened yet.'

'Can I go home now?'

'Of course. Whenever you want. Thank you for doing this, I know it wasn't easy.'

139

Elínborg escorted Unnur and her parents out and saw them off from outside the house, watching the family disappear down the road. They were a sad little company, all three of them victims of unspeakable violence and depravity. Their lives had been devastated, and there was nothing they could do about it except weep in silence.

Elínborg wrapped her coat tightly around her as she returned to the car, wondering if she had another restless, wakeful night in store.

12

Frída bore a strong resemblance to Lóa. She was about the same age, a little stockier, dark-haired, with beautiful brown eyes behind dainty glasses. She was not especially surprised to be visited by the police. She said that she had already been thinking of contacting them, having read about the drug found at the murder scene. She was frank and energetic, and ready to tell Elínborg everything she knew.

'It's awful, reading about it in the papers,' she said. 'I didn't know what to do. It was such a shock. Just think, I once went home with that man. He could have drugged me.'

'Did you go to his place?' asked Elínborg.

'No, he came here. It was only the once, but that was more than enough.'

'What happened?'

'It's just so embarrassing,' said Frída. 'I hardly know how to explain it. I got to know him quite well, but we weren't dating or anything. And it's not something I generally do. Not at all. I . . . but there was something about him.'

'Do what?' asked Elínborg.

'Sleep with them,' said Frída, with an awkward smile. 'Not unless I'm really sure.'

'Sure that what?'

'That they're all right.'

Elínborg nodded as if to say that she understood, but she was uncertain. She looked around at the flat. Frída said she lived alone, with two cats, which were twining themselves around Elínborg's legs. They were determined to show her who was boss. One took a massive leap into her lap. The flat was on the second floor of a block in one of Reykjavík's older districts. From the windows the Bláfjöll mountains could be glimpsed between two more blocks of flats.

'No, I mean, I've used the personal ads, and I go clubbing, and all that,' explained Frída with some embarrassment. 'You do what you can, but the market . . . those guys are nothing to write home about.'

'The *market*?'

'Yes.'

'Was it because of Runólfur that you left your job at the gym?' asked Elínborg.

'I suppose so. It was one of the reasons. I didn't want to risk running into him. Then I heard he'd left and gone to another gym, and I never saw him again, until it was on the news.'

'So he wasn't *all right*, as you put it?' asked Elínborg, shoving at the cat, which jumped down to the floor with a squeal and vanished into the kitchen. The other cat then followed its example and jumped into Elínborg's lap. She did not particularly like cats. They sensed it, though, and would not leave her alone, as if they were trying to win her over. That would not happen any time soon.

'I should never have invited him here,' said Frída. 'He wanted to take me back to his place but I wouldn't go. It annoyed him, although he tried to conceal it.'

'Was he used to getting his own way, do you think? Was that what it was?'

'I don't know. Do you know anything about him?'

'Not a lot,' replied Elínborg. 'Did he talk about himself at all?'

'Very little.'

'We know he was from a small village.'

'He never mentioned it. I assumed he was from Reykjavík.'

'Did he talk about any friends, or family?'

'No. I didn't really know him that well. We used to chat about the gym, and films, that sort of thing. He never said anything to me about his personal life. I know he had a friend called Edvard, but I never met him.'

'What do you make of Runólfur, based on your short acquaintance?'

'He was a narcissist,' said Frída, pushing her glasses up. 'I'm sure he was. He worshipped himself. Like down at The Firm – he was in good shape, and not shy about showing off. He would strut around the place, trying to get the women to notice him, always putting on a show.'

'So he . . .'

'And there was definitely something weird about him,' Frída went on.

'Weird?'

'You know . . . with women.'

'We don't know whether he used the date-rape drug, although it was found at his home,' said Elínborg. She did not mention that Runólfur had also swallowed Rohypnol himself.

'No, that's not what I mean,' said Frída. 'I read about the drug you found – I wasn't surprised.'

'Really?'

'He was really strange, the one time we . . . you know . . .'

'I don't quite follow.'

'No. It's not easy to talk about it,' sighed Frída.

'But you knew him *quite* well, then?' asked Elínborg, trying to work out where the conversation was leading.

'No, not really,' said Frída. 'Not well at all. These guys who come into the gym, they think they're God's gift, but Runólfur was always very polite to me. We would sometimes talk, and he asked me once if I'd like to go out to dinner. I said yes. He was very friendly, that wasn't the problem. He could chat, and be funny and all that, but I still got the feeling that he was unhappy.'

'Did he ever talk about it? Express how he felt?'

'No, not at all. Not to me. When it came to the point, you see, he came over all shy and awkward. And after that he was just creepy.'

'Really?'

'Yeah, he wanted me to . . .'

'What?'

'Um, I don't know.'

'What did he want?'

'He wanted me to play dead.'

'Dead?' echoed Elínborg.

Frída looked at her. 'Dead,' she repeated. 'I wasn't to

move, if you see what I mean. I was supposed to lie still and hardly breathe. Then he started slapping me and shouting at me. I didn't understand why. The words he used! It was as if he was in a world of his own.' Frída shuddered at the memory. 'What a pervert!' she added.

'So it wasn't rape, as such?'

'No. And he didn't injure me, really. He didn't hit me hard.'

'What did you do?'

'I just froze up. That seemed to be what turned him on, and then it was all over. He was pathetic afterwards. He left without a word, and I lay there paralysed, completely at a loss. I didn't tell anyone, it was just too . . . I was embarrassed. It wasn't rape, but I felt as if I had been raped. Looking back, I think that was what he wanted. I think that was the whole point.'

'And you never saw him again?'

'No. I avoided him, and he never got in touch. Just as well. It was as if he'd made his use of me. I would never have agreed to see him again. Never.'

'And then you left the gym?'

'I did. I feel soiled just talking about it, especially after I read about him, what happened.'

'Did you know – or do you know now – about any other women in his life? Did he ever mention any female friends?'

'No, no one,' said Frída. 'I know nothing about him, and I don't want to.'

Elínborg knocked at the door. Berti had finally been persuaded to give her the name of a drug dealer, Valur, who lived in a block of flats in the suburbs with his partner and two children. The investigation had made little progress. Elínborg had uncovered nothing more about the shawl, and no clothes shop in the Reykjavík area had sold T-shirts with a San Francisco design.

A man in his thirties opened the door. With a baby girl slung on his arm, he looked with hostility at Elínborg and Sigurdur Óli in turn. Elínborg had felt that it would be safer not to make this call alone. She did not know much about Valur, who had crossed paths with the Drug Squad from time to time, both as a user and as a dealer, though always strictly small-time. He had once been caught smuggling a small quantity of marijuana into the country, for which he had received a short suspended sentence. Berti might have lied to her: maybe he wanted to get Valur into trouble, had a grudge against him; or perhaps he had just thought of a name in order to placate his beloved Binna.

'What do you want?' the man demanded.

'Are you Valur?' asked Elínborg.

'What's that got to do with you?'

'We need to talk to him,' snapped Sigurdur Óli. 'What do you think?'

'What's your problem?' the man retorted.

'Just calm down, will you, mate,' said Sigurdur Óli.

'Are you Valur?' Elínborg asked again. Perhaps it had been a mistake to bring Sigurdur Óli.

'I'm Valur,' the man replied. 'Who are you?' He transferred the baby over to his other arm, and looked again from Elínborg to Sigurdur Óli.

'We need information about a man named Runólfur,' explained Elínborg, and introduced herself and her colleague. 'Can we come in and talk to you?'

'You're not coming in here,' answered Valur.

'All right,' said Elínborg. 'Did you know this Runólfur?'

'I don't know any Runólfur.'

The baby had a toy in her hand, which she was sucking with intense concentration. She was so endearing, safe in her daddy's arms, that Elínborg had to resist the urge to ask if she could hold her for a minute.

'He was in his own home when his throat was cut,' explained Sigurdur Óli.

Valur looked at him with disdain. 'Doesn't mean I know him.'

'Can you tell us where you were when he was killed?' asked Sigurdur Óli.

'We think you—' Elínborg got no further.

'Do I have to talk to you?' asked Valur.

'We're only looking for information,' said Elínborg. 'That's all.'

'Yeah, well, you can fuck off,' he sneered.

'You can either answer our questions here, or you can come to the station and answer them there,' she said. 'It's up to you.'

Valur was still looking from one detective to the other. 'I've got nothing to say,' he said. As he was about to shut the door in their faces Sigurdur Óli flung himself forward and leaned against it.

'Then you're coming with us,' he said.

Valur stared at them through the gap. He saw that they meant what they said. Even if he refused to let them in this time, they would not leave him alone.

'Wanker,' he said, releasing the door.

'Scumbag,' said Sigurdur Óli and shoved his way in.

'Charming,' said Elínborg, following him in. The place was a mess of dirty laundry, old newspapers and leftover food. There was a nasty sour smell in the air. Valur was home alone except for the younger of his children. He put her down on the floor where she sat still, chewing on her toy and dribbling.

'What do you want?' Valur asked Elínborg. 'Are you accusing me of topping him?'

'Well, did you?' she asked.

'No,' replied Valur. 'I didn't know the man.'

'We think you knew him well,' said Sigurdur Óli. 'Shouldn't you tidy up in here?' he added, looking around.

'Says who?'

'Just look at this place. It's a pigsty,' said Sigurdur Óli.

'Are you retarded, or what?' exclaimed Valur. 'Who says I knew him well?'

'Information received,' said Elínborg.

'Someone's spinning you a line.'

'It's a reliable source,' she replied, trying not to think about Shorty.

'Says who? Who is it?'

'None of your business,' snapped Sigurdur Óli. 'We've been told you knew Runólfur and sold him stuff, supplied him with this and that.'

'Maybe he owed you money,' said Elínborg. 'Maybe you went round to collect, and things got out of hand.'

Valur stared at her, open-mouthed. 'Hey, hang on, what the hell is this? Who says that? I didn't know the bloke, didn't know him at all. Someone's telling lies about me. And you're saying I'm supposed to have killed him? Absolutely not! I had nothing to do with it. Don't even go there.'

The child looked up at her father and stopped chewing.

'We can take you down to the station,' said Elínborg. 'We can lock you up. We can treat you as a suspect and read you your rights. OK, we haven't got much evidence yet, but we have to start somewhere. We can hold you in custody for a few days. You'll need a lawyer, which will cost you. The papers and the telly will report that we've made an arrest, and they'll dig up pictures of you. Information tends to leak out – you know how it is. The tabloids will publish a front-page interview with your girlfriend in the weekend edition: there'll be a photo of her with your little girl here. I can see the headline: *My Valur Is No Killer!*'

'Why do you think I know something?'

'Please,' said Elínborg, and bent down to pick up the baby from the floor. 'You get doctors to prescribe all sorts of drugs for you, which you sell on at a much higher price. Prescription medications. Like roofies. You probably sell them mostly to coke users, who are out of stuff and scared of coming down. We've heard you supply the coke, too. So it's a comprehensive service you provide. Maybe you use coke yourself? You look as if you probably do. Must be expensive. How do you find the cash?'

'What are you doing with the kid?'

'Then there's the odd one who uses roofies to—'

'Give her here,' said Valur, snatching the baby.

'Sorry. Then there's the odd one who uses roofies to spike women's drinks and have sex with them when they're

151

helpless. That's what we call a rapist. The question is: do you sell roofies to rapists?'

'No,' said Valur.

'Quite sure?'

'Yes.'

'How can you be? You haven't a clue what they do with it after you sell it to them.'

'I just do. And I didn't know that Runólfur bloke.'

'Do you use roofies on women yourself?'

'No, what . . . ?'

'Is that your flatscreen telly?' Sigurdur Óli asked, pointing at a brand-new 42-inch plasma screen.

'Yeah,' said Valur, 'it's mine.'

'Got the receipt, have you?'

'Receipt?'

'You must have a receipt for an expensive bit of kit like that.'

'All right,' said Valur. 'I used to sell – you know about it, you've got it on file. But I'm not selling any more, and I never sold much prescription medicine anyway. The last time I sold any roofies was about six months ago. Some idiot I've never seen before, or since.'

'Not Runólfur?' asked Elínborg. She noticed that Valur was willing to talk about anything other than the plasma TV.

'He was really nervous. He said his name was Runólfur.

He was about to shake hands with me, as if we were at some important meeting or something. He said a relative had told him about me. He gave me a name, but I'd never heard of him. It was like he'd never done it before.'

'Did he come back often?'

'No, just that once. I didn't know him. I usually know who they are. The punters. You build up a group of regulars. He was kind of a weirdo.'

'And why did he want the roofies?'

'He said he was buying them for a friend. That's what they all say – when they're new and don't know what sad little losers they are.'

'And it was definitely Rohypnol he bought?'

'Yeah.'

'How much did you sell him?'

'One bottle. Ten pills.'

'Did he come here? To your place?'

'Yeah.'

'Was he alone?'

'Yeah.'

'And was it Runólfur?'

'Yes. No. Look, he said his name was Runólfur but it wasn't him.'

'Not the Runólfur who was murdered?'

'No, it wasn't that bloke whose picture was in the papers.'

'So was he posing as Runólfur?'

'How would I know? Maybe his name was Runólfur too. Maybe it's a coincidence. Do you think I give a fuck?'

'What did he look like?'

'I don't remember.'

'Try.'

'About my height, probably thirty-something. Fat face, balding, with a bit of a beard. I don't remember him very clearly.'

Elínborg looked at Valur. Suddenly she recalled the man she had interviewed in her office, Runólfur's friend. Edvard. The description fitted him well.

'Anything else?' she asked.

'No. I don't know anything else.'

'Thank you.'

'Yeah, whatever. Now fuck off out of here.'

'At least he takes good care of the baby,' sighed Elínborg once they were back in the car. 'Her nappy was dry, and she'd just been fed. She was fine with her daddy.'

'He's a piece of shit.'

'No doubt.'

'Have you heard from Erlendur at all?' asked Sigurdur Óli.

'No, he hasn't been in touch. He said he was going to the east for a few days, didn't he?'

'How long's he been gone?'

'Must be over a week.'

'How much holiday was he taking?'

'I don't know.'

'What was he planning to do there?'

'He's visiting the place where he lived as a boy.'

'Have you heard anything from that woman he's been seeing?'

'Valgerdur? No. I probably ought to give her a ring. See if she's heard from him.'

13

It was evening when Elínborg and Sigurdur Óli pulled up outside Edvard's home, a dilapidated house on the west side of town. Edvard was unmarried, and childless. His car was parked beside the house – a Japanese hatchback, several years old. Elínborg knocked, and they heard movement from within. But nobody came to the door. Lights were visible in two windows and they had noticed the glow of a television, which was suddenly extinguished. They knocked again, then a third time. Sigurdur Óli hammered at the door, and finally Edvard appeared. He recognised Elínborg at once.

'Is this a bad time?' she asked.

'No, well, it's . . . is something the matter?'

'We've got some more questions about Runólfur,' explained Elínborg. 'Can we come in?'

'It's really not convenient now,' answered Edvard. 'I was on my way out.'

'It'll only take a minute,' said Sigurdur Óli.

They stood at the threshold while Edvard stubbornly blocked their way.

'I really can't invite you in at the moment,' he protested. 'I'd appreciate it if you could come back later – maybe tomorrow.'

'Yes, well, no, I'm afraid that won't be possible,' Elínborg replied. 'It's to do with Runólfur, as I said, and we have to speak to you now.'

'What about him?' asked Edvard.

'We'd really prefer not to have this conversation here, on the doorstep.'

Edvard glanced out into the street. The house was cloaked in darkness, with no street lamp nearby and no porch light. It faced straight on to the street without a front garden, but by the wall stood a single tree, a dead alder, whose naked, contorted branches loomed over the roof like the paw of a great beast.

'Yeah, well, come in, then. I don't see what you want from me,' the detectives heard Edvard mumble. 'We were just friends.'

'This will only take a minute,' said Elínborg.

They entered a small living room, sparsely furnished with old, worn furniture. A large, new-looking flatscreen hung on one wall, and on the desk stood a brand-new computer with a huge monitor. Computer games of many kinds were scattered around and arranged on shelves, along with a vast array of films on DVD and video cassettes. Tables and chairs were also piled high with documents, papers and textbooks.

'Marking essays?' asked Elínborg.

'Is that a serious question?' asked Edvard, eyeing the stacks of paper on the table. 'Yes, it's time I handed them back. They do tend to pile up.'

'Do you collect films?' asked Elínborg.

'No, I'm not a collector as such, but I have quite a lot, as you can see. I sometimes buy them from rental shops when they close down. They're sold off dirt cheap.'

'Have you watched them all?' asked Sigurdur Óli.

'No . . . yeah . . . pretty much. Most of them.'

'You said you knew Runólfur very well,' said Elínborg. 'Last time we spoke.'

'Yes, quite well. I liked him.'

'And you shared an interest in films, if I remember correctly.'

'We used to go to the cinema sometimes.'

Elínborg noticed that Edvard was more uncomfortable than at their previous encounter. He seemed uneasy having visitors in his home. He did not look them in the eye, and his hands wandered restlessly over the desk. Finally, he thrust them into his pockets, but before long he was scratching his head or his arm, or fiddling with the DVD cases. Elínborg decided it was time to put him out of his misery. She picked up a film from a chair, one of Hitchcock's early silents, *The Lodger*. Elínborg had prepared carefully, and was about to ask her first question, but Sigurdur Óli was impatient – not for the first time. He was especially edgy with individuals who were vulnerable, or had low self-esteem, and was quick to pinpoint their weaknesses.

'Why didn't you tell us you'd bought a date-rape drug?' he asked abruptly.

'What?'

'Using Runólfur's name. Were you buying it for him?'

Elínborg glared at Sigurdur Óli. She had made it clear to him that she intended to conduct this interview. He was supposed to be there purely for support.

'Why?' Sigurdur Óli went on. He was unsure what to make of Elínborg's enraged expression. He thought he was doing pretty well. 'Why did you pretend to be Runólfur?'

159

'I don't know . . . what?' babbled Edvard, shoving his hands into his pockets again.

'We've got a witness who sold you Rohypnol about six months ago,' said Sigurdur Óli.

'The description fits you,' said Elínborg. 'He said you used the name Runólfur.'

'What description?' asked Edvard.

'He described you to a T,' said Elínborg.

'So?' said Sigurdur Óli.

'So, what?' asked Edvard.

'Is it true?' asked Sigurdur Óli.

'Who says so?'

'Your drug dealer!' barked Sigurdur Óli. 'Aren't you listening?'

'Would you mind just letting me talk to him?' Elínborg said calmly.

'Tell him that if he doesn't cooperate we'll take him to the dealer and get the truth out of him that way,' said Sigurdur Óli menacingly.

'I did it as a favour for Runólfur,' Edvard admitted, intimidated by Sigurdur Óli's threat. 'He asked me to do it.'

'What did he want the drug for?' asked Elínborg.

'He told me he had difficulty sleeping.'

'So why didn't he go to a doctor and ask for a prescription?'

'I didn't really know what this Rohypnol stuff was, not until after Runólfur was killed. I had no idea.'

'Do you expect us to buy that?' asked Elínborg.

'We weren't born yesterday,' growled Sigurdur Óli.

'Honestly, I don't know anything about drugs.'

'How did Runólfur find this drug dealer?' asked Elínborg.

'He didn't say.'

'Apparently you mentioned some relative of yours?'

Edvard thought for a moment. 'The supplier wanted to know. He was very nervous. Demanded to know who I was, how I'd heard about him. He was quite a scary bloke. Runólfur sent me to him and that's why I used his name. I made up the thing about my relative.'

'Why didn't Runólfur just buy the stuff himself? Why did he get you to go?' asked Elínborg.

'We were friends. He said . . .'

'Yes?'

'He said he didn't trust doctors, or patient records. And he confided that he drank a bit and the Rohypnol was helpful for hangovers. He said he didn't want to draw attention to the fact that he was using it, because it was a problematical drug. He was uncomfortable asking a doctor for it. That's what he said. I wasn't really sure what he was on about.'

'But why did he get you to go?'

161

Edvard hesitated. 'He asked me to go as a favour to him,' he said finally.

'Why?'

'I don't know. He was embarrassed to do it himself, and . . .'

'And?'

'I don't have a lot of friends. Runólfur and I were mates, and I wanted to help him out. He came to me with his problem and I said I'd take care of it. That's all there was to it. I wanted to do him a favour.'

'How much did you buy?'

'One bottle.'

'Who else have you bought from?'

'Who else? No one else. It was just that one time.'

'Why didn't you tell me about this when we spoke the other day?'

Edvard shrugged abjectly. 'I thought I'd get dragged into something that was nothing to do with me.'

'Don't you think it might have something to do with you, if you've bought Rohypnol for someone who might have been a rapist?'

'I didn't know what he was going to do with it.'

'Where were you when Runólfur was killed?'

'Here. At home.'

'Can anyone corroborate that?'

'No. I'm alone at home most evenings. You're not seriously alleging that I did it?'

'We're not alleging anything,' replied Elínborg. 'Thank you for your help,' she added curtly.

Elínborg and Sigurdur Óli returned to the car. Elínborg was apoplectic. 'What the hell was that?' she snapped, and started the car.

'What do you mean?'

'You ruined it, you bloody idiot. I've never seen anything like it. You played right into his hands. Now we have no idea whether he really was buying for Runólfur! You've got no evidence! How could you say that? You handed it to him on a silver platter!'

'What are you talking about?'

'It's the perfect get-out for Edvard.'

'Get-out? You don't really think he was buying it for himself?'

'Why not?' asked Elínborg. 'Maybe the pills Runólfur used were Edvard's. He could be an accessory. Maybe he attacked Runólfur.'

'That wimp?'

'There you go again. Can't you treat people with a bit of respect?'

'He wouldn't have needed any help from me to make

up a story like that. I bet he came up with it ages ago –
that is, if he *is* lying to us.'

'Why won't you ever admit you've made a mistake?'
asked Elínborg. 'You screwed up. Royally.'

'Hey, steady on.'

'He picked up on what you said. I think everything he
said after that was a lie.' Elínborg sighed heavily. 'I've never
had a case like this before.'

'Like what?'

'Every single person I speak to seems to be a viable
suspect.'

14

Elínborg's father was resting in the bedroom. It was Monday, his bridge night, and he would be going out to one of his friends' homes. He had been playing bridge on Monday evenings with the same group for as long as Elínborg could remember. Year had followed uneventful year in a blur of bids and slams. They had grown old gracefully, those young men who had once patted her on the head and teased her and played cards, and consumed the snacks served by her mother. They had a quiet dignity, a friendliness, and an inexhaustible eagerness to explore the mysteries of bridge. Elínborg had never learned the game, nor had her father shown any interest in teaching her. He was a good player and had taken part in tournaments, occasionally bringing home a minor trophy, which he would put away in a drawer. But age had its consequences and these days, if he was to be alert for an evening at the card table, he needed to take a nap in the afternoon.

'Hello, dear!' said Elínborg's mother as she opened the door. Elínborg had her own key and let herself in.

'Just thought I'd look in.'

'Is everything all right?'

'Yes. How are you?' asked Elínborg.

'I'm well. I'm thinking of doing a bookbinding course.' Her mother was sitting in the living room, reading an advert in the paper. 'My friend Anna is doing it, and she says I should try it too.'

'That's a good idea, isn't it? You can take the old man with you.'

'I don't think so. He can never be bothered to do anything. How's Teddi?'

'He's fine.'

'And what about you?'

'Fine. Busy.'

'I can see that – you look a bit tired. I've been reading about this awful murder in Thingholt. I just hope you're not involved with that. It's not the kind of thing normal people can cope with.'

Elínborg had heard it all before. Her mother was disappointed that she had 'finished up' in the police, as she put it. She thought the job was beneath her daughter. Not because it was unimportant – far from it – but she simply could not bear to think of her Elínborg dealing with crooks. She imagined other people – nothing like her daughter – pursuing criminals, arresting them, questioning them and locking them up. Her daughter just wasn't that kind of woman.

Elínborg had long ago given up defending her profession. She understood that most of her mother's objections stemmed from fears of her daughter being surrounded by the dregs of humanity. Elínborg did what she could to protect her mother by playing down her role in apprehending violent criminals and giving her a sanitised impression of the job. Perhaps she had gone too far. Sometimes Elínborg felt her mother was in a state of denial about her line of work. 'Really, there are days when I can't help wondering what I'm doing in this job,' Elínborg said.

'Of course you do,' her mother answered. 'Would you like some hot chocolate?'

'No, thanks. I just wanted to check that you were both all right. I'll be off home now.'

'Now, now, dear, it will only take a minute. No need to rush away – they're all old enough to look after themselves. Sit down for a minute and relax.'

Quick as a flash, her mother had placed a saucepan on the stove, with a little water in the bottom and a bar of dark chocolate that was melting in seconds.

Elínborg sat at the kitchen table. Her mother's handbag was hanging from the back of a chair. She remembered how she had always liked the fragrance of her mother's bag when she'd been a little girl. Whenever she was under pressure and needed a brief respite from her day-to-day routine she found it comforting to visit her childhood home and ground herself again in her old surroundings.

'It's not so bad,' said Elínborg. 'Sometimes we achieve something worthwhile. Arrest people, stop violence, help victims.'

'Of course,' said her mother. 'But I don't understand why *you* should have to do it. It never occurred to me that you would stay in the police for so long.'

'No,' said Elínborg. 'I know, but somehow it worked out that way.'

'Not that I ever understood the geology thing either. Or that Bergsveinn.'

'His name's Bergsteinn, Mum.'

'I don't know what you ever saw in him. Teddi's entirely different, of course. Reliable. He'd never let you down. And what about Valthór, how is he?'

'All right, so far as I know. We don't talk much these days.'

'Is it still because of Birkir?'

'I don't know. Maybe he's just at a difficult age.'

'Yes, of course, he's growing up. He'll come back to you. He's such a fine lad, Valthór. And intelligent.'

So is Theodóra, thought Elínborg, but did not say anything. Valthór had always been a favourite with his grandmother. The other children sometimes felt left out, and Elínborg had mentioned it to her. 'Nonsense!' had been the old lady's response.

'Do you ever hear from Birkir?' she enquired.

'Occasionally. Hardly ever.'

'Doesn't he keep up with Teddi?'

'No more than with me.'

'I know Valthór misses him terribly. He always says he needn't have left.'

'Birkir wanted to go,' answered Elínborg. 'I don't know why Valthór goes on about it. I think we're all over it now. We're on good terms with Birkir, even though he doesn't contact us often. He's fine. He and Valthór are in touch, although I don't get to hear much about it. Valthór never tells me anything. I hear it from Teddi.'

'I know Valthór can be a bit pig-headed, but . . .'

'It was Birkir's decision to go and live with his father,' said Elínborg. 'It was nothing to do with me. He tracked his father down, although the man had never acknowledged him in any way, never asked about him, in all these years. Not once. And all of a sudden he was the central person in Birkir's life.'

'Well, he *is* his father.'

'What about us? What were we, then? Childminders?'

'Youngsters that age always want to break out and go their own way. I remember well how eager you were to leave home.'

'Yes, but this is different. It's as if we had never been his parents, as if he'd just been a guest in our home. And that's not how we treated him. He called you Gran. Teddi and I were his mum and dad. And then one day it was all over. I was angry with him, and so was Teddi. It was no problem that he wanted to get to know his father – of course that was natural – but when he cut us off completely it was awful. I told him so, but he wouldn't listen. I don't know what went wrong.'

'Perhaps nothing went wrong. Things just happen. You can't always control them.'

'Maybe we didn't do enough, didn't devote enough time to them. One fine day they become complete strangers, all because we didn't spend enough time with them. We no longer mean anything to them. They learn to take care of themselves, not to need us. Then they move out, and they're gone. Never talk to you again.'

'That's only right,' answered her mother. 'They have to learn to look after themselves. They must become self-reliant, not dependent on others. Can you imagine what it would be like if you still lived here? It's bad enough, having your dad around the house all day.'

'So why do I always feel guilty that I don't do enough for them?'

'I think you've done a fine job with them, my dear. Don't worry yourself about it.'

The bedroom door opened and Elínborg's father appeared. 'Hello, darling,' he said, pushing back his tousled hair. 'Have you caught the killer yet?'

'Oh, stop it!' exclaimed her mother. 'As if our Elínborg's out chasing murderers!'

From her parents' house Elínborg went back to the station where she worked late into the evening. She did not get home until past ten o'clock. Teddi had taken the children out for burgers, followed by ice cream, so they were in high spirits. She looked in on Valthór to ask how he was. He was watching TV and simultaneously surfing the net, and seemed fully occupied. Aron was with him in his room, watching TV. He hardly answered his mother's greeting. Distractedly they informed her that Teddi had gone to a meeting.

Theodóra was in bed. Elínborg peeked into her room. A small reading lamp shone from the bedside table but Theodóra was asleep. Her book had fallen from her hand

and lay open on the floor. Silently Elínborg approached the bed, intending to switch the light off. Theodóra was absolutely self-sufficient. She never had to be reminded to tidy her room – unlike her brothers. She tidied it every day, and even made her bed before leaving for school. Her dozens of books were kept in perfect order in a large bookcase, and her little desk was always as neat as a pin.

Elínborg picked the book up. It was one of her own from childhood. She'd passed it on to her daughter: an adventure story by a well-known British writer whose language was probably a little ornate for modern children. It was one of a long series of books which were great favourites with Theodóra. Elínborg remembered reading them voraciously as a child, and waiting impatiently for each new story. She turned the thick yellowed pages with a smile of remembrance. The spine was damaged and the cover tattered by the many young hands through which it had passed. She noticed that she had written her name in clumsy joined-up script on the title page: *Elínborg, class 3G*. The thrilling events were illustrated by excellent drawings, and Elínborg paused over one image; she had a feeling that there was something important in the picture. She stared at it for a long time until she identified what had caught her attention. After gazing at the drawing again, she woke her daughter up.

'I'm sorry, sweetheart,' she apologised, once Theodóra's

eyes were open. 'Your gran sends lots of love. Can I ask you something?'

'What?' asked Theodóra. 'Why did you wake me up?'

'This book – I don't remember, it's such a long time since I read it. Look, this man, in the drawing, who is he?'

Theodóra screwed up her eyes and peered at the illustration. 'Why are you asking about him?' she asked.

'I just want to know.'

'Did you really have to wake me up to find out?'

'Yes, I'm sorry, darling. But you'll drop straight off to sleep again. Just tell me, who's the man in the story?'

'Did you go to Grandma's?'

'Yes.'

Theodóra squinted at the picture again. 'Don't you remember who it is?' she asked.

'No,' replied her mother.

'That's Robert,' explained Theodóra. 'He's the villain.'

'Why does he have that thing on his leg?' asked Elínborg.

'He was born that way,' said Theodóra. 'He wears the brace because he was born with a twisted foot.'

'Yes, of course,' Elínborg recalled. 'It was a deformity.'

'Yes.'

'Can I borrow your book? I'll give it back to you by tomorrow evening.'

'What for?'

'I want to show it to a lady called Petrína. I think she

may have seen a man with a brace on his leg, like that one, walking down her street. What was it that this Robert did in the story?'

'He's horrible,' said Theodóra, yawning. 'They're all scared of him, the children, and he tries to kill them. He's the malefactor.'

15

Petrína did not recognise Elínborg. She stood at the half-open door of her flat, looking sceptically at Elínborg as she tried to explain who she was and what she wanted. She reminded Petrína that she had called on her a few days ago to ask about a man in the street outside her home.

'What man?' asked Petrína. 'From the power company? They haven't been here.'

'They haven't come round yet?'

'They haven't turned up, those men,' said Petrína, and took a deep breath. 'They're not interested in me,' she added sadly.

'I'll ring them for you. Can I come in for a minute and talk to you about the man you saw the other day?'

Petrína gazed at her. 'All right, come in,' she said.

Elínborg followed her inside and closed the door behind her. She entered the same fug of cigarette smoke as before. She glanced towards the room lined in aluminium foil, but the door was closed. The two rods that Petrína had used to detect the electromagnetic field in the flat lay on the living-room floor, as if she had flung them down there. Elínborg regretted that she had been so dismissive of the old lady's story; in a case where clues were few and far between, days had been wasted. The lame man whom Petrína had spotted from her window might be an important witness: perhaps he had seen something significant, heard something, noticed someone. It was possible that the 'aerial' Petrína had described on his leg was simply some form of brace, fitted due to an accident or a physical disability. Petrína was so obsessed with her massive electromagnetic waves and uranium that she had interpreted it in her own fashion.

Petrína looked more weary than at their first encounter. She was less vehement than before, as if her zeal had faded in the past few days and she had given up the battle with the electromagnetic waves. Perhaps she was worn out by waiting for the men from the power company, who Elínborg suspected would never visit the poor woman.

She remembered that she had intended to call Social Services to check on Petrína's situation but had not yet got around to it. The woman appeared intensely vulnerable, with nowhere to turn for protection against the invisible waves that threatened to engulf her. Elínborg noticed that she had now wrapped her television in aluminium foil. Then she saw another, smaller, foil-wrapped package on the kitchen counter: a radio, she deduced.

'I'd like to show you a picture in a book of mine,' said Elínborg, producing Theodóra's adventure story.

'A picture in a book?'

'Yes.'

'Is the book for me?'

'No, I'm afraid not,' said Elínborg.

'Yes, no, you're afraid not?' Petrína was offended. 'No, of course you can't be bringing me anything. Who do I think I am?'

'I'm sorry, it's my daughter's . . .'

'You're the policewoman?'

'That's right,' said Elínborg. 'So you do remember me.'

'You promised to hurry them up, at the power company.'

'I will. I'm afraid I forgot,' Elínborg said, embarrassed at letting Petrína down. 'I'll ring them as soon as we've finished.'

Elínborg opened the book and flicked through the pages until she found the picture of the villainous Robert. One of his legs was fitted with a strange device from the knee down to the ankle. The brace comprised two metal bars that were fixed to his shoe and fastened with leather straps.

'You told me that you saw a man walk past the house during the night, at a time when a serious crime was being committed in the next street. You were at the window, waiting for the men from the power company.'

'They never turned up.'

'I know. You said the man walked with a limp and had something on one leg, like an aerial, and it transmitted massive waves.'

'Oh, yes, massive waves,' agreed Petrína, with a smile that revealed small nicotine-stained teeth.

'Was the fitting on his leg anything like this?' asked Elínborg, passing her the open book.

Petrína put down her half-smoked cigarette, took the book, and carefully examined the illustration. 'What book is this?' she asked at last.

'It's an adventure story that my daughter's reading,' replied Elínborg, gagging on the cigarette smoke. 'That's why I can't give it to you. I'm sorry. Is that like the aerial you saw on the man's leg, here outside the house?'

Petrína took her time considering the question. 'It's

not exactly the same,' she concluded finally. 'He had a sort of clamp here, one that reached up over the knee.'

'Did you have a clear view of it?'

'I did.'

'So it wasn't an aerial?' asked Elínborg.

'Yes, I'm sure it was like an aerial. Is this an old book?'

'Could it have been a plaster cast on his leg?'

'No, absolutely not. Plaster cast? Who said so?'

'Did it look as if he might have a club foot?'

'Club foot? Nonsense!'

'Did it look as if he'd had an accident, and the brace had been fitted for that?'

'That leg was much bigger,' said Petrína. 'Definitely bigger. Probably to receive the signals. I heard them.'

'You heard the signals?'

'Yes,' answered Petrína firmly. She took a long drag on her cigarette.

'You didn't say anything about that when we talked before.'

'You didn't ask.'

'What did you hear?'

'None of your business. You think I'm daft.'

'No, I don't. I never said that. I don't think you're daft at all,' asserted Elínborg, striving to sound sincere.

'You never rang the power company. You said you

would. You think I'm a silly old woman, talking nonsense about electric waves.'

'I've been polite to you. I wouldn't dream of being so disrespectful. Many people worry about electromagnetic waves – and microwaves, mobile phones and so on.'

'Mobile phones will boil your brain. Boil it like an egg, until it's all hard and useless,' said Petrína, thumping her skull with a fist. 'They whisper at you. Whisper all sorts of evil stuff.'

'Oh, yes, they're the worst,' Elínborg agreed hastily. She grabbed Petrína's hand to stop her banging at her head.

'I couldn't hear it properly, because he was in a hurry, although he wasn't able to walk fast. He walked by here, limping on his aerial like a scalded cat. It was . . .'

'Yes?'

'It was as if he was running for his life, that man.'

'And what did you hear?'

'Hear? I couldn't hear anything he said.'

'You said you heard some signal from him.'

'That may well be, but I didn't hear anything he said on the telephone. I just heard a humming. That was the waves. I didn't hear anything he said. I couldn't. He was in such a hurry. Running as fast as he could. I didn't hear anything.'

Elínborg contemplated the woman, trying to make sense of what she had said.

'What?' asked the old lady when Elínborg continued to stare at her in silence. 'Don't you believe me? I didn't hear anything he said.'

'He had a mobile phone?'

'Yes.'

'Was he talking on the phone?'

'Yes.'

'Do you know what time this was?'

'It was night-time.'

'Can you be any more precise?'

'What for?'

'Did he seem agitated when he was talking on his mobile?' Elínborg asked, weighing every word.

'Oh, yes, it was obvious. The man was in a tearing hurry. I noticed it clearly, but I'm sure he couldn't go as fast as he wanted – because of his leg.'

'Do you know where the crime took place, in the next street down? Do you know which house it was?'

'Of course I do. It was number 18. I read it in the paper.'

'Was he heading that way?'

'He was. He certainly was. With his leg, and his mobile phone.'

'Did you see him get out of a car? Did you see him come back the same way? Did you see him again?'

'No, no, and no. This book your daughter's reading – is it good?'

Elínborg did not hear her question. She was thinking about escape routes from number 18. She recalled a path that led into the adjoining garden, then down into the next street. 'Do you have any idea how old he was?' she asked.

'No, no idea. I don't know the man. Do you think I know him? I don't know him at all. I don't know how old he was.'

'You said he was wearing a woolly hat?'

'Is it a good story?' Petrína asked again. She did not answer Elínborg's question, but handed the book back. She was tired of this. She wanted to talk about something else, do something else.

'Yes, it's very good,' answered Elínborg.

'Would you mind reading me a bit of it?' asked Petrína, with an imploring look.

'Reading?'

'Would you mind? Just a few pages. It needn't be much.'

Elínborg hesitated. While her police career had involved countless experiences, she had never been asked a favour more humbly.

'I'll read to you,' she said. 'Of course I will.'

'Thank you, my dear.'

Elínborg opened the book at the first page and started

reading about the children's adventures, and their dealings with the crippled Robert who had a brace on his leg and a terrible secret on his conscience, and tried to destroy them all.

Before Elínborg had been reading for five minutes Petrína was asleep in her chair, apparently at peace and free of all anxieties about electromagnetic waves and massive amounts of uranium.

When Elínborg returned to her car she rang the power company and was put through to a woman who specialised in home appliances and electromagnetic fields. It was not uncommon for her to receive phone calls from customers concerned about electromagnetism in their homes, she remarked. She was familiar with Petrína and her problems; she said she had visited her several times and had suggested rewiring the flat. The expert admitted that, as a matter of fact, the readings she had taken did not indicate high levels of electromagnetic waves in the flat. In her view, Petrína was 'a sweet dotty old thing'.

When Elínborg contacted Social Services she learned that Petrína was one of many people living alone whom they kept an eye on. A social worker visited her regularly, and although Petrína was eccentric in her ways she was quite lucid and largely able to take care of herself.

Elínborg was about to make a third call, to her home, when the mobile rang in her hand. It was Sigurdur Óli.

'I don't like the look of this creep Edvard,' he said. 'Have you got time to pop into the station?'

'What's this about?'

'See you in a minute.'

16

It took Elínborg only a few minutes to drive from Thingholt down to police headquarters, where Sigurdur Óli was waiting for her with a colleague from CID, a veteran detective named Finnur. The two men had been chatting in the cafeteria when the murder investigation came up. Sigurdur Óli mentioned Edvard, who claimed to have bought the Rohypnol for his friend Runólfur.

'So?' asked Elínborg, as she took a seat at their table. 'What's this about Edvard?'

'If he's been dealing in Rohypnol, we're certainly

interested,' said Finnur, 'whether it was for himself or someone else.'

'Why? Have you got anything on him?'

'You knew all about the case – you were with us at the start of the investigation,' he said, with a look at Elínborg. 'Erlendur was always interested. Though we never did succeed in finding the girl. She was nineteen, disappeared from her home, out west in Akranes. The local police called us in.'

'Akranes?'

'Yes.'

Elínborg glanced at Finnur, then at Sigurdur Óli. 'Hang on . . . are you talking about Lilja? *That* missing-person case in Akranes?'

Finnur nodded.

'It turns out that Edvard knew her,' said Sigurdur Óli. 'He was teaching at Akranes Comprehensive College at the time she disappeared. Finnur interviewed him. He remembered Edvard as soon as I mentioned his name, but he didn't know he'd been buying a date-rape drug on the black market.'

'If he got in touch with Valur he must have done his homework, because Valur keeps a very low profile,' Finnur observed. 'He's very cautious, trusts nobody. The word is he's not dealing any more, but we reckon he's fencing stolen goods and still selling all sorts of dope. I don't see some ordinary bloke walking in off the street and buying dope from Valur – prescription medicine or anything else. There's more to it than that.'

'Valur said he'd never seen him before,' said Elínborg.

'You can't trust a word Valur says,' replied Finnur. 'They could have been best mates, met every day.'

'But the description fits. He described Edvard to us.'

'Maybe he wants us to take him out of circulation, sees Edvard as a threat. You ought to go back to Valur, talk to him again – the two of them may know each other better than they're admitting. Get him to make a formal identification and tell you more about his dealings with him.'

'I can't imagine anyone seeing Edvard as a threat,' said Sigurdur Óli. 'He's such a loser.'

'Do you think Edvard was involved in Lilja's disappearance?' asked Elínborg.

Finnur shrugged. 'He was interviewed during the investigation – but then, we talked to almost everyone there.'

'Did he teach her?'

'Not at the time she disappeared, but he'd taught her the previous year,' said Finnur. 'He might have had no involvement. I'm not saying he did. We got nowhere with the case, couldn't even reach a conclusion about whether a crime had been committed, or whether the girl might have taken her own life for reasons we knew nothing about. Or it could have been an accident. We found nothing.'

'How long ago was it? Six or seven years?'

'Six. It was in 1999. I remembered Edvard when Siggi told me about him. We spoke to all the teachers, and I did that interview myself. I remember he lived here in Reykjavík and drove up there every day. Siggi says he's teaching at the Breidholt College here in town now.'

'He left Akranes College four years ago,' said Sigurdur Óli. 'And don't call me Siggi.'

'They were friends, Edvard and Runólfur,' said Elínborg. 'According to Edvard they were great mates.'

Elínborg went over in her mind the case of the missing girl, Lilja. The Akranes police had been contacted by the girl's mother, who was worried because she had not seen or heard from her daughter for more than twenty-four hours. Lilja, who lived with her parents, had left the house to visit a friend, telling her mother they planned to go to the cinema and that she might stay the night at her friend's place, as she often did. It was a Friday evening. Lilja had no mobile phone. On the Saturday afternoon Lilja's mother called the friend's house. The girl told her that she and Lilja had intended to see a film, but in the event she had not heard from her. She had assumed that Lilja had gone to visit her grandparents on their farm in the country.

On the Sunday there was still no trace of the missing girl. The media were informed and a photo was circulated, but without result. An extensive search and investigation yielded very little. Lilja was a student at the comprehensive college and lived an unremarkable life: she attended her classes, and went out at the weekends with friends, or spent time with her maternal grandparents who ran a horse farm in nearby Hvalfjördur. She loved horses, helped out on her grandparents' farm in the summer holidays, and dreamed of working with them full-time in the future. There was no evidence of alcohol or drug abuse. She had no boyfriend but was one of a close-knit group of friends; the other girls were devastated by her disappearance. Search parties were sent out and townspeople combed the area around the little town. Lilja was never found, nor did any clue to what had become of her that Friday evening ever come to light.

'Didn't the girls know anything?' asked Elínborg.

'No,' Finnur replied. 'Only that they didn't believe she'd killed herself. They found that a ridiculous suggestion. They thought it more likely that she'd had an accident, or even been murdered. We came up empty-handed.'

'I don't suppose you remember what Edvard said at the time?' asked Elínborg.

'You can look it up. All the reports and statements are on file,' said Finnur.

'I shouldn't think he said any more than the rest of them – the other teachers: she was a good, conscientious student and they had no idea what had happened to her.'

'And now it turns out that Edvard was trying to get his hands on a rapists' drug?'

'I just wanted to pass on what I know,' said Finnur. 'I think there's something a bit dodgy about the connection to your Runólfur. The bloke was working at Akranes when the girl went missing and he's been buying Rohypnol. It's worth looking into.'

'You're absolutely right,' said Elínborg. 'Thanks for the tip – we'll be in touch.'

'Let me know what comes of it,' said Finnur, and left.

'I think . . .' started Elínborg, but then she drifted off into her own thoughts in mid-sentence.

'What?' asked Sigurdur Óli.

'It puts a new twist on everything,' said Elínborg. 'The two of them, Runólfur and Edvard, and the girl from Akranes. What if there's a link?'

'What link?'

'I don't know. Could Runólfur have known or found out something about Edvard, something that backfired on him? Meaning that Edvard had to get rid of him? Could the drugs at Runólfur's place have belonged to Edvard? Maybe Runólfur took them off him. Maybe Runólfur had no intention of using them?'

'And there was no woman with him on the night his throat was cut?'

'What if it was some kind of dispute between the two of them?'

'You mean Runólfur and Edvard?'

'What if Runólfur was threatening to go to the authorities? Could he have been blackmailing Edvard?'

'Edvard can spin us any story he likes, of course,' said Sigurdur Óli. 'He knows the Rohypnol was found at Runólfur's place. It's been on the news. It's dead easy for him to claim that Runólfur asked him to get hold of it.'

'With a little help from you . . .' observed Elínborg, unable to resist the dig.

'No – as I said, he must have worked out his story long before we turned up. Shall we go and bring him in?'

'No, not yet,' answered Elínborg. 'We need to do a bit more groundwork – talk to Valur again. I'm going to look up the records about the missing girl. Then we'll go and have another word with him.'

Elínborg dug out the police records about Lilja's disappearance. According to the file, Edvard had taught maths and sciences at Akranes Comprehensive College. His statement was short and provided no leads. He said he had no knowledge of where Lilja had been on the Friday of her disappearance. He remembered her clearly, having taught her the previous year. She was not an outstanding student, he said, but a pleasant, quiet girl. He said he had finished teaching early that Friday, and gone home to Reykjavík.

17

The search for the limping man whom Petrína had seen hurrying towards house number 18 had yielded meagre results; the witness was unreliable, to say the least, and the description of the lame man was questionable. It occurred to Elínborg to consult an orthopaedic specialist, who might be able to shed some light on the question of the apparent leg brace. It might mean no more than that he had broken his leg, yet it could be something far more significant.

The orthopaedist, whose name was Hildigunnur, invited Elínborg to call in at her surgery. Hildigunnur was fortyish, fair-haired and fit, a walking advertisement for a healthy lifestyle. She was intrigued by Elínborg's line of enquiry, which she had briefly explained over the phone.

'So what kind of leg support is it, precisely, that you're looking for?' asked Hildigunnur, once she and her visitor had sat down.

'We don't really know, that's the thing,' said Elínborg. 'The description's rather vague, and our witness isn't awfully reliable, to tell the truth. More's the pity.'

'But your witness said she may have seen metal rods, isn't that right?'

'What she actually said was that she had seen an "aerial" but I think she might have meant some sort of brace, maybe metal, which was fixed to the man's leg. He was wearing jogging trousers, with the leg open up to the knee.'

'Was he wearing orthopaedic shoes? Was it that kind of limp?'

'Possibly. We don't know.'

'If the person has a physical disability, I'm thinking it could perhaps be a club foot. Special shoe attachments are used for that. Another possibility is a degenerative disease leading the muscles to atrophy. Or he could have undergone surgery, possibly an arthrodesis.'

The last word meant nothing to Elínborg.

'Perhaps you're talking about a full-length leg brace?' Hildigunnur suggested.

Elínborg looked at her. 'Sounds about right,' she said.

'And of course it could just be a fracture,' Hildigunnur pointed out, with a smile.

'We've checked that angle,' said Elínborg, 'but we came up with nothing useful. We've examined reports of broken legs and other leg injuries going back several weeks, but no joy there.'

'Well, let's go on brainstorming. Leg deformities – caused by polio, for instance – are a known phenomenon here in Iceland. The brace was only on one leg, wasn't it?'

'Yes, so far as we can tell.'

'Do you know how old he is?'

'Not exactly, unfortunately.'

'The last polio epidemic here was in 1955 and an immunisation programme started the following year. After that the disease was eliminated.'

'So if it does relate to polio, then he's over fifty?'

'Yes, but then there's also the Akureyri Disease, as it's called.'

'Akureyri Disease?'

'It was an infectious disease that had various polio-like symptoms. It was believed to be a variant of polio. The first case was diagnosed up north near Akureyri in 1948. If I remember correctly, about seven per cent of the population of the town fell ill, including some of the boarding students at Akureyri High School. But I don't think it caused permanent physical handicaps. I may be wrong about that, though.'

'Are there any files about patients who got polio, for instance?'

'I'm sure there must be. A lot of them were sent to the Isolation Clinic in Reykjavík. You could get in touch with the Ministry of Health – they may still have records.'

Elínborg did not make it home for dinner. She rang Teddi to say she did not know when she would be back. He was used to these calls, and simply told her to take care. They spoke briefly. Elínborg asked him to make sure that Theodóra took her knitting to school in the morning. She was supposed to knit fifteen rows for the class, but Theodóra detested all handiwork lessons at school, whether needlework or carpentry. Her current project, a woolly hat, had largely been knitted by her mother.

Elínborg rang off and put her mobile in her pocket, then pressed the doorbell. She heard it ringing inside. A long time passed, and nothing happened. She rang again and heard a rustling before the door was finally opened by a dishevelled woman in a white dressing gown.

'Good evening,' said Elínborg. 'Is Valur in?'

'Who are you?'

'I'm from the police. My name's Elínborg, I spoke to him a couple of days ago.'

The woman looked Elínborg up and down, then called out to Valur that someone wanted to see him.

'Does he sell from here?' asked Elínborg bluntly.

The woman looked at her as if she did not understand the question.

Valur appeared. 'You again?' he remarked.

'Would you mind coming for a short ride in the car with me?' asked Elínborg.

'Who is this?' the woman asked.

'It's nothing,' replied Valur. 'Go inside – I'll deal with it.'

'Oh, yeah, you deal with everything!' she sneered and went back into the flat, where a baby could be heard crying.

'Why don't you leave me alone?' said Valur. 'Are you on your own? Where's that wanker who was with you before?'

'This won't take long,' said Elínborg. She hoped she hadn't woken the baby by ringing the doorbell. 'Just a quick drive, that's all.'

'What drive? What's this fucking bullshit?'

'You'll see. You could earn some brownie points. I expect someone like you needs them.'

'I don't work for you,' said Valur.

'Really? I've heard that you do, actually. I'm told you can be quite cooperative, despite giving me such a rude reception. My friend on the Drug Squad says you tell them all sorts about other dealers. He said if I mentioned it you might be less bloody-minded. Or I can go and get him, and all three of us can go together. But I'd rather not disturb him unless it's absolutely necessary. He's a family man, like you.'

Valur gave the matter some thought. 'What do you want me to do?' he said.

Elínborg waited for Valur in the car, and when at last he came out she drove him to Edvard's small house. On the way she explained what was expected of him. It was an easy task – all that was required was that he should tell the truth. She did not want to summon Edvard down to the station and have him identified by Valur as the man who had bought Rohypnol, using Runólfur's name. She did not want to tip Edvard off and make him anxious and agitated, but she did need confirmation that it was he who had bought the drug from Valur. She had had another talk with her friend on the Drug Squad, who admitted after a little persuasion that the Squad occasionally found that its interests coincided with Valur's. Both he and Elínborg were eager to reduce the number of dealers on the streets of Reykjavík, although for different reasons. Elínborg's colleague resolutely denied that the Squad was turning a blind eye to Valur's little ways. That was out of the question.

'But you know he's selling date-rape drugs,' Elínborg said.

'That was news to us.'

'Come on. You know all there is to know about this guy.'

'He's not selling any more, we know that. But he's still well connected in the business. We have to weigh up the benefits. It's not cut and dried – you should know that as well as I do.'

Elínborg pulled up near Edvard's home and switched off the engine. Valur was in the passenger seat.

'Have you been here before?' she asked.

'No,' replied Valur. 'Can we get this over with?'

'The man who called himself Runólfur lives here. I need you to confirm that we're talking about the same person. I'm going to get him to come to the door. It should be easy for you to see whether you recognise him.'

'Then can we get the fuck out of here?'

Elínborg walked over to the house and knocked at the door. The glow of a television was visible through the threadbare curtains. She had noticed them when she had called on Edvard with Sigurdur Óli. They had once been white, no doubt, but now they were brown with years of accumulated filth. She knocked again, harder, and waited patiently for a response. Edvard's wreck of a car was parked outside, as before.

Finally the door opened, revealing Edvard.

'Hello again,' said Elínborg. 'I'm sorry to disturb you. I'm afraid I might have left my bag here when I was here yesterday. It's a leather satchel, a sort of handbag, brown?'

'Your bag?' asked Edvard in astonishment.

'I've either lost it or it's been stolen. I just don't understand. I've checked everywhere else I've been. I don't
suppose you've noticed it here?'

'No, sorry,' Edvard replied. 'It's not here.'

'Are you absolutely sure?'

'Yes, quite sure. Your bag is not here.'

'Would you . . . would you mind taking a look? I'll wait
here.'

Edvard eyed her sceptically. 'There's no need. It's not
here. Was there anything else?'

'No,' answered Elínborg glumly. 'I'm sorry to inconvenience you. There wasn't much money in it, but I'll
have to cancel all my cards and replace my driving licence
and . . .'

'Yes, well. As I said . . .' replied Edvard.

'Thank you.'

'Bye.'

Valur was waiting in the car.

'Do you think he spotted you?' asked Elínborg as she
drove off.

'No, he didn't see me.'

'Well, was that him?'

'Yeah, it's the same guy.'

'The one who came to you using the name Runólfur,
and bought Rohypnol from you?'

'Yeah.'

'You said you only saw him once, about six months ago. You said you didn't know him, that you'd never seen him before. You said a relative of his had put him in touch with you. That's a lie, isn't it?'

'No.'

'It's most important that you tell me the truth about it.'

'Leave me alone. I've got nothing more to say about it. Whatever you're investigating has got nothing to do with me. I don't give a fuck what's important for you and what isn't. Now take me home.'

They drove the rest of the way in silence. When they reached Valur's block of flats, he got out without a word and slammed the car door behind him.

Elínborg drove home, deep in thought. A pop song was on the radio, sung by a female singer who had long been a favourite of hers: *I whisper your name, but there's no answer* . . . She thought about Edvard and the girl from Akranes, Lilja. Might he know something about her disappearance, six years before? She had checked it out earlier. Edvard had no criminal record. His relationship with Runólfur might prove to be the key to what had happened in Runólfur's flat, but she was wary of reading too much into Edvard's use of his friend's name when he'd bought the Rohypnol. Had Edvard been supplying Runólfur with prescription drugs? When had that started? And what for? Or was Edvard using the stuff himself? Who was the man Petrína had seen hurrying through Thingholt, towards number 18? Elínborg felt that Petrína's information about the man was reliable, even though some of her statements were hard to fathom. Why was the man in such a hurry? Did he see something? Did he have a connection with the tandoori woman who had apparently been in Runólfur's flat? Was he more than just a potential witness? Perhaps he was Runólfur's assailant?

Elínborg parked outside her home and sat in the car for a while, considering various questions but finding no answers. She was feeling guilty for neglecting her family recently. As if it weren't enough that she was hardly ever home her mind was invariably on her job, even during the very limited time she did spend with them.

Unhappy though she was about the situation, she could not help herself. That was the way with the difficult cases – they were relentless.

As the years went by, Elínborg increasingly craved the safe haven of her family life with Teddi. She wanted to sit with Theodóra and help her with her knitting. She wanted to know Valthór better, and understand how he was growing into a young man who would soon be leaving home. Then he would probably be largely lost to her, except for the odd awkward phone call, neither of them knowing what to say. A visit now and then. Perhaps she had neglected him when he'd been younger because, in spite of everything, her work had always come first – morning, noon and night. Perhaps she had given it more thought than she had to her own flesh and blood. She understood that she could not turn the clock back but she could still try to make up for it. Or maybe it was too late. Maybe in the future she would only have news of her son from his blog? She no longer knew how to approach him.

She had checked Valthór's blog earlier in the day when she'd been at work. He was describing a football match he had seen on TV, and a political debate on a popular chat show about conservation – apparently aligning himself with big-business interests. He also sounded off about a teacher at college against whom he apparently had a grudge; and, finally, he mentioned his mother: she wouldn't leave him alone, he wrote, just like she had never left his brother alone, which had led to him leaving the country to live with his real dad in Sweden. 'I'm consumed with envy of him,' blogged Valthór. 'I'm thinking of renting a place,' he went on. 'I've had enough of this.'

This? This what? wondered Elínborg. We haven't spoken for weeks. She clicked on *Comments (1)*, where she saw two words:

Mums suck.

18

The man observed Elínborg as she stood at his door in a block of flats in Kópavogur. He was unwilling to invite her in, so she had to explain what she wanted out on the landing and she was not handling it particularly well. She had acquired a list of over a dozen individuals who had spent time at the Isolation Clinic in Reykjavík. They were the last patients to have contracted polio before the introduction of the immunisation programme in the 1950s.

The man seemed wary, standing half-hidden behind his front door, so Elínborg could not tell whether he was wearing a leg brace. She told him that the police were trying to trace a group of people who had been in the

Isolation Clinic in their youth. The enquiry concerned a crime that had been committed in Reykjavík – in fact, in Thingholt.

The man listened, then asked exactly what they were looking for. She told him: a man who might still need a leg brace.

'Then I can't help you,' he said, opening the door wide so that both his legs were visible. He wore no brace.

'Do you remember any other boy at the Isolation Clinic who might have had to use a brace? In later life, I mean.'

'None of your business, my dear,' said the man. 'Goodbye now.'

That was the end of the interview. The man was the third one that Elínborg had spoken to who had been in the Isolation Clinic. Hitherto she had received friendly responses but had got nowhere.

The next name on Elínborg's list was that of a man who lived in a townhouse in the eastern suburbs. When he heard what Elínborg wanted he was more helpful than her last interviewee had been. He welcomed her warmly and invited her in. He wore no brace, but she noticed that his left arm was withered.

'People all over the country caught polio in that epidemic,' said the man, whose name was Lúkas. He was in his sixties, slim and lithe.

'I was fourteen, living in Selfoss. I shall always remember how terribly ill I was, you know. My whole body ached, like with a bad case of flu, and I was paralysed from head to toe. I couldn't move a muscle. I've never felt worse in my life.'

'It must have been an awful illness,' said Elínborg.

'It didn't occur to anyone that it could be polio,' Lúkas explained. 'Never even considered it. They assumed it was just the usual flu epidemic. But it turned out to be much, much worse.'

'And they took you to the Isolation Clinic?'

'Yes, they put me in quarantine once they realised what was really going on, and they took me to that house, the one they called the Isolation Clinic. There were people there from all over the country, mostly children and youngsters. I think I was lucky. I made a pretty good recovery, thanks to the rehabilitation at the clinic, but my arm's been useless ever since.'

'Do you remember any man or boy at the Clinic who had to use a brace – a leg brace, perhaps? – I don't know much about these things.'

'And I don't know how they did in the end, the lads I met there. You lose touch, you see. So I don't suppose I can tell you anything useful. But there's one thing I will say: the youngsters I was with there, there was no way they were going to give up.'

'I'm sure people dealt with their problems in different ways,' said Elínborg.

'As I often say, our futures were put on hold for a while,' Lúkas continued. 'But we were determined to pick up and go on, and that's what we did. I think we were all determined not to let it break us. It never occurred to us to give up. Never crossed our minds.'

Elínborg took the tunnel under Hvalfjördur and drove up to Akranes. A brisk northerly wind was blowing. She had arranged to meet the parents of Lilja, the girl who had vanished six years before. She had spoken to the mother, who still contacted the police occasionally to ask if any progress on the case had been made. When she first heard from Elínborg, the mother had thought initially that there might be a new lead, but the detective was quick to disabuse her and say that, regrettably, she had no new evidence. She only wanted to review the events and establish whether Lilja's parents might have anything new to contribute to the investigation.

'I thought the case was closed,' the woman had said on the phone.

'No, nothing new has come up, we don't know any more than we did then.'

'So what do you want?' asked Hallgerdur, Lilja's mother. 'What are you ringing me for?'

'I gather that you get in touch with us now and then to ask about the case,' said Elínborg. 'A colleague mentioned Lilja the other day. I played a small part in the investigation at the time, and it occurred to me that you might be prepared to refresh my memory, run through the events. We try to learn from cases like Lilja's. We're always learning something new.'

'Absolutely,' replied the woman.

She was waiting for her visitor and had opened the front door before Elínborg was out of her car. They shook hands in the chilly breeze, and Hallgerdur ushered her in. She was some years older than Elínborg, very slender, and appeared to be highly strung. She was clearly tense about being visited by the police. She said she was alone in the house. Her husband, an engineer on a fishing boat, had gone out to sea that morning. The couple lived in an old detached house with a large garden which showed the ravages of autumn weather. In the living room Elínborg saw a large photograph of Lilja, taken about two years before her disappearance. She recognised it as the photo that had been published in the media at the time of the search. It showed the cheery face of a young girl with dark hair and pretty brown eyes. The photograph was displayed in a heavy black mourning frame on top of a fine chest of drawers. In front of it a votive candle flickered.

'She was just a normal child,' said Hallgerdur, when

they had taken their seats. 'A really lovely girl. She was so interested in all sorts of things, and loved being with her gran and grandad in Hvalfjördur. She spent all her time there with the horses. But she had a lot of friends here in town: you could speak to Áslaug – the two of them were inseparable, ever since infant school. She works in the bakery now, she's got two children of her own. Married a good lad from nearby. Áslaug's a treasure. She always stays in touch, pops in for a chat. She brings her two little girls, such pretty children.'

Elínborg detected a fleeting, delicate tinge of regret in Hallgerdur's voice.

'What do you think happened?' asked Elínborg.

'I've been torturing myself all these years, and all I know for sure now is that it was God's will. I know now that she must be dead and I've accepted it, and I know she's with God. As to what happened to her, I have no idea. No more than you do.'

'And she intended to stay the night with a friend, did she?'

'Yes, with Áslaug. They'd been talking about meeting up that evening and seeing a film. They often stayed the night with each other, without planning it specifically. Sometimes Lilja would ring to say she was at Áslaug's and was going to stay over, and the same went for Áslaug when she came here. They didn't necessarily decide in advance, but this time Lilja had said she meant to go to Áslaug's that evening.'

'When did you last speak to her?'

'It was that Friday, the day she disappeared. *See you*, she said. It was the last thing she ever said to me. *See you*. There was nothing special about the conversation. Just a routine call, to let me know. No more than that. I said a proper goodbye, I think. *Bye, sweetheart*, I said. That was a comfort to me, afterwards. That was all there was to it. *Bye, sweetheart*. That was all.'

'So she hadn't been feeling depressed in the days before, or seemed unhappy about something?'

'Not at all. Our Lilja was never depressed. Always cheerful, and positive, and willing to help. She was pure in heart, an innocent, as really good people are. She treated others well and they treated her well in return. That was the way it was. She was trusting, didn't see evil in anyone, because she'd never encountered it. She had only ever known good people.'

'There's a lot of talk now about bullying in schools, and ways to prevent it,' said Elínborg.

'No, there was nothing like that going on,' Hallgerdur replied.

'And was she happy at school?'

'Yes. Lilja was a good student. Maths was her favourite subject, and she used to talk about doing something scientific at university – physics or maths. She wanted to go abroad to study, to America. She said their universities were the best for those subjects.'

'Was the science teaching good at the college?'

'So far as I know. I never heard anyone complain about it.'

'Did she ever talk about the teaching? Or the teachers – anything like that?'

'No.'

'Did she ever mention a teacher called Edvard?'

'Edvard?'

'He taught her science subjects,' Elínborg explained.

'Why are you asking about him?'

'I . . .'

'Did he know my daughter, or something?'

'He taught her during the school year before she disappeared. He's an acquaintance of mine, that's all. I know he was teaching here around that time.'

'She never mentioned any Edvard. Is he from here? I don't remember her ever talking about him specifically, no more than any other teacher.'

'No, no, of course. I just thought of asking, because I know him slightly. Edvard lives in Reykjavík. He used to commute by car. He was quite young then. He has a friend named Runólfur. Do you remember Lilja ever saying anything about them?'

'Runólfur? Is he a friend of yours too?'

'No,' answered Elínborg, realising that she had got herself into an awkward position. She could not bring herself to tell Hallgerdur the truth, or explain her suspicion – really no more than a hunch – that a link might exist between Lilja and a suspected rapist in Reykjavík. She did not want to add to the woman's distress any more than necessary, especially since she had so little to go on, but she wanted to float the names in case Hallgerdur had any relevant knowledge.

'Why are you asking about Lilja now, and why are you asking about those men?' asked Hallgerdur. 'Is there new evidence you don't want to tell me about? What are you after?'

'I'm sorry,' said Elínborg. 'Perhaps I shouldn't have brought up any names. They have nothing to do with Lilja's disappearance.'

'I don't know them.'

'No, I didn't expect you to.'

'Runólfur? Isn't that the name of that man who was murdered in Reykjavík?'

'Yes, it is.'

'Is that him? The one you're asking about?'

Elínborg hesitated. 'Edvard knew Runólfur,' she said.

'Knew Runólfur? Is that why you're here? Is this Runólfur involved with my daughter's case?'

'No,' replied Elínborg. 'Nothing new has come to light. All we know is that Edvard and Runólfur were friends.'

'I don't know them – I've never heard those names.'

'No, I didn't expect so.'

'What's their connection with Lilja, then?'

'Nothing.'

'But didn't you come here to ask about them?'

'I just wanted to find out if you might recognise the names. That was all.'

'It's good to know that Lilja's case isn't forgotten.'

'We do our best.' Elínborg hurriedly changed the subject, asking Lilja's mother more about their daily routine and assuring her that the police were receptive to information, even after so many years. Elínborg sat with her for some time, and when she took her leave dusk was falling. Hallgerdur came out to the car with her and stood in the sharp northerly wind, apparently not noticing it.

'Have you lost anyone close to you in this way?' she asked Elínborg.

'No, not in the same way, if you mean . . .'

'It's as if time stands still, and it can't start again until we know what happened.'

'Of course it's a terrible experience.'

'The tragedy is that it never ends. We can't say goodbye to her, because we don't know anything,' said Hallgerdur, smiling faintly and with her arms crossed across her chest.

213

'When Lilja vanished, a part of us went with her which we will never get back.'

She ran a hand through her hair. 'Maybe we lost ourselves.'

The bakery where Áslaug worked was quiet. A bell hung against the door, and it jangled harshly when Elínborg called in on her way out of town. The northerly wind was rising and Elínborg found herself almost physically blown inside the shop. Inside she was met with the comforting aroma of freshly baked bread. A young woman wearing an apron was handing change to a customer. She closed the till and smiled at Elínborg.

'Do you have any ciabatta?' asked Elínborg.

The woman scanned the shelves. 'Yes, we've got two left.'

'I'll take them, and a sliced wholemeal loaf, please.'

The assistant put the ciabatta in a bag and placed the wholemeal loaf on the counter. They were alone in the shop.

'Here you are,' said the young woman.

Elínborg handed over her credit card. 'I gather that you were a good friend of Lilja?' said Elínborg. 'You're Áslaug, aren't you?'

The woman looked at her. She did not appear surprised. 'Yes,' she replied, tapping her name badge with a finger. 'My name is Áslaug. Did you know Lilja?'

'No, I'm from the Reykjavík police, just passing through. I met some colleagues here and we got talking about Lilja and how she vanished. They said you were her best friend.'

'Yes,' said Áslaug. 'I was. We were . . . she was such a nice girl. So you were talking about us?'

'Lilja's disappearance came up in conversation,' answered Elínborg as Áslaug passed back her card. 'Lilja was planning to stay over with you, wasn't she?'

'Yes, that was what she said to her mum. I thought she'd changed her mind and gone to see her grandparents. She often did. I didn't think any more of it. I'd spoken to her that morning – we were thinking of going to the cinema in the evening, and then back to my place. We were planning a trip to Denmark. Just the two of us. Then . . . then it happened.'

'It was as if she disappeared into thin air,' said Elínborg.

'It was just so unbelievable,' said Áslaug. 'So ridiculous. So ridiculous that it could happen. I just know she didn't kill herself. She must have had some freak accident and . . . She often used to go down to the seashore. All I can imagine is that maybe she slipped and fell, and was knocked unconscious, then drowned when the tide came in – or something like that.'

'You're sure it couldn't have been suicide?'

'Absolutely not. That's a daft suggestion. She was trying

to find a birthday present for her grandad. She mentioned it to me that morning, and she was seen in a sports shop that sells riding equipment. Her grandad loves horses. That was the last sighting. Then she disappeared. And nobody has any idea what happened to her.'

'But apparently the shop didn't have what she wanted?' said Elínborg, who had read the witness statements.

'No.'

'And that's the end of the trail.'

'As I say, it doesn't make any sense. I never thought to get in touch when I didn't hear from her that evening. We hadn't made any firm plans, and she often went out to the farm without telling anyone beforehand. I just assumed she'd gone there.'

The bell rang and a new customer entered. Áslaug sold him a Danish pastry and some rolls. Another customer arrived, and Elínborg waited patiently.

'How have her parents been coping?' she asked when they were alone again.

'They're up and down,' said Áslaug. 'It put a great strain on their marriage. Hallgerdur became very religious and joined a fundamentalist church. Lilja's dad, Áki, is quite different. He just doesn't mention it.'

'You were at school together, weren't you?'

'For as long as we could remember.'

'And at the comprehensive college too?'

'Yes.'

'Was she happy there?'

'Yes, very much so. We both were. She was brilliant at maths. Physics and the other sciences were her favourite subjects. I was more on the languages side. We had even considered going to Denmark to study. That would have been . . .'

'Apparently she also talked about going to America.'

'Yes, she wanted to try living abroad.'

The door opened once more. Áslaug served four customers before Elínborg could ask her about Edvard. She was grateful to Áslaug for not talking about Lilja when other people were in the shop. 'Did she have any favourite teacher?' she asked. 'At the college?'

'No, not that I know of,' said Áslaug. 'They were all really nice.'

'Do you remember a teacher called Edvard? He taught science subjects, I think.'

'Yes, I do. He left ages ago. He never taught me. He taught Lilja, though, I'm sure of that.'

'Did she ever talk about him?'

'No, not that I can remember.'

'Yet you recall him clearly?'

'Yes. He once gave me a lift into town.'

'Town? Do you mean the town centre here?'

Áslaug smiled for the first time during their

217

conversation. 'No,' she said. 'Edvard lived in Reykjavík, and he once offered me a lift there. To Reykjavík.'

'Recently?'

'No, no. It was years ago, when he was teaching here. It must have been before Lilja vanished, because I remember telling her. He was very nice. Why do you ask?'

'Then what? Did he drop you off when you got to Reykjavík?'

'Yes, I was waiting for the bus when he stopped and offered me a lift. I was going shopping in Reykjavík and he drove me to the Kringlan mall.'

'Did he often give people lifts?'

'I don't know,' Áslaug replied. 'But he was very friendly. Invited me to come round, if I wanted.'

'Come round to his home?'

'Yes. What is it? Why are you asking about him?'

'And did you go round?'

'No.'

'Did he ever give Lilja a lift?'

'I don't know.'

The door opened to admit another customer, followed by yet another, and before long the bakery was crowded. Elínborg picked up her loaves, called goodbye to Áslaug and left the bakery with the noise of the shop bell ringing in her ears.

* * *

Elínborg drove back to Reykjavík, arriving at the Asian food shop just before it closed. Jóhanna was not there and the shop was being minded by a girl who said she sometimes covered for her. Elínborg did not recall seeing her there before. She explained that she knew Jóhanna well, and had hoped to speak to her. The young woman, Jóhanna's twenty-five-year-old niece, was friendly and helpful. She had been helping Jóhanna out with the shop more and more over the past year, she said, as her aunt's health had been declining. The cause was not clear – probably exhaustion, she observed frankly, adding that her aunt worked too hard and did not take proper care of herself. Elínborg had the impression that it had been a slow day in the shop, and the girl was pleased to have someone to talk to.

'If you're often here, maybe you can help me,' said Elínborg. 'I've discussed it with Jóhanna. She knows I'm with the police, and I've told her I'm trying to trace a young woman, with dark hair, who may be a customer of yours. She probably buys tandoori spices, could have bought a tandoori pot.'

The girl was deep in thought.

'She might have been wearing a shawl,' said Elínborg. 'I can show it to you but I haven't got it with me now.'

'A shawl?' the girl asked. 'Wasn't Jóhanna able to help you?'

'She was going to look into it for me.'

'I've only sold one tandoori pot this autumn,' said the girl. 'And it wasn't to a young woman with a shawl. It was to a man.'

'So you don't remember any regular customer – a dark-haired woman? Who's interested in Indian cookery, or any kind of Asian food, spices? Maybe she's been to the Far East?'

The girl shook her head. 'I wish I could be more help,' she said.

'Of course. This man who bought the tandoori pot, was he alone? Do you remember?'

'He was. There was no girl with him. I remember him particularly because I helped him take the pot out to his car.'

'Yes?'

'He didn't want to be a nuisance, but I assured him it was no problem.'

'He needed assistance, did he?'

'He walked with a limp,' the girl explained. 'There was something wrong with his leg. He was very nice, and awfully grateful.'

19

The family had done well for themselves. The husband, Elínborg had learned, was a qualified economist and a head of department at the Ministry of Agriculture. The wife worked in a bank. They lived in a townhouse in a prosperous district of the city, furnished with leather sofas, an oak dining table, and new-looking kitchen fittings. The floors were parquet, and on the walls hung two fine oil paintings and a number of drawings. Photographs of the family at different ages: three children, from infancy to college graduation. Glancing casually around, Elínborg took all this in as she was shown into the living room.

She had decided to make this visit alone. She did not

want to make the man uncomfortable. Jóhanna's assistant at the shop had dug out the credit-card slip for the tandoori pot that he had bought in the late summer. He had written his name clearly and firmly on the receipt: this was no illegible scribble, like so many credit-card signatures. This man's signature was neat, controlled, confidence-inspiring.

In trying to trace him, Elínborg had first spoken to two men of the same name, both of them mystified to be contacted by the police. At her third attempt she had struck lucky. The man asked whether she wanted him to come to the station, but she allowed him to meet her on his own territory and she had the impression that he was relieved. She had told him she was a police officer, looking for witnesses in the Thingholt murder case. 'A man was seen near the scene of the crime, with some kind of support on his leg – as if he had a broken leg, or an injury or disability,' she had said.

'Oh?'

'He had a brace on one leg. We've been trying to identify him, and we're wondering if you're the right man.'

He was silent. Then he said he was aware of the case, and he recalled that he had been in Thingholt at about that time. 'What . . . how can I help you?' He was uncertain how to address a police officer. This was evidently a new experience for him.

'We're trying to find witnesses, but there are very few,' explained Elínborg. 'I'd just like to speak to you, to find out if you noticed anything unusual when you were in Thingholt.'

'By all means come round,' the man answered courteously. 'But I don't know that I can contribute anything.'

'No, no, of course. That remains to be seen,' said Elínborg.

And now she was sitting with him in his living room. His wife was not yet back from work. The children had all left home now, he told Elínborg, unprompted.

'This is just a routine enquiry,' announced Elínborg. 'I hope I'm not intruding.'

'You said there weren't many witnesses,' he answered. Konrád was sixtyish, not tall but sturdily built, with a head of thick greying hair, cropped short, and a broad face with laughter lines around the mouth. He had powerful shoulders and big hands. He walked slowly, because he had a brace on one leg. Elínborg recalled Petrína's fantastical description: to the old lady, buzzing with radiomagnetism at her window, the metal rod on the brace might well resemble an aerial. Konrád was wearing a comfortable pair of tracksuit bottoms zipped open over the calves. They flapped as he walked, revealing the brace.

'Have you been trying to reach me at work?' asked Konrád.

'No, I only rang here,' answered Elínborg.

'Good. I've had a touch of flu recently. So you've been looking for me?'

'Yes, actually, we have. As I said, a man with a leg brace was seen near a house in Thingholt where a man was murdered. We thought that might indicate a physical disability, so we contacted an orthopaedist, who mentioned polio as a possibility. We looked back at the records of the Isolation Clinic and compiled a list which includes your name.' Elínborg decided not to mention at this stage the line of enquiry about tandoori cuisine.

'Yes, I was at the Isolation Clinic, that's right. I caught polio in the last epidemic here in Iceland, in 1955, and this is what I got out of it,' said Konrád. He patted the brace. 'I never regained full strength in my leg. But you must know all this, of course.'

'You were unlucky. The immunisation programme started the following year.'

'Yes, that's true.'

'So you were in the Isolation Clinic for a while?' asked Elínborg. She sensed that he was slightly uneasy. 'Can't have been much fun for a young lad.'

'No,' replied Konrád politely. 'It was a difficult experience. Really quite difficult. But that's not why you're here.'

'I'm sure you must have heard about what happened in Thingholt,' said Elínborg. 'We're trying to gather as much information as we can, from all possible sources. You were there, weren't you?'

'Yes, I was, but I didn't go anywhere near that house, the one on the news. I'd parked my car nearby earlier that evening and I was reluctant to leave it there overnight. It was a Saturday and my wife and I had gone out for the evening. Then I went to fetch the car. I might have had one too many – we'd been to a number of bars. I know you're not supposed to drink and drive, but I really didn't want to leave my car where it was.'

'It's a bit of a walk from Thingholt into the centre of town, isn't it?'

'I suppose I wanted to be sure that the car wouldn't be vandalised. It can be a bit dodgy downtown from that point of view – nothing seems to be safe unless it's nailed down.'

'Oh, yes, there are plenty of vandals about,' said Elínborg. 'So you went out for a few drinks, did you?'

'I suppose you could put it like that.'

'And then you went to get the car?'

'Yes.'

'Couldn't your wife have gone? You're the one with the bad leg, after all.'

'She'd had more to drink than me,' replied Konrád, with a smile. 'I preferred to go myself. Please don't get the idea that this is something we make a habit of. And it wasn't far. We stayed near the centre, on Bankastræti and Laugavegur.'

'And you walked back alone to collect the car?'

'Yes. Did someone see me hobbling along, then?' Konrád smiled as if he had said something amusing. Elínborg noticed that he smiled a lot. She wondered if his smile was a mask, intended to deceive. Should she tell him about the Asian food shop and the tandoori pot, the shawl smelling of Indian cuisine that had been found at the scene of the murder? She decided to leave that line of questioning for now. Elínborg did not enjoy interrogating witnesses. She disliked misleading people, catching them out in their lies. She was quite certain that most of what Konrád had told her was a carefully constructed fabrication, and that she would have to trick him into admitting whatever it was that he was striving to conceal. If she asked random and irrelevant questions she might be able to trip him up and induce him to reveal something important that would give her a handle on the case. She saw her interrogation technique as being like one of those party games in which questions had to be answered without using the words *yes* or *no*, *black* or *white*, and so on. If her instinct was correct, both she and Konrád knew there were certain things he must not say, and as the game progressed she would make it more and more difficult for him to maintain his focus.

'It's a small world,' said Elínborg, evading his question. 'Didn't you think to get in touch with us, given that you were in the neighbourhood when the crime took place?'

'I didn't really think about it,' answered Konrád. 'I suppose I would have done if I'd believed I could help you in any way. But I'm afraid I haven't anything to contribute.'

'So you just strolled calmly along towards your car, did you?'

'Yes, I think so. I don't know what your witness saw. I'd be interested to know. I was trying to be as quick as possible, because of my wife. She rang me when I was on the way.'

'So she's the person you were speaking to on the phone?'

'Yes, I was on the phone to her. Is there something particular you want to know? Some specific questions you want to ask me? I didn't realise this was all going to be about me.'

'I'm sorry,' said Elínborg. 'We have to check the reliability of all witnesses. It's just procedure.'

'I see,' said Konrád.

'And please bear in mind that anything could be important, even if it seems to you to be quite insignificant. What time was it that you were there?'

'I didn't notice exactly. It was about two when we got home.'

'Did you notice anyone else around, someone we might be able to trace?'

'No, I didn't. I didn't see a soul. The street lighting around there isn't all that good, and I wasn't parked very near the place where I understand these terrible events occurred. I was quite some distance away, in fact.'

'We may be looking for a young woman in connection with the murder.'

'So I've read in the papers.'

'So you didn't see any young woman around that night?'

'No.'

'Or a young woman with a man?'

'No.'

'She could have been alone. We don't have a precise time of death, and it's entirely possible that the crime was committed around two.'

'All I saw was a deserted street as I was hurrying along it. I'm afraid I didn't notice anything in particular. No doubt I'd have been more observant if I'd known I would be a witness in this case.'

'Where exactly did you park?'

'It wasn't on the street you're interested in. I took a short cut. The car was in the next street down the hill. That's why I can't help you. I was never on the road where the murder happened.'

'Did you hear any noises? Anything unusual?'

'No, I don't remember anything like that.'

'Are these your children?' asked Elínborg, changing tack abruptly. On a small table three photographs of young people at their high-school graduations were arranged: two young men and a young woman, all smiling into the camera.

'Yes – those are my boys and my daughter,' replied Konrád. He seemed relieved at the change of subject. 'She's the youngest, always competing with her brothers. The elder boy went into medicine, the younger into economics, like me, and my daughter's doing engineering.'

'A doctor, an economist, and an engineer?'

'Yes, they're good kids.'

'I've got four children,' said Elínborg. 'One of my boys is at the Commercial College.'

'My daughter's at the University of Iceland. Our doctor son is about to finish his training in San Francisco and he'll be coming home next year. He's specialising in cardiology.'

'San Francisco?' asked Elínborg.

'He's been there three years. He's very happy there. We . . .' Konrád fell silent.

'Yes?' asked Elínborg.

'No, nothing.'

Elínborg smiled. 'Everyone says San Francisco's a wonderful city. I've never been,' she said.

'It is,' said Konrád. 'Yes, indeed.'

'What about your daughter?'

'What about her?'

'Did she go with you?'

'Yes, she did, actually,' answered Konrád. 'The second time we visited. She came with us and fell in love with the place, just as we did.'

Outside Konrád's home, Elínborg's phone rang. It was Sigurdur Óli.

'You were right,' he said.

'So Runólfur did call on her?' asked Elínborg.

'According to the records, he went to her home about two months ago, on two consecutive days.'

20

Elínborg was in no hurry. She did not contact Konrád to arrange a second interview until the following day. He answered the phone himself and said she was welcome to call on him around midday – he was not planning to go anywhere. He asked why she found it necessary to speak to him again, but she simply said she had a few more questions. He sounded quite calm. Elínborg had the impression that he knew what to expect.

She did not tell Konrád that she had made arrangements to ensure that neither he nor any member of his immediate family could leave the country. She doubted whether it was strictly necessary but she did not want to take any risks with the case she was building. Elínborg also ensured that Edvard would be apprehended if he tried to flee.

During the night she lay awake for a long time, thinking about a conversation with Valthór. When Elínborg had come home she had entered his room and sat down. Teddi had been asleep, as were Theodóra and Aron, but Valthór, as usual, had been at his computer. The television had also been on. When Elínborg had said she needed to talk to him he said nothing.

'Are you OK, dear?' she asked.

'Yeah,' he replied brusquely.

Elínborg was worn out after a long day. She knew Valthór was a good boy at heart. Over the years they had been close, but as a teenager he had entered a rebellious phase of ferocious independence and his hostility seemed to be directed mainly at her.

After several attempts to get a response, Elínborg switched off the TV. Valthór stopped what he was doing.

'I want to talk to you for a minute. How can you be on the Internet and watch telly at the same time?'

'Easy,' answered Valthór. 'How's the hunt going?'

'All right. Look, I don't want you blogging about me. I don't want you writing about our private business. This family's private business.'

'So don't read it,' he snorted.

'Whether I read it or not, it's on the net. Theodóra's

uncomfortable with it, too. You go too far on your blog, Valthór. You write about things that are nobody's affair but ours. And who are these girls you're always writing about? Do you think it's any fun for them to read that stuff about themselves?'

'Jesus,' said Valthór. 'You just don't get it. Everyone does it, it's no problem. Nobody thinks anything of it – it's just a joke, no one takes it seriously.'

'You could write about something else.'

Valthór suddenly changed the subject: 'I'm thinking of moving out.'

'Moving out?'

'Kiddi and me thought we'd rent a place together. I told Dad earlier.'

'And where will the money come from?'

'I'll get a part-time job.'

'What about your schoolwork?'

'I'm going to see how it goes. I know I won't have any trouble finding work. And Birkir moved out. He went all the way to Sweden.'

'You're not Birkir.'

'No.'

There was a note in his voice Elínborg did not like. 'What do you mean, *no*?'

'Oh, forget it. You don't want to hear it, anyway.'

'What don't I want to hear?'

233

'Nothing.'

'I told Birkir that if he wanted to meet his natural father, that was absolutely fine. Of course it was. But it was an awful shock when he suddenly decided to go and live with his father. In Sweden! I thought we were his family but he obviously didn't agree with me, or with your dad. In the end Birkir went his own way.'

'You forced him to leave.'

'That is just not true, Valthór.'

'That's what he says. And he's dropped out of touch. We hardly hear from him, and he never speaks to you. You think that's OK, do you?'

'Birkir was at a difficult age, just like you are now. Do you really believe it's all my fault? I hope he's changed his opinion now that he's older.'

'He told me he never felt like one of the family.'

Elínborg was dumbstruck. 'What?'

'Birkir felt the difference.'

'What difference?'

'You never treated him the same as the rest of us. He always felt he was in the way. As if he was just a visitor.'

'Did Birkir say that? He never said anything about it to me.'

'Do you think he'd say something like that to *you*? He told me when he left, and said I must keep my mouth shut.'

'But that's nonsense. He has no right to talk like that.'

'He can say what he wants.'

'Look, Valthór, you know perfectly well that Birkir was always one of the family. I know it was hard on him, losing his mum. It wasn't easy for him to come here to live with his uncle – and with me, who he didn't know at all. And then you kids came along. I always understood the position he was in and I always, always did my best to make him happy. We never treated him any differently from you three. He was one of our children. You can't imagine how much it hurts to know that he says that about us.'

'I wish he hadn't left,' said Valthór.

'So do I,' said Elínborg.

Elínborg lay in bed, wide awake. She glanced at her alarm clock: 02.47.

She started counting down: 9,999. 9,998 . . .

She really must sleep.

Konráð led her into the living room, as he had done the day before. He limped ahead of her, apparently quite calm and unruffled. Elínborg was alone; she was not expecting any trouble. She had been delayed slightly at the station when the DNA results for the hairs found on the shawl and in Runólfur's bed came in.

'I thought I'd told you everything I know yesterday,' said Konráð once they were seated.

'We're always receiving new information,' answered Elínborg. 'Perhaps I could start by telling you about a man . . .'

'Would you like coffee?'

'No, thank you.'

'Quite sure?'

'Yes. I just want to tell you about the man who was killed in Thingholt,' she said. Konráð nodded. He placed his bad leg up on a footstool and listened. She told him the known facts. Runólfur had been born in a little coastal village just over thirty years ago. His mother still lived there, while his father had died in an accident several years before. The community was dying: the young generation were all moving away, and Runólfur himself had left as soon as he had the chance. He did not have a close relationship with his mother, who had a reputation as a harsh woman and a strict disciplinarian and, on the rare occasions that he returned, he barely visited her. He settled in Reykjavík where he trained at technical college, and once he was qualified he started work as a telecoms engineer. He did not marry or have children and his only known relationships with women were one-night stands. He lived in rented flats and apparently moved quite frequently. Through his work he came into contact with a lot of people, in their homes and workplaces, and was invariably regarded as hard-working and reliable. He seemed to have had an interest in comic-book and film superheroes. Nothing was known of any other interests.

Konrád listened in silence. She wondered whether he grasped what she was doing by presenting these facts to him. He might have asked *What's all this got to do with me?* but he said nothing. He merely sat there, frowning, as Elínborg continued with her account of Runólfur.

'We believe – and we have evidence of this – that Runólfur, having met women through his work, sometimes ran into them later at bars around town. It's possible that the women were of a similar type: young, single, and dark-haired. Perhaps he encountered them by chance, but we do know of one case where he had found out from the woman in question which bar she generally went to.

'Runólfur had acquired a date-rape drug, Rohypnol, and he was carrying it when he was murdered – when his throat was slashed with a razor-sharp blade. The pills were found in his pocket. We have a theory about how he got hold of them. It appears very likely that Runólfur had been with a young dark-haired woman when he was killed. She left a shawl at his home.'

The police had been waiting for the results of the DNA tests, which showed that the hairs from the shawl matched the hairs from Runólfur's bed.

'I've got the shawl here,' Elínborg continued. She opened her bag, removed the shawl, and spread it out.

237

'It's beautiful. When it was found it had a very strong smell, which is almost gone now. A smell of Indian cuisine – tandoori.'

Konrád did not say a word.

'We're pretty sure that there was a woman with Runólfur when he was killed. We think he met her in the same way as he did other women, by setting up a supposedly chance encounter at a bar. We believe he initially went to her home to install telephone or TV equipment, a fibre-optic connection or broadband, whatever telecoms engineers do. He may have returned shortly afterwards on the pretext that he had left some small thing behind, like a screwdriver or a torch. He had a pleasant manner and would have made conversation easily. They were of a similar age. They would have chatted about this and that, and he would have steered the conversation towards certain subjects in order to elicit information from her. She told him which were her usual bars and he also learned that she was unattached, lived alone and was a university student. That background knowledge made it easier to approach her later in public. By that time she must almost have felt she knew him.'

'I don't know why you're telling me all this,' said Konrád. 'I can't see that it has any relevance to me.'

'No,' replied Elínborg. 'I understand, but I still want to ask your opinion. We have various small clues that I want to ask you about. Runólfur persuaded the woman to go home with him. He had the drug in his pocket, and it's very likely that he slipped something in her glass while they were still at the bar. Or he may not have drugged her until they got to his flat.' Elínborg glanced at the graduation photo of Konrád's daughter, which she had examined the day before. 'We don't know what happened there,' she said. 'What we do know is that Runólfur was killed, and the young woman who was with him left the scene.'

'I see,' said Konrád.

'Do you know anything about it?'

'As I told you, I didn't notice anything when I passed through. I'm sorry.'

'How old is your daughter?'

'She's twenty-eight.'

'Does she live alone?'

'She rents a place near the university campus. Why do you ask?'

'Is she interested in Indian cookery?'

'She's interested in all sorts of things,' answered Konrád.

'Do you recognise this shawl?' asked Elínborg. 'You can pick it up if you like.'

'There's no need,' said Konrád. 'I don't recognise it. I've never seen it before.'

'It smelt strongly of tandoori spices. I recognised the

smell, because I'm keen on Asian cuisine myself. I have a special tandoori pot, which I use a lot. It's essential for cooking those dishes. Does your daughter have a tandoori pot?'

'I really couldn't say.'

'We know you bought one last autumn – I can show you a copy of the receipt if you like. Was it for your own use?'

'Have you been investigating me?' asked Konrád.

'I need to know what happened in Runólfur's flat when he was killed,' said Elínborg. 'If you can tell me, then you're the person I've been looking for.'

Now Konrád stared at his daughter's photograph.

'This hasn't been made public, but when Runólfur's throat was slit he was wearing a T-shirt,' said Elínborg. 'It looks like a woman's garment and I believe it was your daughter's. You said she went to San Francisco with you, on your second visit. I believe she bought the T-shirt there. It has the words *San Francisco* on the front.'

Konrád's gaze remained fixed on the photograph.

'You were observed near the scene,' said Elínborg. 'You were hurrying, and talking on your mobile. I think you went to her aid. Somehow she managed to make a phone call and tell you where she was. When you got there and saw what had happened, when you realised what had been done to your daughter, you lost it, grabbed a knife . . .'

Konrád shook his head.

'. . . that you had brought with you, and you went for Runólfur.'

Konrád looked steadily at Elínborg.

'Did Runólfur visit your daughter's home twice, about two months ago?' she asked.

He made no reply.

'We have a record of Runólfur's call-outs. It lists all the homes and businesses he went to and it shows that he called twice within a few days at the home of Nína Konrádsdóttir. I think I'm right in saying she's your daughter?'

'I don't keep tabs on exactly who calls on my daughter.'

Elínborg sensed that the man's confidence was dwindling. 'Did she ever mention his name?'

Konrád dragged his gaze from the graduation photo and turned to Elínborg.

'What are you trying to say?'

'I think you killed Runólfur,' she said quietly.

Konrád sat staring at Elínborg, as if he were trying to work out what he should say, what he could say, to make the detective accept it and go away, so the problem would be over with once and for all and nobody would ask any more awkward questions. But he could find no words. He could not speak. Seconds ticked past and before long his features expressed defeat, followed by helplessness, as he spoke haltingly:

'I . . . I can't do this any more.'

'I know it must be hard—'

'You don't understand,' he interrupted. 'You can't possibly understand how awful it is. What a nightmare it's been for all of us. Don't even try to understand it.'

'I didn't mean to . . .'

'You don't know what it was like. You don't know what happened. You can't imagine.'

'Tell me.'

'He raped her. That's what happened. He violated her! He raped my daughter!' Konrád took a deep, shuddering breath. He avoided meeting Elínborg's gaze. He reached for the photo, held it in his hands and studied his daughter's face, her dark hair, her pretty brown eyes, and her happy face on that sunny day.

Then he groaned. 'I wish it *had* been me that killed him.'

21

Konrád would never forget the phone call from his daughter that night. He saw her name on the screen: *Nína*, followed by three little hearts. His mobile had been on the bedside table and he'd answered at the first ring.

When he'd seen what time it was he had been taken aback.

And when he heard the pain in her voice, his blood had run cold.

'Oh, God,' he moaned. He was still clutching his daughter's photo. 'I . . . I've never heard anything like it in my life.'

Konrád and his wife had had no particular anxiety

about their daughter. Not any more, at least. When she was younger, and they knew she was out on the town with her friends, they were always a little uneasy. And the same was true when she first left home and rented her own flat. News reports of brutal attacks in the city centre, growing violence in connection with drug use, and rapes were not calculated to reassure them, and they urged her always to carry her mobile. If anything happened, she was to ring home. They had been just as uneasy about their sons when they had first started going out at night.

Nothing serious had befallen any of them before. A wallet had been stolen on a foreign holiday, and a couple of years ago their younger son had caused a minor road accident. The family had lived a fairly uneventful life, and that was what they wanted. They had maintained their standards and treated others with consideration and respect. The couple were close and united in all they did, had a wide circle of friends, and enjoyed travelling both in Iceland and abroad.

They had made a good life for themselves, were happy with what they had achieved and were proud of their children. Both sons were now settled: the elder one, who lived in San Francisco, was married to an American woman who was also a doctor doing postgraduate training. They had a child, a little girl named after her Icelandic grandmother. For the past two years the younger son had been living with a woman who worked in the corporate division of one of the major banks. Nína was in no hurry to settle down. She had lived with a young computer scientist for a year but since then she had been single.

'She's always been reserved and self-sufficient,' Konrád said to Elínborg as he replaced the photo on the table. 'She's never been any trouble. Although she has a lot of friends, I think she's happiest on her own. That's just the way she is. And she would never hurt a fly.'

'They don't care about that,' said Elínborg.

'No,' said Konrád, 'that's for sure.'

'What did she say when she called?'

'It was impossible to understand her. A stifled howl of anguish – terror and weeping and fear, all at the same time. She couldn't say a word. I knew it was Nína's phone because I saw the caller ID, but I thought at first it was some stranger who had stolen it. I didn't even recognise her voice. Then I heard her say *Daddy*, and that's when I knew something terrible had happened. That she must have experienced some unspeakable horror.'

'Daddy.' The voice was racked with sobbing.

'Now, now,' Konrád spoke into the phone. 'Try to calm down, sweetheart.'

'Daddy,' his daughter wept. 'Can you come? Please . . . please . . . please come.'

Her voice cracked. Konrád heard his daughter keening at the other end of the line. He was out of bed now. He walked down the hall and into the living room. His wife followed anxiously.

'What's happening?' she asked.

'It's Nína,' he replied. 'Are you there, darling?' he asked. 'Nína? Tell me where you are. Can you do that for me? Tell me where you are, and I'll come and get you.' He could hear nothing but crying. 'Nína! Tell me where you are.'

'I'm at . . . at his . . . his place.'

'*Whose* place?'

'Dad, you've got to come. You mustn't call the police.'

'Where are you? Are you hurt? Are you injured?'

'I don't know what I've done. It's awful. It's . . . so awful. Daddy!'

'Nína, what's wrong? What's happened? Have you been in a car crash?'

His daughter was whimpering again. Konrád could hear nothing but her stifled wailing.

'Speak to me, sweetheart. Can you tell me where you are? Can you do that? Just say where you are and I'll come and fetch you. I'll come right away.'

'There's blood everywhere, and he's lying . . . lying on the floor. I'm scared, I'm scared to go . . .'

'What house is it, darling?'

'We walked. We walked here. Dad, you can't come here. I don't know what to do. You have to come alone. Just you! You've got to help me.'

'I'll come and get you. Do you know the name of the street?'

Konrád dressed hurriedly in tracksuit bottoms and shrugged on a jacket over his pyjama top.

'I'm coming with you,' said his wife.

He shook his head. 'She wants me to come alone. You stay here. Are you there, sweetheart?' he asked.

'I don't . . . don't know the name of the street.'

'What's the name of the man who lives there? Maybe I can find him in the phone book.'

'His name's Runólfur.'

'Do you know his surname?'

Silence.

'Nína?'

'I think . . .'

'Yes?'

'Dad? Are you there?'

'Yes, my dear.'

'I think . . . I think he's dead.'

'All right. Don't worry. It's all right. I'll come and get you, and everything will be all right. But you've got to tell me where you are. Which way did you go?'

'There's blood everywhere!'

'Try to be calm, now.'

'I can't remember anything. Not a thing.'

'All right.'

'I went into town for the evening.'

'Yes.'

'And I met this man.'

'Yes.'

Konrád heard that his daughter was becoming less hysterical.

'We passed the High School. And then the American Embassy, round that way,' she said. 'You must come alone. And make sure no one sees you.'

'All right.'

'I'm so scared, Dad. I don't know what happened. I only know I must . . . must have attacked him.'

'Where did you go next, darling?'

'I don't remember anything – but it's not that I was drunk. I didn't drink anything. And yet I can't remember. I don't know what's wrong with me . . .'

'Can you see any bills lying around, something with his name on, which might show the address?'

'I don't . . . don't know what's going on here.'

'Have a look around, dear.'

Konrád opened the garage door, got into the car and started the engine. He reversed out into the street and drove off. His wife had refused to be left at home and she sat in the passenger seat, devoured by anxiety as she listened to the conversation.

'Here's a bill. It's addressed to Runólfur. And there's an address.' Nína read it out.

'That's my brave girl,' Konrád said. 'I'm on my way. I'll be with you in five minutes, at most.'

'You must come alone.'

'Your mother's with me.'

'No! God, no! She mustn't come. You and Mum mustn't be seen here. I don't want anyone to see. I just want to go home. Please, please don't bring Mum . . .' Nína was sobbing uncontrollably. 'I can't do this,' she moaned.

'All right,' her father said. 'I'll come by myself. I won't park at the house. Is that all right? Don't worry. Mum'll wait in the car.'

'Be quick, Daddy. Be quick.'

Konrád turned off the Ring Road, up Njardargata, then made a left turn. He parked a short distance away and, leaving his wife in the car, set off towards the house where Nína was waiting for him. He hurried towards her with his phone to his ear, doing his best to calm her as he walked. The streets were empty and so far as he could tell nobody had noticed his presence. On arrival he started up the steps to the front door. But he saw that the name on the doorbell was not Runólfur's, so he turned back and followed the path around to the back garden. There, above the postbox, was the name he was looking for.

'I'm here, my dear,' Konrád said into the phone. The door stood slightly ajar. He pushed it open and stepped inside. He saw a man lying on the floor in a pool of blood. Nína was wrapped in a bedspread, huddled against the wall, clutching her knees to her chest. She was rocking back and forth, her phone clasped to her ear. Konrád switched his mobile off, went to her, and gently helped her to her feet. She collapsed, shaking, into his embrace.

'What have you done, my child?' he murmured.

Konrád concluded his account. For a long time, lost in thought, he looked at the brace on his leg. Then he turned to Elínborg.

'Why didn't you call the police?' she asked him.

'I should have rung you immediately, I know that,' he replied. 'But we just gathered up her clothes and left. We didn't go back the same way. We went out through the garden, down into the next street to the car, then drove home. I know I did the wrong thing. I just wanted to protect my daughter – protect us and our lives – but I'm afraid I've just made things worse.'

'I'll need to speak to her,' said Elínborg.

'Of course,' said Konrád. 'I told her and my wife that you were here yesterday. I think we're all relieved.'

'You have difficult times ahead, I'm afraid,' said Elínborg as she stood up.

'We haven't felt able to tell her brothers about it yet. Our sons. We're at our wits' end. How can we tell them that their little sister cut a man's throat? A man who had raped her.'

'I do understand that.'

'Poor child. What she's been through!'

'We should go to her now.'

'We just want her to be treated justly,' said Konrád. 'That man defiled her and she retaliated. That's how we believe you should see the situation. It was self-defence. She had to defend herself. Simple as that.'

22

Nína lived in a small rented flat in the west of town. Konráð phoned to say that he was on his way there, with the police. He spoke to his wife, who was with their daughter, and asked her to tell Nína. The pretence was over. He drove over to the university district, followed by Elínborg, and stopped in front of a small block of flats. They went up to the first floor. Konráð rang the doorbell and a woman of his own age answered. She looked at Elínborg with an expression of deep distress.

'Are you alone?' she asked. 'I didn't see any police cars.'

'Yes,' said Elínborg. 'I'm not anticipating any need for them.'

'No,' the woman replied, and shook Elínborg's hand. 'Come in.'

'Is Nína here?' Elínborg asked.

'Yes, she's waiting to see you. We're just glad it's at an end, this absurd charade.'

The two women entered the living room, followed by Konrád. Nína stood with her arms crossed, her eyes swollen with weeping.

'Hello, Nína,' said Elínborg, offering her hand. 'I'm Elínborg, from the police.'

Nína shook her hand. Her grip was clammy and weak. She made no attempt to smile.

'All right,' she said. 'Has my father told you what happened? How it all was?'

'Yes, he's told me his side. Now we need to talk to you.'

'I have no idea what went on,' said Nína. 'I don't remember anything.'

'No, that's all right. We've got plenty of time.'

'I think he drugged me. You found drugs there, didn't you?'

'Yes. Your parents can come to the station with you, but then you and I have to talk, just the two of us. Do you understand? Are you all right with that?'

Nína nodded.

Elínborg glanced into the kitchen. The flat smelt not unlike her own home: a fragrance of herbs and spices

253

from faraway lands, of cuisine so familiar to her yet always exotic. On the counter by the sink stood a tandoori pot. 'I like Indian cookery, too,' she remarked, with a smile.

'Do you?' said Nína. 'I had a dinner party that evening, before . . .'

'I've got your shawl,' Elínborg said. 'The one you were wearing. I thought from the smell that you must have been cooking Indian food.'

'We left it behind by accident,' Nína explained. 'Dad picked up everything of mine he could see, but I didn't think of the shawl.'

'And the T-shirt.'

'Yes, the T-shirt, too.'

'We'll have to speak to the boys,' said Konrád. 'Before anything happens. Before the media get hold of it.'

'You can call them from the station if you like,' Elínborg told him.

Nína and her parents followed Elínborg's car to police headquarters. When they arrived Nína was shown into an interview room, while her parents waited in Elínborg's office.

Word spread fast that the police had a suspect in the Thingholt Murder, as the media were calling it, and soon reporters started ringing to ask for details. A request for remand in custody had been sent down to the District Court. Konrád had found a lawyer. He had looked into the matter in advance and knew who to contact. The lawyer he engaged, well known as a successful criminal defence counsel, had put his other cases aside and was present, as was the prosecutor, when the custody request was submitted to the judge. The younger of Nína's brothers met his parents in Elínborg's office, thunderstruck by what his mother had told him on the phone. Disbelief and astonishment soon gave way to anger, directed initially at his parents for not confiding in him and then at Runólfur.

Elínborg felt heartily sorry for Nína who sat hunched in the interview room, awaiting her fate. She did not look like a cold-hearted killer but a bewildered victim who had been through a horrifying experience only to face another ordeal.

She was eager to speak, now that the truth about her encounter with Runólfur was out and it was known that she was the woman who had been with him when he died. She seemed glad to be able to tell the truth at last and get the story off her chest, so that she could embark on her long journey towards understanding and closure.

'Did you know Runólfur before you met him on the night in question?' asked Elínborg, once all the formalities had been completed and the interview could begin.

'No,' said Nína.

'But he'd been to your home two months before, hadn't he?'

'Yes, but I still didn't know him.'

'Can you tell me what happened?'

'Nothing. Nothing happened.'

'You had called in an engineer, hadn't you?'

Nína nodded.

Nína wanted to move the TV into the bedroom, so she needed the aerial cable extended through the wall. She had also switched to a different telephone company and was having some problems with her Wi-Fi connection. She wanted to be able to use her laptop anywhere in the flat. When she rang the helpline she was put through to customer services, and later that day an engineer turned up. That had been on a Monday.

The engineer was friendly and engaging, maybe two or three years older than Nína. He got straight to work and she did not pay much attention to what he was doing. She heard the noise of an electric drill coming from the bedroom, and he had to pull out a skirting board. She did not have the impression that he spent an excessive amount of time in the bedroom. It did not even cross her mind until later, after the event.

He helped her get online and then wrote out an invoice, which she paid on the spot, using a card. He talked to her about this and that – superficial chat between strangers – then left.

The following day the engineer came back to complete the job and later on he reappeared at her door, asking if she had seen the drill bit that he had used when he drilled the hole through the bedroom wall. She had not noticed it.

'Do you mind if I come in and have a look?' he asked. 'I'm on my way home. I thought I might have left it here. I can't find it anywhere. It's a nuisance, because I use it all the time.'

Nína accompanied him into the bedroom and helped him search. The cable passed through a wardrobe, which she opened. He checked the windowsill and looked under the bed before giving up.

'I'm sorry for the inconvenience,' he said. 'I'm always mislaying things.'

'I'll get in touch if it turns up,' she replied.

'No problem,' he said. 'I had a bit of a heavy weekend. Spent too long at Kaffi Victor on Saturday night.'

'I know the place,' she said smiling.

'Do you ever go there?'

'No, we mostly go to Kráin.'

'We?'

'My friends and I.'

'So you'll let me know if you find the drill bit?' the engineer said as he was leaving. 'Perhaps we'll meet again some time.'

*　*　*

Nína was known as a good cook, and she liked inviting her girlfriends over to try out new recipes. She had become interested in Indian cuisine after working at an Indian restaurant in Reykjavík, where she had got to know the chefs well, learning from them and gradually assembling her own collection of herbs and spices, and recipes using pork and chicken. Like Elínborg, she experimented with substituting Icelandic lamb for other meats in Indian dishes. On the evening when she met Runólfur she had cooked lamb for her friends, using the tandoori pot that her father had given her for her birthday. It was nearly midnight when they all left her flat to go into town. They had soon split up, and Nína was thinking of going home when she ran into Runólfur.

As she had not had much to drink, she was mystified to have so little memory of that night until she read that Rohypnol had been found in Runólfur's flat. She had had a Martini with her friends before dinner, and red wine with the Indian lamb dish, followed by some beer, as the spicy dish had made her thirsty.

She was unable to say much about what happened after she had met Runólfur in the bar. She remembered him coming over to her and talking about San Francisco. She had told him that she had visited her brother there. She finished her drink, and Runólfur offered her another – by way of compensation for the ridiculously expensive bill the other day, he said. She accepted, and while he was ordering the drinks she glanced at her watch. She did not intend to stay long.

Her recollection of their walk back to his flat in Thingholt was fragmentary. She seemed to be blind drunk: she was uncoordinated and completely helpless.

Nína regained consciousness gradually. It was the middle of the night. On the wall above her she saw Spider-Man, ready to pounce.

Initially confused, she thought she was at home. Then she realised that could not be right, and thought she must have fallen asleep at the bar.

But that made no sense either. Slowly she understood that she was lying in an unfamiliar bed, in a room that she had never seen before. She felt sick, dazed and weary. She did not know how she came to be there. When she had been lying there for some time she realised that she was stark naked. She looked down at her body and found the situation absurd. She did not even think to cover herself. Spider-Man was watching her. She imagined he might come and help her. She smiled at the idea. Her, and Spider-Man!

When Nína woke up again she felt cold. She jerked awake, trembling. She was naked, in a strange bed.

'Oh, God,' she moaned, seizing the bedspread from the

floor and wrapping it around her. The room was unfamiliar. She called out 'Hello?' but heard only an empty silence. She inched her way out of the bedroom into the living room, and felt for the light switch. A man was lying on his back on the floor, and she thought that she had seen him somewhere before. But could not place where.

Then she saw the blood.

And the gash across the throat.

Nína gagged. She saw the man's deadly-white face, and the gaping red wound. His eyes were half-open and she felt that he was looking at her, accusing her of something.

'I found my phone, and rang home,' said Nína. The tape recorder hummed in the quiet of the interview room. Elínborg watched her. Her account, though patchy towards the end, was credible. She did not appear defensive – until she had to describe waking up in a strange place and finding Runólfur's body.

'Why didn't you call the police?' asked Elínborg.

'It was such a shock,' Nína replied. 'I didn't know what to do. I wasn't thinking straight. And I felt awful. I don't know if that was the drug wearing off, or what. I was . . . I was sure I must have done it. Absolutely certain. And I was terrified. All I could think of was to ring home, and then try and conceal what had happened. Hide the horror. I didn't want anyone to know I'd been there. That I'd done it. I . . . I couldn't face it. Dad took my side. I told him to conceal everything. You've got to understand – he was just thinking of me. He's not a dishonest man. He did it for me.'

'Are you convinced that Runólfur drugged your drink?'

'Yes.'

'Did you see him do it?'

'No. I wouldn't have drunk it if I had, would I?'

'I suppose not.'

'I don't do drugs. I don't take anything. And I hadn't had that much to drink. This was different.'

'If you'd called us that night we might have been able to prove you'd been given Rohypnol. Now we can't corroborate your story. Do you understand?'

'Yes,' answered Nína. 'I know.'

'Did you see anyone else in the flat?'

'No.'

'Did you notice anyone when you were in town, someone who might have been with Runólfur?'

'No.'

'Quite sure? Another man?'

'I don't remember any other man,' said Nína.

'And there was no one with Runólfur at the bar?'

'No. Like who?'

'Never mind that for now,' said Elínborg. 'Do you know what you did with the knife you used?'

'No. I don't know anything about the knife. I've gone over it again and again in my mind, and I don't remember attacking him.'

'He had a set of knives on a magnetic strip in the kitchen. Do you recall anything about them?'

'No, nothing at all. I woke up in a strange flat with a man I didn't know, who was lying on the floor with his throat cut. I know I probably must have done it. I don't suppose anyone else could have done it, and I realise the circumstances don't look good for me, but that night is a blank.'

'Did you have sexual intercourse with Runólfur?'

'No.'

'Are you sure? That's another factor we can no longer prove.'

'I'm quite sure,' Nína said. 'That's a ridiculous way to put the question. It's a ridiculous question.'

'Why?'

'We didn't have sexual intercourse. He raped me.'

'So penetration took place?'

'Yes, but it wasn't sexual intercourse.'

'Do you remember it?'

'No. But I know. I don't want to go into it. I know he raped me.'

'That's consistent with our evidence. We know he had sexual intercourse shortly before he died.'

'Don't say *sexual intercourse*. It wasn't sex. It was rape.'

'Then what happened?'

'I don't know.'

Elínborg paused. She was not sure how much pressure the young woman could withstand during this first round of questioning. But dozens of urgent questions jostled in the detective's mind. If Nína felt she was under duress, that was too bad. Elínborg decided to change her approach.

'Are you covering for someone?' she asked.

'Covering?'

'Maybe you rang your father much earlier than you claim? When you realised Runólfur had you cornered in the flat?'

'No.'

'Maybe you told him where you were, and said you were in danger? Did he come and rescue you?'

'No, absolutely not.'

'You claim not to remember anything, but you remember that?'

'I . . .'

'Isn't it just as likely that your dad killed him?'

'Dad?'

'Yes.'

'You're trying to confuse me.'

'We'll see,' said Elínborg, relenting. 'That's all for now.'

She went out into the corridor and entered her office. Nína's parents were hovering anxiously.

'Is she all right?' Konrád asked.

'Aren't you forgetting something?' asked Elínborg, ignoring his question.

'What?'

'Your part in all this.'

'My part?'

'Why should I believe your little story? Your account and your daughter's are a bit too consistent. Why should I accept what the two of you say?'

'Why not? My part? What do you mean?'

'Why couldn't *you* have slashed Runólfur's throat?'

'Are you mad?'

'We can't dismiss the possibility that you killed him. Your daughter rings you, you hurry to her, slit Runólfur's throat, and the two of you flee the scene.'

'You can't think it was me!'

'You deny it?'

'Of course I do! Are you insane?'

'Was there any blood on your daughter when you arrived?'

'No, not that I noticed.'

'Shouldn't there have been, considering the nature of the murder?'

'Perhaps. I wouldn't know.'

'There was no blood on her,' Nína's mother said. 'I remember that.'

'What about your husband?' countered Elínborg. 'Was there any blood on him?'

'No.'

'I assure you that we will find the clothes he was wearing that night. Or did you burn them?'

'Burn them?' said Konrád.

'Nína has a far better case than you have,' Elínborg went on. 'She could get off on self-defence, but you would go down for murder. You and your daughter have had plenty of time to get your story straight, after all.'

Konrád stared at Elínborg as if he could not credit what he was hearing. 'I can't believe you're making such an allegation!'

'There's one thing I've learnt from play-acting like yours,' Elínborg said. 'It's almost always based on a lie.'

'Surely you don't think I'd kill someone and lay the blame on my own daughter?'

'I've seen worse.'

23

Elínborg was sitting in her car near Edvard's house, nibbling at a sandwich and sipping at a cup of coffee that was now stone cold. She listened to the evening news on the radio, which included a report about the arrest of a father and daughter who were suspects in Runólfur's murder and had been remanded in custody.

The news team speculated freely about what had happened in Runólfur's flat, what had led to his death at the hands of the man and his daughter, precisely how the events had unfolded. Some of the ideas put forward were accurate, while others were nonsense. A theory was proposed that the woman now in custody had been raped by Runólfur and had then taken her revenge. The police had issued no information on the arrests and had avoided answering questions, which the media were now eagerly trying to answer for themselves. Not wanting to be caught up in the circus, Elínborg had left the station.

The sandwich was disgusting, the coffee was now undrinkable, and she was getting very uncomfortable in the car. Soon she would knock at Edvard's door and ask him about Lilja, the young girl from Akranes who had disappeared six years ago. The car was chilly but she did not want to keep the engine running and risk drawing attention to her presence. She was also reluctant to pollute the atmosphere more than necessary. She never left the engine running when the car was stationary – it was practically the only cast-iron rule she observed as a driver.

Though Elínborg normally shunned fast food, she was hungry and had stopped at a snack bar on her way to Edvard's. She had searched for something healthy to eat but there had been little choice and she had to settle for a tuna sandwich. The coffee, which had been stewing for hours on a hotplate, was revolting.

She thought about Valthór, who maintained that she had discriminated amongst her children and that Birkir had felt excluded. Before leaving for Sweden, Birkir had told her that he had been happy living with her and Teddi but that he wanted to get to know his father. She had asked him if that was the only reason, and he assured her that it was. She had taken him at his word but could not shake the suspicion that he was shielding her from the truth. Birkir was a quiet, self-effacing boy – like a shy guest at the party of his own life. He had been like that ever since he had come to live with them. Valthór demanded much more attention, as did Aron, and then along came the baby girl, Theodóra, the apple of her mother's eye. Had Birkir really been left out? He did not seem to harbour any resentment against Teddi. Maybe it was different for men: so long as they could talk about cars and football they had no need for intimacy.

Sighing heavily, Elínborg got out of the car. She had no answers.

Edvard had stopped being surprised to see Elínborg on his doorstep.

'What did you forget this time?' he asked when he came to the door.

'I'm sorry to inconvenience you again,' she said. 'May I come in? It's about Runólfur – and some other matters. You may have heard that we've made two arrests in connection with the murder.'

'I saw it on the news,' replied Edvard. 'So the case is solved, then, isn't it?'

'Yes, I expect it is. But there are a few loose ends I

thought you might be able to help us with, since you knew Runólfur better than anyone. If I could sit down with you for a minute?' she added doggedly.

Edvard scowled but then gave way. Elínborg followed him into the living room. He lifted a stack of papers off a chair and placed them on top of a pile of old films. 'You can sit here if you want. I don't suppose I can refuse, but I don't see how I can be any more help to you. I don't know anything.'

'Thank you,' said Elínborg, taking the seat. 'You know we've located the woman who was with him that night?'

'Yes – that was on the news, too. They said he might have raped her. Did he?'

'Did you know about Runólfur's ways?' asked Elínborg without replying to Edvard's question.

'That's what I'm saying – I didn't know anything,' answered Edvard. His annoyance at Elínborg's presence was palpable. 'I don't understand why you keep coming here.'

'By his *ways*, I mean to ask whether you knew about how he behaved towards women – drugging them and then abusing them.'

'I have no idea what he did in his own home.'

'You said he had trouble sleeping and that was why he wanted the Rohypnol. That he didn't want to ask a doctor to prescribe it because it was a problematic drug. Yet you helped him get hold of it. To be quite frank, I don't think you've given us a true picture of your relationship with Runólfur. Do you understand what I'm getting at?'

'I didn't know he was a rapist,' said Edvard.

'So you just decided to take everything he said at face value?'

'I didn't know he was lying.'

'Do you know of any other victims he raped?'

'Me? I'm telling you, I don't know anything else.'

'Did he ever talk about other victims, other women he'd got to know, women who came to his home?'

'No.'

'How many times did you buy Rohypnol for him?'

'Just that one time.'

'Have you ever used it yourself, for your own purposes?'

Edvard stared at her. 'What do you mean?' he asked.

'Did both of you get up to nasty tricks with women?'

'What are you talking about? I don't know what you mean.'

'You claim you were at home alone the night Runólfur was killed,' said Elínborg, discreetly gripping her mobile phone. 'No one can confirm your story. You said you were watching TV. Were you in fact at Runólfur's place?'

'Me? No.'

'Did you slash his throat?'

Edvard jumped to his feet, agitated. 'Are you out of your mind?'

'Why shouldn't it be you?' asked Elínborg.

'I had nothing to do with it! I was here, at home, and I just saw it on the news. You've got the killers. Why are you questioning me? I haven't done anything. Why would I kill Runólfur?'

'I don't know,' said Elínborg. 'You tell me. Maybe you and he had some secrets. Maybe he knew something about you, something discreditable, that you didn't want known.'

'What? Like what? What are you suggesting?'

'Calm down. I want to ask you about another matter.'

Edvard hesitated, then sank back slowly into his seat.

His stare was fixed on Elínborg. She had succeeded in confusing him and sapping his confidence. She was not afraid of him. She had met people who scared her, but Edvard was not one of them. It had been her decision to confront him alone, reckoning that he would find a one-on-one less intimidating. Unafraid though she was, she had nevertheless taken steps to ensure her own safety. She had little idea who this man really was, or how he might react if he felt threatened. A patrol car was nearby and all she had to do to summon support was press a single button on the mobile she was holding. She wanted to provoke Edvard, to shake him up and see how he responded.

'You used to teach in Akranes,' Elínborg said, 'at the comprehensive college. I gather you taught science. Is that correct?'

Edvard looked at her, puzzled. 'Yes.'

'That was several years ago. Then you left, and started teaching here in Reykjavík. There was an unexplained event when you were teaching in Akranes: a young girl, a student at the college, vanished – and has never been heard of again. Do you remember that?'

'I remember when she disappeared,' answered Edvard. 'Why are you asking me about that now?'

'Her name was Lilja. I gather you taught her during the previous school year. Is that correct?'

'I taught her for one school year,' said Edvard. 'What's going on here? What's she got to do with me?'

'What can you tell me about the girl – about Lilja? What do you remember about her?'

'Nothing,' said Edvard, a tone of uncertainty in his voice now. 'I didn't know her at all. I taught her, but, after all, I taught dozens of students. I was there for several years. Have you questioned other members of staff? Or are you only questioning me?'

'I'm going to question others, and actually I've already made a start,' answered Elínborg. 'I want to re-examine the case, and it occurred to me to ask you because your name came up.'

'*My* name?'

'The police interviewed you at the time. I've read the report. You used to drive from Reykjavík to Akranes and back every day, morning and evening. That was in the report. You finished early on Fridays, if I remember correctly?'

'Yes, that must be right if it's in the report. I don't remember.'

'What kind of girl was Lilja?'

'I told you, I didn't know her.'

'Did you have a good car back then?'

'The same one I drive now. It's parked outside.'

'Did you ever give your students a lift to Reykjavík? If they had something to do in town, or if they were going out for the evening?'

'No.'

'You never offered anyone a lift?'

'No.'

'Never?'

'No, I didn't.'

'What if I tell you I know a girl you once drove to Reykjavík and dropped her off at the shopping mall?'

Edvard thought about this. 'Are you saying I'm lying?' he asked.

'I don't know,' answered Elínborg.

'If I ever gave anyone a lift, then that would have been quite exceptional. Maybe if someone had asked me. Another member of staff, perhaps. I don't remember any students asking me.'

'The person I'm talking about didn't have to ask you. You picked her up in Akranes. You stopped and offered. Do you remember now?'

Edvard's face flushed red and his hands, which had been fiddling restlessly with papers and video cases on the desk, now lay motionless before him. His forehead was beaded with perspiration. He kept the house very warm. Elínborg passed her phone from hand to hand.

'No. Someone's been telling you lies.'

'She was waiting for the bus.'

'I don't recall anything like that.'

'She speaks well of you,' said Elínborg. 'You dropped her off at the shops. She was going into Reykjavík. I can't see why she would invent it.'

'I don't remember that at all.'

'She was a student at the college.'

Edvard offered no response.

'Lilja disappeared on a Friday, a day when you got off early and drove back to Reykjavík. You finished at midday, apparently. You weren't asked at the time – but *did* you go straight back to Reykjavík? That lunchtime?'

'Are you alleging that I killed both that girl *and* Runólfur? What's the matter with you?'

'I'm not alleging anything,' Elínborg replied. 'Answer the question, please.'

'I don't see why I should answer such ridiculous

questions,' Edvard retorted. He was pulling himself together, trying to show that he would not be bullied.

'That's up to you. I have to ask these questions. You can answer now, or you can answer later. Did you see Lilja in Akranes that Friday, when you left for Reykjavík?'

'No.'

'Did you offer her a lift to town?'

'No.'

'Do you know anything about Lilja's movements that Friday?'

'No. Please leave now. I've no more to say to you. I don't know why you won't leave me in peace. I knew Runólfur, that's all. He was a good friend of mine. Does that make me a guilty party in all these cases of yours?'

'You made contact with a known drug dealer and bought drugs for Runólfur.'

'So what? Does that make me a killer?'

'That's your word, not mine.'

'Why do you keep coming here? It's not my word at all!'

'I haven't said anything about you harming either of them,' said Elínborg. 'You're the one who keeps going on about it. I'm simply asking you whether you gave Lilja a lift into Reykjavík on the day she disappeared. Nothing else. You had a car. You commuted by car. You knew who Lilja was, having taught her. Are my questions at all unreasonable?'

Edvard did not answer.

Elínborg stood up and put her phone away in her pocket. Edvard was not going to be a problem. He seemed more taken aback than anything else, and came across as edgy and neurotic by nature. Elínborg could not decide whether he was lying.

'Lilja may well have gone to Reykjavík that day, and disappeared there,' she said. 'That's one possibility. I thought you might know something about her movements. I haven't been implying anything about your role in her disappearance. You've drawn your own inferences.'

'You're just trying to confuse me.'

'You taught Lilja science – you said she wasn't an outstanding student.'

'That's right.'

'Her mother says that she was especially good at science, and that maths was her favourite subject.'

'Is this relevant?'

'If she was a good student, then you might have noticed.'

Edvard was silent.

'But you kept quiet after she disappeared – you probably didn't want to attract attention from the police.'

'Leave me alone,' said Edvard.

'Thank you for your help,' said Elínborg.

'Leave me alone,' repeated Edvard. 'Just leave me alone.'

24

Formal questioning of Konrád and Nína began early the following morning.

Elínborg was in charge. Nína was brought first into the interview room where the detective was waiting. Her father would be questioned afterwards. The young woman appeared composed when she greeted Elínborg. She had been to the rape-trauma centre for tests and had been offered counselling.

'Did you manage to sleep?' asked Elínborg.

'Yes, a bit. The first time for days,' answered Nína, who was accompanied by her lawyer, a middle-aged man. 'How about you? How did you sleep?' she asked sarcastically.

'My father didn't do anything wrong, you know. He just came to help me. He's innocent.'

'I hope so,' replied Elínborg. She did not add that she had indeed slept well, having taken a sleeping pill. She did so very rarely, and only as a last resort since she disliked using any kind of medication. But she had slept badly for several nights in a row and had been struggling to work on minimal rest. She knew that she could not go on like that, so when she lay down in bed she had placed a little tablet under her tongue – and slept blissfully until morning.

As before, Elínborg started by taking Nína through the events leading up to her encounter with Runólfur. Nína's account was entirely consistent with what she had said previously. She spoke clearly and confidently, as if she was finally prepared to deal with everything that had happened, her present situation, and the court case that lay ahead. She seemed less depressed than the day before, as if the half-remembered nightmare, the denial and the fear had given way at last to a reality that had to be confronted.

'When your father – Konrád – came to help you, as you said, how did he get into the flat?' asked Elínborg.

'I don't know. I think the door was open, or unlocked. He just appeared.'

'You didn't let him in?'

'No, I didn't. I don't think so. I don't remember. I was caught up in this horrific experience. I'm sure he can tell you how he got in.'

Elínborg nodded. According to Konrád, the door had been ajar when he arrived. 'Perhaps you'd got out of bed before he arrived, and opened it?'

'I don't think so.'

'Maybe you intended to run away, and changed your mind when you got to the door?'

'It's possible. I remember I found my mobile and rang Dad.'

'Do you think it was Runólfur who opened the door?'

'I don't know,' said Nína, raising her voice. 'I swear, I can hardly remember anything that happened. He'd drugged me – with a drug that affects the memory. What do you want me to say? I can't remember anything!'

'Do you think you might have managed to ring your father before Runólfur was dead? Perhaps your father defended you by attacking Runólfur?'

'No.'

'How can you be sure?'

'I told you: I woke up alone in the flat, and went into the other room, and there was Runólfur lying on the floor. That's when I rang Dad. Why won't you believe me? That's all I remember. I must have attacked Runólfur and . . .'

'There's not much evidence of a struggle in the flat,'

Elínborg pointed out. 'The murder was neat and tidy, so to speak – except for all the blood, of course. So you would have had to creep up on him and slash his throat quite skilfully. Do you think you'd have been capable of that?'

'Maybe. If I'd had no alternative, if I'd had to defend myself. If I'd been drugged.'

'But there was no blood on you, according to your mother.'

'I don't remember anything about that. I took a shower when we got home, although that's not clear in my mind either.'

'After you got to Runólfur's place, did you see him drink anything – or take any pills?'

'I seem to be saying the same thing over and over again. I don't remember arriving there. I remember a little bit about walking home with him, and my next memory is of coming to in his bed.'

'Did you give him Rohypnol before he died? So that it would be easier to kill him?'

Nína shook her head in confusion, as if she did not understand the question.

'Did I give him . . . ?'

'We know that before he died he'd taken the same drug he used on you. The Rohypnol would have made him incapable of defending himself. So there's something you're not telling us. Something you're still concealing. Maybe you're covering for your father – or perhaps for someone else? But you're still hiding behind your parents and playing games with us. I think you're covering for your father. Am I right?'

'I didn't drug that man. I'm not covering for anyone.'

'When you came out of the bedroom and saw Runólfur's body you didn't call the police. Why not?'

'I told you.'

'Was it to conceal what your father had done?'

'No. There's nothing to conceal. He didn't do anything.'

'But . . .'

'You can't think that Dad killed him,' Nína protested anxiously. 'Dad could never do a thing like that. Never. You don't know him, what he's been through, ever since he was a boy.'

'You mean the polio?'

Nína nodded. Elínborg remained silent.

'I shouldn't have rung him,' said Nína. 'If I'd known he would be a suspect, I never would have.'

'So can you explain to me more clearly why you and your father didn't call the police?'

'I was ashamed,' Nína said. 'Ashamed of being there. Of having gone there, having no memory of it, and waking up naked in a strange bed. Of being raped. I knew at once what he'd done to me. I felt . . . I felt humiliated. I didn't want anyone to know. It was just so disgusting. I saw the condom on the floor, imagined what people might say. What if I'd come on to him? Was it somehow all my fault? Had I brought this on myself, brought it on my family? When I saw him dead on the floor, I think I went mad for a moment. I don't know that I can describe it any better than that. I was scared – scared of what I had seen, and scared of the shame. I could hardly force myself to tell my own father what I was doing there, alone and naked with a complete stranger. How could I tell the police?'

'There's no shame in being raped. It's the rapist who is shamed,' said Elínborg.

'I understand them better now,' mumbled Nína. 'God, how well I understand them.'

'Them?'

'The victims. I think I appreciate now what they go through. You hear about these rapes but there are so many horrors on the news that you tune them out, including the rapes. Now I know that behind every news story about rape there's a revolting experience like mine. They're women like me, women who've suffered horrific violence. And those men! What kind of beasts are they? I . . .'

'What?'

'I know I shouldn't be saying this, and especially not to you. Especially not here, in this place. But I don't care. When I think of what he did to me, it just makes me so angry. How he treated me. Drugged me and then raped me!'

'What is it that you're trying to say?'

'And the sentences they're given! It's an outrage. The legal system doesn't punish the bastards – it pats them on the back.' Nína took a deep breath. 'Sometimes . . .' She struggled to suppress her tears. 'There are times when I'd like to remember cutting his throat.'

About an hour later it was Konrád's turn. Like his daughter, he was calm to start with, sitting in the interview room with his lawyer. He was tired, remarking that he had not slept at all. His wife had taken on the unenviable task of telling their son in San Francisco about the misfortunes that had overtaken his family. Konrád was worried about his daughter.

'How is Nína?' were the first words out of his mouth.

'She's not happy, of course,' said Elínborg. 'We want to get this over with as quickly as possible.'

'I don't understand how you could possibly think I was involved in the man's death. I know I said that I would rather it had been me and not my daughter that killed him. But any father in my position would say that. I imagine you'd say the same yourself.'

'This isn't about me,' Elínborg replied.

'I hope you're not taking what I said as some kind of confession.'

'Why didn't you call the police when you saw what had happened at Runólfur's home?'

'It was a mistake,' said Konrád. 'I know that. We could never have gone on concealing the truth. We realised that almost at once. I know it's hard for you to understand, but put yourself in our shoes. I felt that Nína had been through enough, and I thought it would be all right so long as you – the police – didn't know about her. They'd met at a bar that evening. She hadn't told anyone where she was or who she was with. I did my best to take all her things away but I missed the shawl.'

'Can we discuss how you got into Runólfur's flat? I'm not clear about that.'

'I simply walked in. The door was not quite closed. Nína probably opened the door – she was expecting me. We might have talked about it on the phone as I made my way over – how I was to get in. I'm not quite sure.'

'She doesn't remember, either.'

'Well, the state she was in – and I wasn't much better myself. I had the impression he'd been burning something, that man. I noticed a smell like that.'

'Burning?'

'Or . . . do you know if he had any paraffin around the place?'

'Paraffin?'

'You didn't find any paraffin there?'

'No. Nothing like that.'

'Didn't anyone notice a smell? A sort of paraffin smell?'

'We didn't find any paraffin,' said Elínborg. 'There was nothing of that sort in the flat.'

'Well, there was a smell of paraffin when I got there,' said Konrád.

'There was nothing to indicate that he'd been burning anything except for some tea-light candles, that was all. What did you and your daughter do with the knife?'

'What knife?'

'The one your daughter used to kill Runólfur.'

'She didn't have any knife when I arrived. I gave no thought to it. She must have got rid of it somehow, during all the commotion.'

'How do you shave? What do you use? An electric shaver? Safety razor? Straight razor?'

'I use a safety razor.'

'Do you own a straight razor?'

'No.'

'Have you ever owned one?'

Konrád thought about it.

'We've got a warrant to search your home,' said Elínborg. 'And your daughter's.'

'I've never owned a straight razor,' said Konrád. 'I don't

even know how to use one. Is that what was used to kill him? A razor?'

'There's another thing that puzzles us,' said Elínborg. 'Your daughter, Nína, claims to have attacked Runólfur, although she has no memory of doing so. She says it's the only possible explanation. So far as she knows, the two of them were alone in the flat. Do you think she could subdue a man like Runólfur on her own? Especially if he'd drugged her, and she was incapacitated?'

Konráð considered the question. 'I'm well aware of the state she was in,' he said.

'She might have been capable of it, if she was in fact fully conscious and acted quickly and quietly, and took Runólfur by surprise,' said Elínborg. 'But first she would have had to get hold of the weapon. She had to be prepared.'

'I suppose.'

'Was she?'

'What do you mean?'

'Was she prepared, when she went home with Runólfur?'

'How could she have been prepared? She didn't know the man. What are you talking about?'

'I'm talking about premeditated murder,' said Elínborg. 'I'm saying your daughter went there with the express intention of killing Runólfur. I want to find out why. What was her motive? Who did she get to be her accomplice?'

'I have never heard such a load of nonsense,' said Konrád. 'Surely you don't mean that seriously?'

'Runólfur didn't just lie down and die,' said Elínborg. 'We can also consider the events from a different viewpoint. We haven't disclosed the fact that Runólfur himself had ingested Rohypnol shortly before he died. And I don't think he took it of his own accord. Someone must have compelled him. Or slipped it to him, just as he drugged your daughter.'

'He took the stuff himself?'

'We found traces in his mouth. He took a considerable quantity. That puts a different light on the story you and your daughter are telling, don't you think?'

'What are you getting at?'

'Someone forced him to swallow the pills.'

'Not me.'

'If your daughter's telling the truth, I can't see how she would have been able to do it. And there aren't a lot of other candidates. I think you took revenge for his rape of your daughter. To me it looks like a classic payback killing. Nína managed to phone you and ask for help. You hurried over to Thingholt, and she opened the door for you. Perhaps Runólfur was asleep by then. When you saw what had happened, what he had done to her, you went wild. You gave him a taste of his own medicine, and then you slashed his throat – in front of your daughter.'

287

'That's ridiculous. It wasn't me!' Konráð exclaimed.

'So who was it?'

'It wasn't me, and it wasn't Nína,' he said. 'I know she could never hurt anyone. She's simply not like that – even if he'd drugged her and she wasn't herself.'

'You shouldn't underestimate what people will do in self-defence.'

'She didn't do it.'

'Well, *someone* made him swallow the pills.'

'Then it must have been someone else. Some other person there, in the flat with them.' Konráð leaned forward over the table between Elínborg and him. 'Nína couldn't do it. And I didn't do it, I know that. So there's only one other possibility. There must have been someone else there with Runólfur. Someone other than my daughter!'

25

The idea that a third person could have been present at Runólfur's place was not new to the police. Elínborg had twice questioned Edvard about his whereabouts on the night of Runólfur's death and he gave the same answer both times: he had been alone at home watching television. His story could not be corroborated. It was not impossible that Edvard was lying, but the police were not aware of any motive for him to have killed his friend. And Elínborg's assessment of him was that he would hardly have been capable of such a drastic act. Her theory that he was involved in Lilja's disappearance was tenuous: there was no evidence that he had given the girl a lift to town, and even if he had that was not proof of anything. He could claim to have dropped her off anywhere, after which she had disappeared. Yet Elínborg could not let go of Edvard.

She spent the day questioning Nína and Konrád, whose accounts remained unchanged throughout repeated interviews. Nína was more convinced than ever that she must be responsible for Runólfur's death; she almost seemed to hope that she had done it. Konrád, on the other hand, was tending in the opposite direction; he felt that his daughter was fundamentally incapable of the deed, and he steadfastly denied having killed Runólfur himself. No test could now confirm whether Nína had been drugged and had therefore been physically incapacitated. The police had only her word for it, that she had no memory of the events. It was entirely possible that she had been fully conscious the whole time.

And then there was the matter of Runólfur. He could hardly have taken the Rohypnol voluntarily. Someone must have compelled him – someone who wanted payback. Was it possible that Nína had forced the drug down his throat? So many questions remained unanswered. To Elínborg's way of thinking, Konrád and Nína were the most likely suspects. Nína had not confessed directly but Elínborg was expecting to elicit a full confession before long, after which she thought the father and daughter would tell her where the murder weapon was.

Not that she was pleased about it. Runólfur had dragged down good people to flounder in the filth of his unsavoury world.

Later that afternoon Elínborg parked, yet again, some distance from Edvard's house to observe what went on there. His car was parked in its usual place. Elínborg had checked the website of the college he taught at and had found his timetable: he generally finished around three o'clock. She was not sure what she expected to gain by keeping an eye on Edvard. Perhaps her sympathy for Konrád and his daughter was making her a little biased and unduly keen to exonerate them.

From where she sat Elínborg could see the dry dock of the old harbour, soon to make way for new residential developments on the former dockside. History would be erased at a stroke. She thought of Erlendur, who clung to the old ways. She did not always agree with him – after all, progress demanded space. Erlendur had ranted on about one particular building, the Gröndal House, which was to be moved from its location in the old town to the open-air museum on the outskirts of the city. Why, he had fumed, shouldn't it stay where it was, in the heart of the old town where it belonged, in the context of its history? The building was important, he said, bearing the name of the nineteenth-century writer Benedikt Gröndal who had written his autobiography – Erlendur's favourite book – under that very roof. The Gröndal House was one of only a handful of nineteenth-century buildings remaining in Reykjavík: 'And so they're going to uproot it,' Erlendur had grumbled, 'and dump it in the middle of nowhere!'

Elínborg had been sitting in the car for nearly two hours when at last the door opened, and Edvard emerged and drove off. She followed him. He made his way first to a cut-price supermarket, after which he called at a laundry and then at a video-rental shop that was closing down. On the front of the shop was a sign: EVERYTHING MUST GO. CLOSING-DOWN SALE. Edvard spent a long time inside before reappearing loaded down with videos, which he put in the boot of his car. He stood outside for a long time talking to the owner before driving off.

His next port of call was a telephone company – the same one that had employed Runólfur. Through the window Elínborg watched Edvard examining mobile phones. A shop assistant came over to him and they discussed the phones at length, until Edvard made his selection and bought one. He drove back towards his home, stopping on the way at a burger joint. He took his time over his meal and Elínborg almost decided to abandon her surveillance. She did not know what she expected to find out; she was probably tailing an innocent man.

She rang home, and Theodóra answered. They spoke

briefly. Theodóra had brought two friends home from school and did not have time to chat with her mum. Teddi was not home yet, and Theodóra had no idea where her brothers were.

Edvard finished eating and returned to his car. Elínborg said goodbye to her daughter and followed him again. He was heading westwards towards his home, along by the old harbour. At the old dry dock he slowed down and pulled over to park with his wheels up on the pavement. He seemed to be looking out over the dry dock and across the bay to Mount Esja. Elínborg was in a quandary. She could not pull in behind him so she went on and stopped in the next car park, where she waited until Edvard drove slowly past towards his home.

Elínborg parked in her usual spot and switched off the engine. Edvard carried his clean laundry, groceries and videos inside, and shut the door behind him. It was evening now and Elínborg felt guilty about neglecting her family, who these days were surviving mostly on takeaways provided by Teddi. She resolved that she must give more priority to her home life; she must be there for Theodóra and the boys, and make time for Teddi, who tended to spend his evenings in front of the television. He claimed to watch mostly documentaries, wildlife programmes especially, but that was rubbish. She had often come home to find him absorbed in mindless drivel such as American reality TV – weddings, models or castaways, it was all the same. Those were Teddi's new 'wildlife documentaries'.

Elínborg saw one of Edvard's neighbours come out and open his garage door. Inside was an old car, which he set to waxing and polishing. It was a classic car, unfamiliar to Elínborg: a large, flashy vehicle dating from the 1950s, with baby-blue bodywork, shiny chrome fittings, and tall, dramatic fins at the rear. Teddi adored that kind of car, especially Cadillacs: Caddies, he said, were the best cars ever made. Elínborg had no idea whether this was a Cadillac, but she knew exactly how to strike up a conversation with the owner. She got out of her car and walked over to him.

'Good evening,' she said as she looked in at the garage door. The owner of the car looked up from what he was doing and returned her greeting. He was fiftyish, with a friendly, cherubic face.

'Is this your car?' asked Elínborg.

'Yes,' replied the man. 'Yes, it's mine.'

'It's a Cadillac, isn't it?'

'No, actually it's a Chrysler New Yorker, '59 model. I got it sent over from America a few years back.'

'Oh, a Chrysler?' responded Elínborg. 'Is it in pretty good nick?'

'It's in very good condition,' the man replied. 'It doesn't need any work, just a bit of spit and polish now and then.

Do you like classic cars? You don't meet a lot of women who are interested.'

'No, not exactly. It's my husband who loves them. He's a motor mechanic and he had a car like this once, but he sold it in the end. He'd like this one.'

'Oh, well, send him over to see me, by all means,' the man said. 'I'll take him out for a spin.'

'Have you lived here long?' enquired Elínborg.

'Since my wife and I were married. Must be about twenty-five years now. I like to be near the sea. We often go for a walk along the shore here, around by the harbour.'

'I hear it's all going to be cleared for new construction at the old dock. What do the locals feel about that?'

'I'm not happy,' said the man. 'I don't know about anyone else. I feel we shouldn't always be chucking out our history, and the traditional ways of life and work. It's not as if we've got much left: all the businesses that used to be down by the harbour are forgotten now. And the dry dock will go next.'

'I don't suppose your neighbours are pleased.'

'No, probably not.'

'Do you know them well?'

'Reasonably.'

'I was passing through and thought I recognised the man in the yellow house over there, the one with the alder tree growing over it. Do you happen to know his name?'

'Do you mean Edvard?' asked the man.

'Yes, Edvard, that's right!' exclaimed Elínborg, as if she had been racking her brains. 'That's him. I used to work with him,' she said. 'Is he still teaching, or . . . ?'

'Yes, he's a teacher. At one of the secondary colleges – I don't remember which one.'

'We used to teach together at Hamrahlíd High School,' Elínborg said. She felt bad about lying to her new acquaintance but she was reluctant to admit she was a police officer. The word would spread quickly through the neighbourhood and soon get back to Edvard himself.

'Right,' said the man. 'I don't see much of him. He keeps himself to himself, and you hardly notice him.'

'I know. He's a bit of a mystery. Has he lived here long?'

'I think he moved in about ten years ago. He was still a student back then.'

'But he could afford to buy a house?'

'I wouldn't know anything about that,' the man said. 'But I think he used to have a lodger for a while, a few years ago. Maybe that helped towards the mortgage.'

'Yes, I remember him mentioning that,' Elínborg lied. 'Didn't he teach in Akranes at one time?'

'Yes, that's right.'

'Did he drive up there every day?'

'Yes, he did. He had the same car he's driving now. It's

296

pretty decrepit. As I say, I don't know Edvard very well even though we're neighbours. He's more of an acquaintance, really. I don't know much about him.'

'Is he still single?' asked Elínborg, trying to feel her way forward.

'Oh, yes. Edvard doesn't seem to have much to do with women. Not that I've noticed, at any rate.'

'He was certainly no party animal when I knew him.'

'That hasn't changed, then. I never see anyone at the house at weekends,' said the man, with a smile. 'Or at all. He's pretty much a loner.'

'Good luck with the Chrysler,' said Elínborg. 'She's a beauty.'

'Yes,' the man replied. 'She's a real humdinger.'

As Elínborg was pulling up outside her home, her mobile rang. She turned the engine off and glanced at the screen. She did not recognise the number and was in two minds about answering. It had been a tiring day and she longed for a few hours of peace and quiet at home. She looked at the number, trying to place it. The children sometimes used her phone, and occasionally one of their friends would ring her number by accident. The ringing was irritating but she was reluctant to turn it off. She decided to answer.

'Good evening,' said a woman's voice. 'Is that Elínborg?'

'Yes, I'm Elínborg,' she snapped.

'I'm sorry to call so late.'

'That's all right. Who is this?'

'We haven't met,' said the woman. 'I'm a bit worried, although I probably shouldn't be. He can look after himself, and he likes to be alone.'

'Excuse me, who is speaking?'

'My name is Valgerdur,' the woman replied. 'I don't think we've spoken before.'

'Valgerdur?'

'I'm a friend of your colleague Erlendur. I've tried to contact Sigurdur Óli but he's not answering.'

'No,' said Elínborg. 'He won't pick up if he doesn't recognise the number. Are you all right?'

'Yes, thank you. I just wanted to find out if Erlendur has been in touch with either of you. He's gone to the East Fjords and I haven't heard from him.'

'No, I haven't either,' said Elínborg. 'How long is it since he went to the east?'

'Nearly two weeks now. He'd been working on a difficult case, which I think he found very distressing. I'm a bit worried about him.'

Erlendur had not said goodbye to Elínborg or Sigurdur Óli when he left – they had simply found out at the station that he had taken a leave of absence. Just before that he had discovered the bodies of a man and woman who had been missing for twenty-five years. He had also been pursuing another case on his own time but had been unable to uncover enough evidence for a prosecution.

'I should think Erlendur just wants to be left alone,' said Elínborg. 'Two weeks isn't all that long, if he was planning to stay in the east for a while. I know he's been working very hard lately.'

'Perhaps. Either he's turned his mobile off, or he's in some dead spot.'

'He'll turn up,' said Elínborg. 'He's gone off before without telling anyone.'

'Well, that's good to know. If he does get in touch, perhaps you'd let him know I was asking after him?'

26

Theodóra was still awake. She moved over in bed and Elínborg lay down next to her. They lay quietly together for a while without speaking. Elínborg's mind was on Lilja, who had vanished from Akranes. She thought of the young woman dumped by the road in Kópavogur who had locked herself away in her misery. She recalled Nína in tears in the interview room: imagined her, knife in hand, slashing Runólfur's throat.

The house was silent. The boys were out and Teddi was at the garage, working late over his accounts.

'Don't worry, Mum,' said Theodóra. She sensed a restlessness in her mother, who was tired and distracted. 'Not about us, anyway. We know you sometimes have to work a lot. Don't worry about us.'

Elínborg smiled. 'I think I have the best daughter in the world,' she said.

They did not speak for a while. The wind was rising, howling at the windows. Autumn was gradually giving way to winter, and to the cold and darkness it would bring.

'What is it you must never do?' Elínborg asked Theodóra after a few minutes. 'Never?'

'Never accept a lift from a stranger,' replied Theodóra.

'That's right,' said Elínborg.

'No exceptions,' recited Theodóra, using the words she had long since been taught by her mother. 'No matter what they say, whether it's a man or a woman. Never get into a car with a stranger.'

'It's a pity to have to say it . . .' Elínborg said.

Theodóra, who had heard these words many times before, finished the sentence for her: '. . . because the majority of strangers are perfectly good people, but there are always a handful who can't be trusted. And that's why you must never get into a car with strangers. Even if they say they're police officers.'

'That's my girl, Theodóra,' Elínborg said.

'Are you investigating a case like that?'

'I don't know,' answered Elínborg. 'Perhaps.'

'Did someone accept a lift?'

'I don't want to tell you about what I'm doing at present,' said Elínborg. 'Sometimes it's no fun to talk about work when you get home.'

'I read in the paper that two people are being held – a man and his daughter.'

'Yes.'

'How did you find them?'

'I followed my nose,' said Elínborg smiling and pointing at her nose. 'I think it was my sense of smell that broke the case. The daughter likes tandoori cookery, like me.'

'So is there a spicy smell in her house, like here?'

'Yes, much the same.'

'Were you in danger?'

'No, sweetheart, I wasn't in any danger. They're not that kind of people. I've told you, police officers are rarely at any risk.'

'But the police are often attacked. On the streets.'

'Those assailants are just hoodlums, the dregs of society,' said Elínborg. 'Don't you worry about low life like that.'

Theodóra gave that some thought. Her mum had been in the police all of Theodóra's life, but she had very little sense of her job because Elínborg did not want her to know too much about it while she was so young. Theodóra's friends generally had some sense of what their parents did at work, but not Theodóra. She had occasionally been to police headquarters, when Elínborg had no option but to take her along. She would sit in a small office, waiting for her mother as she hurriedly finished some task. Men and women, some in uniform, others in plain clothes, would look around the door and say hello, smiling and expressing amazement at how big she was getting. All except one man, wearing an overcoat, who frowned at her and asked Elínborg brusquely what she thought she was doing with a child in a place like this. Theodóra never forgot the words the man had used: *a place like this*. She asked her mum who he was, but Elínborg shook her head and told her daughter to forget it – the man had his problems.

'What *is* your job, Mum?' asked Theodóra.

'It's just like an ordinary office job, darling,' her mum replied. 'Nearly finished!'

But Theodóra knew perfectly well that it was no ordinary office. She knew about some of the things police officers did in their work, and she was well aware that her mum was a police officer. Just as Elínborg finished speaking, a great commotion broke out in the corridor, where a man, handcuffed between two policemen, had gone berserk. Punching and kicking in all directions, he headbutted one of the policemen, who collapsed with blood pouring down his face. Elínborg shepherded Theodóra back into the little office and shut the door.

'Maniacs,' she hissed under her breath, with an apologetic smile at her daughter.

Theodóra remembered what Valthór had said, late one evening when their mum was still at work. He said she was dealing with some of the worst criminals in the country. It was one of very few occasions when Theodóra sensed that her older brother was proud of their mother.

As Theodóra lay in bed with her mother beside her, she asked the question again:

'What *is* your job, Mum?'

Elínborg did not know how to respond. Theodóra had always been interested in what she did at work: curious about the details, what Elínborg was doing, what kind of people she had to deal with, who her colleagues were. Elínborg had done her best to answer Theodóra's questions without touching on murder and rape, violence against women and children, brutal assaults. She had witnessed so much that she would have preferred not to see, and it was impossible to tell a child about it.

'We help people,' she said finally. 'People who need our help. We try to make sure they can live their lives in peace.' Elínborg stood up and smoothed the quilt over her daughter. 'Was I not kind enough to Birkir?' she asked.

'Yes, you were.'

'So what went wrong?'

'Birkir never thought of you as his mother,' said

Theodóra. 'He told Valthór, but you mustn't say I told you.'

'Valthór tells you all sorts of odd things.'

'He said Birkir had had enough of us, his foster family.'

'Could we have done anything differently?' asked Elínborg.

'No, I'm sure we couldn't.'

Elínborg kissed her daughter's forehead. 'Goodnight, sweetheart.'

The questioning of Konráð and Nína continued after Elínborg left. They were asked repeatedly about their movements on the night of the attack, and their story remained unchanged. Their accounts were very consistent but, as Elínborg pointed out, they had had plenty of time to agree on a story. The witness who had reported seeing a woman in the passenger seat of a car in Thingholt when he was walking home that night was brought in to identify Konráð's wife. He was sure that she was the woman he had seen.

The next afternoon Elínborg entered the interview room where Konráð was being held. Konráð was clearly worn down by being locked up and bombarded with questions, and by his anxiety about his family, especially Nína. He asked Elínborg how his daughter was, and she assured him that Nína was managing as well as could be expected. Everybody wanted this process to be over. 'Wouldn't you expect to find blood on my daughter's clothes, or on her hands?' demanded Konrád in response to a barrage of questions about Nína's part in Runólfur's death. 'I didn't see any bloodstains on her – not on her clothes, not on her hands. There was no blood.'

'You said you didn't notice.'

'I remember now.'

'Can you prove it?'

'No, I can't prove it. I know I should have called the police right away, got them to come, let them see the evidence, and shown them that Nína could not have killed him. And I was wrong not to take Nína to the rape-trauma centre and arrange counselling. We should have done all those things, I realise that. We shouldn't have run away. It was wrong, and it's rebounded on us. But you must believe me. Nína could never have done it. Never.'

Elínborg looked at the police officers who were conducting the interview. They beckoned her to join them.

'I think your daughter is ready to confess,' she said. 'Nína has all but told me she killed Runólfur. Her only regret is that she doesn't remember cutting his throat.'

'He raped her,' said Konrád. 'That bloody bastard raped her.'

Elínborg had not heard Konrád swear before. 'That gives us all the more reason to believe that when she came round she slipped him the same drug that he had used on her, overpowered him, and then slit his throat. Perhaps she tricked him – spiked his drink, then washed the glass. A lot of evidence points to that.'

'This makes me sick,' countered Konrád.

'Unless it was you?' said Elínborg.

'Who was this Runólfur?' asked Konrád. 'What kind of a man was he?'

'I don't know how to answer that,' replied Elínborg. 'We never had any dealings with him while he was alive. You must appreciate our problem. Although your daughter says she was raped, we have no evidence. Why should we believe her? Why should we believe *you*?'

'You can believe everything she says.'

'I want to,' said Elínborg. 'But there are problems with her story.'

'I've never known her to lie. Not to me, not to her mother, nor to anyone else. It breaks my heart to see her caught up in this awful mess, this nightmare. It's appalling. I'd do anything for it to be over. Anything at all.'

'You know he was wearing Nína's T-shirt?'

'I realised that later. I took my jacket and wrapped it around Nína, then picked up her clothes. I ought to have been more careful. I knew you were on to us as soon as you asked me about San Francisco. That was no routine enquiry.'

'You said you wished it had been you that killed him. Nína says she wishes she remembered cutting his throat. Which of you did it? Are you prepared to tell me now?'

'Does Nína say she did it?'

'Virtually.'

'I'm not confessing to anything,' said Konrád. 'We're innocent. You should believe us, and put a stop to all this.'

27

Elínborg spent the rest of the day shopping. She bought a selection of healthy foods, which she was forever trying to encourage her sons and their father to eat but with limited success. She bought a steak; she was planning to keep her promise to serve Valthór his favourite. He liked his meat rare, but Elínborg was not keen on bloody meat. She relaxed as she shopped, and tried not to think about the case which was weighing so heavily on her. Into the trolley went a jar of artichoke hearts, Colombian coffee, Icelandic yoghurt.

When she got home she soaked in a hot bath, and unwound so completely that she fell fast asleep. She had not realised how tired the strain of the last few days had left her. She awoke to hear someone moving around the house – one of the children, home from school. She tried in vain to keep her mind off her work. Edvard kept entering her mind. His squalid little house, the rusty old banger parked outside, and the twisted branches of the tree that loomed over the roof like eerie claws. The more she thought about Lilja, the more repulsive she found the house and its owner, Edvard, who shuffled around the rooms, hunched, unshaven, with unkempt hair, nervy and graceless. She could not honestly imagine him hurting anyone, but that proved nothing. Edvard's character could not be judged by outward appearances, except for the obvious fact that he was a slob.

Elínborg wanted to go back up to Akranes, to talk to more people who had known Lilja and Edvard. His colleagues on the college staff might have information that they regarded as unimportant, but could be useful to her. She wanted to re-interview Lilja's mother, who had taken refuge in religion. She might also have to question the girl's father, who had dealt with his grief by withdrawal and silence. It would be difficult to interview them without anything firm to go on, and Elínborg was not sure how far she ought to push it. She did not want to give them false hope. That would be no help to anyone.

She wanted to find out more about Runólfur, too.

Konrád had asked her who the man was, and what the police knew about him, and the answer was: not much. Perhaps she should fly back to his village and interview more of the locals.

Elínborg changed out of her work clothes, and went into the kitchen. Theodóra had brought two friends home and they were in her room. Valthór too was in his room: she decided not to disturb him. She wanted to avoid conflict for the rest of the evening.

Before turning her attention to the steak, Elínborg unpacked two cuts of lamb to which she had treated herself for one of her culinary experiments. She went out into the back garden and lit the barbecue, to give it enough time to get good and hot. She took out her tandoori pot and mixed a marinade using Icelandic herbs. She cut the lamb into chunks, which she plunged into the marinade and set aside for half an hour. The grill was very hot when she lifted the tandoori pot on to it along with several large potatoes, which she baked among the coals to serve with the steak. She called Teddi, who said he was on his way home.

Whenever Elínborg focused on her cooking she attained a rare state of calm. She permitted herself to slow down and retreat from the stressful daily round, to concentrate on something other than work and take a break from the family. She emptied her mind of everything but the consideration of different ingredients, and how she could apply her insight and artistry to producing perfection from chaos. In her kitchen she found an outlet for her creativity: she took the ingredients and transformed their nature, taste, texture, aroma. For Elínborg the three stages of cookery – preparation, cooking, and eating – were a recipe for life itself.

She was planning a new cookery book so she made careful notes of all she did. Her first, *More than Just Desserts*, had sold well; she'd been invited to appear on a TV chat show and had been interviewed in the press. She hoped the next book would enjoy equal success.

She heard Teddi come in. She recognised the sounds of each member of the family: Valthór would slam the door behind him, kick off his shoes, chuck his bag on the floor and disappear into his bedroom without so much as a hello. Aron had been tending to do the same lately; after all, he was a teenager now and strove to be just like his big brother. He invariably dumped his coat on the hall floor, however many times he was reminded to hang it up. Theodóra entered quietly, closing the door softly behind her, hung up her coat, and if her parents were at home she would join them in the kitchen for a chat. Teddi sometimes made a noisy entrance via the garage: invariably cheerful, he often came in humming a song that had been on the radio as he drove home. He cleared up as he went – hung the boys' coats up, put their bags away, arranged their shoes on the rack – before coming into the kitchen to greet Elínborg with a kiss.

'Hey! You're home!' he said.

'I promised to cook the kids a steak ages ago,' she said. 'And there's tandoori on the barbecue for us. Would you mind putting the rice on?'

'So have you solved the case?' asked Teddi as he searched out a packet of rice.

'I don't know. We'll find out soon enough.'

'What a clever girl you are,' remarked Teddi, pleased to have Elínborg home at a reasonable hour. He had become a regular customer at various unappetising fried-chicken places at this time of the evening, and he had been missing his wife and her home cooking.

'What do you say? Shall we have a drop of red wine to celebrate?'

Elínborg's mobile started to ring in her coat pocket in the hall.

Teddi's smile faded. He recognised the ringtone of her work phone. 'Aren't you going to take that?' he asked, reaching for a bottle.

'Don't I always?' answered Elínborg, making for the hall. She would have liked to switch the device off and actually considered doing so as she dug it out of her pocket.

Teddi's jacket was lying over a chair in the hall.

'Are you at home?' asked Sigurdur Óli.

'Yes,' snapped Elínborg. 'What do you want? What's up?'

'I was just going to congratulate you, but if you're going to bite my head off I might as well—'

'Congratulate me?'

'He confessed.'

'Who?'

'The man you took into custody,' said Sigurdur Óli. 'Your mate with the wonky leg. Hopalong Cassidy. He's confessed to killing Runólfur.'

'Konrád? When?'

'Just now.'

'So was it all straightforward?'

'Yeah. They were finishing up for the day, and he said he gave up. I wasn't there but that's the gist of it. He confessed. He said he went crazy when he saw what had happened. He claims he didn't force Runólfur to swallow anything but he did notice that he was under the influence of something. He used one of the kitchen knives, apparently, and threw it in the sea on the way home. Can't remember exactly where.'

Elínborg was not convinced. 'The last thing he told me was that they were both innocent.'

'He must have just had enough. I can't read his mind.'

'Does his daughter know about his confession?'

'No, she hasn't been told. I don't suppose we'll tell her till tomorrow.'

'Thanks,' said Elínborg.

'Well, it's all down to your good work, *pardner*,' said Sigurdur Óli. 'Who'd have believed your Indian spices and sauces would solve the case? I wouldn't.'

'See you tomorrow.'

Elínborg broke the connection and absent-mindedly picked up her husband's jacket. The garment smelt strongly of the motor workshop where he worked and a smell of lubricants and tyres filled the hall. Teddi usually took care not to bring the grime of his work into the house but this time he had forgotten. Maybe because he was so pleased to find her at home, thought Elínborg. She carried his jacket into the garage, hung it up, then returned to the kitchen.

'What was the call about?' Teddi asked.

'We've got a confession,' said Elínborg. 'In the Thingholt case.'

'Ah,' said Teddi, a wine bottle in his hand. 'I wasn't sure whether to open it.'

'Yeah, go ahead,' said Elínborg flatly. 'You left your jacket in the hall.'

'Sorry, I was in a bit of a hurry. What's the matter? The case is solved, isn't it?'

He drew the cork from the bottle, with a loud pop.

Teddi poured two glasses of wine and handed one to his wife. 'Cheers!' he said.

Elínborg toasted him back, her attention elsewhere. Teddi could see that she was distracted as she watched the rice boiling in the pan. He took a sip and watched her. He did not want to interrupt her train of thought.

'Could it be?' exclaimed Elínborg.

'Could what be?'

'He's got it all wrong,' said Elínborg.

'What?' asked Teddi, bewildered. 'Is there something wrong with the rice?'

'Rice?'

'Yes – I just did the usual amount.'

'He thought it was paraffin, but he was wrong,' said Elínborg.

'What?'

Elínborg stared at Teddi. Then she went out to the garage and fetched his jacket. She brought it back and handed it to him. 'Can you tell me what this smell is, exactly?'

'The smell on the jacket?'

'Yes. Is it paraffin?'

'No, not exactly . . .' said Teddi as he sniffed at the garment. 'It's engine lubricant. Oil.'

'*Who was this Runólfur?*' said Elínborg under her breath. '*What kind of a man was he?* Konrád asked me that today,

316

and I had no answer for him, because I don't understand him. But I should.'

'What should you understand?'

'Konrád didn't smell paraffin. Dear God! We should have found out more about him. I knew it. We should have paid far more attention to Runólfur.'

28

Elínborg sat in the car for a while before she entered the filling station. Busy as she was, she allowed herself the time to listen to the closing minutes of a radio programme playing golden oldies. Her first husband, Bergsteinn, had been a devotee of classic popular songs. He would often wax lyrical about the good old days of simple, innocent dance tunes, which had given way to raw, angry, confrontational music.

These familiar songs reminded her of Erlendur, who had gone east to where he had lived as a boy. In his desire to be left alone, it looked as if he had left his phone behind and severed all contact with the outside world. On the rare occasions when he took time off to go to the east, that was what he did as a rule. She wondered what he got up to over there. She had taken the liberty of asking about him at the guest house in the village of Eskifjördur, but he had not been seen there. She had hesitated to make the call: she knew Erlendur at least as well as anyone else and she was well aware that he loathed any such interference.

Elínborg walked into the filling station. By trawling through old reports of fatal road accidents she had traced the driver of the lorry that had collided with Runólfur's father's car, killing him. The man had worked for a haulage company in Reykjavík. Elínborg had gone to the company offices to ask about the driver and had spoken to the manager:

'I was wondering if Ragnar Thór was available. I've only got a mobile number and he's not answering,' said Elínborg, after introducing herself.

'Ragnar Thór?' the manager said. 'He hasn't worked here for years.'

'Oh? Who's he driving for now?'

'Driving? No, Ragnar doesn't drive any more. Not since the accident.'

'The accident where the other driver died?'

'Yes – he gave up driving after that.'

'Because of the accident?'

'Yes.' The manager was standing in his office, flicking through bills of lading. He had scarcely looked up from his paperwork.

'Do you know where he's working now?'

'Yes – he's at a filling station in Hafnarfjördur. I saw him last a couple of months ago. He's probably still there.'

'So it affected him badly, did it?'

'Yes. Like I said, he quit driving. Stopped there and then.'

Elínborg had left the haulage company to drive straight to the filling station that the manager had mentioned. It was a quiet time of day and the place was peaceful. A man was standing at a pump, filling the tank himself to save a few *krónur*. Inside, at the till, were a woman of about thirty and an older man. The woman ignored Elínborg, looking out at the forecourt, but the man stood up, smiled, and asked if he could help.

'I'm looking for Ragnar Thór,' said Elínborg.

'Yes, that's me,' the man replied.

'Your mobile doesn't seem to be working.'

'Oh, were you trying to get hold of me? I haven't got round to buying a new one.'

'Could we speak in private?' asked Elínborg, looking at the woman on the till. 'I need to ask you something. It won't take long.'

'Of course,' said the man. He also looked at the woman. 'We can step outside. Who are you?'

They went outside, and Elínborg explained that she was a police officer, working on a delicate case. To cut a long story short, she wanted to ask him about the accident he had been in some years ago, when he'd collided head-on with a car whose driver was killed.

'The crash?' replied Ragnar Thór cautiously.

'I've read the reports,' said Elínborg. 'But I know things get left out of the written versions. I gather you stopped driving after that?'

'I . . . I don't see how I can help you,' said Ragnar Thór, stepping away from her. 'I've never discussed it.'

'I understand. It must have been an awful experience.'

'With all due respect, you can't understand it unless it happens to you. I don't think I can help you, so please leave me alone. I've never talked to anyone about it and I'm not going to start now. I hope you'll respect that.' He made as if to go back to his work.

'The case I'm investigating is the Thingholt Murder,' Elínborg said. 'Have you heard about it?'

Ragnar Thór halted. A car pulled up at one of the pumps.

'The young man who was killed – had his throat cut, in fact – was the son of the man who died in the accident.'

Ragnar Thór looked at her, baffled. 'His son?'

'Runólfur was his name. He lost his father in that crash.'

The driver who had stopped at the pump sat in his car, waiting to be served. The woman on the till did not move.

'It wasn't my fault,' muttered Ragnar Thór. 'The accident wasn't my fault.'

'I think that's generally accepted, Ragnar. He swerved across in front of you.'

The waiting driver tooted his horn. Ragnar Thór glanced over at him. The woman on the till was ignoring them. He went over to the car. The driver lowered his window and, without a word, handed him a 5,000-*krónur* note, then closed the window again.

'What do you want to know?' asked Ragnar Thór, when he had started the pump.

'Was there anything odd about the accident? Something you didn't mention in your statement? Something to explain how it happened? The report only reaches the conclusion that Runólfur's father seems to have lost control of the vehicle.'

'I know.'

'His wife says he fell asleep at the wheel. Is that true? Or did something else happen? Maybe something distracted him? Did he drop a cigarette on the seat?'

'That lad in Thingholt was his son?'

'Yes.'

'I didn't know that.'

'Well, now you do.'

'If I tell you what I left out of my statement, you mustn't tell anyone else.'

'I won't. You can rely on me.'

Ragnar Thór finished filling the car. They stood by the pump. It was midday, a chilly day. 'It was suicide,' said Ragnar Thór.

'Suicide? How do you know?'

'You can't breathe a word of this.'

'No.'

'He smiled at me.'

'Smiled?'

Ragnar Thór nodded. 'He was smiling when the lorry hit him. He had picked me out – my rig, because it was a big juggernaut with a trailer. He pulled over right in front of me, with no warning. There was nothing I could do. I had no time to react. He steered his car head-on into me and just before the vehicles collided he smiled – from ear to ear.'

The half-empty plane took off from Reykjavík's domestic airport in the afternoon, climbing fast to its cruising altitude. There was talk of abolishing this route unless the government stepped in with an even larger subsidy for the service. Departure had been delayed by fog at their destination, and it was past two p.m. when conditions improved sufficiently for the plane to take off. The captain greeted the passengers over the public-address system: he apologised for the delay, told them when he expected to land, and informed them that there was low cloud at their destination, with a strong breeze. The temperature there was minus four degrees Centigrade. He wished them a pleasant journey.

Elínborg tightened her seat belt, and recalled her last flight, a few days ago. She thought she recognised the captain's voice. They flew above the clouds for most of the way, and Elínborg enjoyed having the sun on her left. It had not broken through the clouds very often during the overcast autumn days in Reykjavík.

Elínborg had brought the case file with her and was reading a transcript of Konráð's confession. He was standing by it and swore that he did not want to change anything. Elínborg knew that being held in custody could have strange and unpredictable effects on people.

'I want to see my daughter,' said Konráð, according to the transcript. 'I won't answer any more questions until you let me see her.'

'That's not going to happen,' was the police officer's reply. Elínborg thought it was probably Finnur, who had tipped them off about the possible connection between Edvard and Lilja.

'How is she?' asked Konráð.

'We think she's on the point of breaking. It's just a matter of time.'

Elínborg grimaced. Konrád was always asking after his daughter and Elínborg felt that the police officer was attempting a rather simplistic form of psychological intimidation.

'Is she all right?'

'She's all right. For now.'

'What do you mean, *for now*?'

'Oh, I don't know. It's no picnic for her, being held in custody, of course.'

A little while later Konrád gave up all resistance. He was being questioned about how he got into the house. The questions were repeated over and over again until he put his foot down. Elínborg pictured him in the interview room, straightening up where he sat and sighing heavily: 'I can't go on like this. I don't know how I thought I could get away with it. I should have contacted you at once, after I cut him. Then Nína wouldn't have had to go through all this, for nothing. It was a stupid mistake but I maintain I did it in self-defence.'

'Are you . . . ?'

'I killed him. Now leave Nína alone. It was me. I'm just sorry I dragged her into my lies. It was my fault. All my fault. When I saw the state Nína was in, and what had been done to her, I was overcome with rage. She had rung me, told me where she was, where the man lived. I received that horrific call for help from her and hurried over. Nína had managed to open the door for me. I went inside and the first thing I saw was the knife on the table. I thought he'd threatened Nína with it. I didn't understand the situation. Nína was sitting on the floor, with a half-naked man standing over her. I'd never seen him before. I thought he was going to harm my daughter so I grabbed the knife and cut his throat. He never saw me. I picked up what I could find of her clothes and then took her out, through the garden, down to the next street and to the car. I stopped the car on the way home to throw the knife in the sea. I don't remember exactly where. That's what happened. That's the truth.'

The police had interviewed Konrád's wife that morning. If his confession was to be relied upon, she was an accessory. She confirmed that he had returned to the car with their daughter, but claimed not to remember Konrád pulling over to dispose of the murder weapon. She, like her husband and daughter, had been in a state of shock so she was not sure whether she had the correct order of events, or even if she remembered everything that had happened. It did not seem necessary at this point to take her into custody.

The plane hit a patch of turbulence and Elínborg gasped as it plunged and juddered. She grasped the armrests and her papers slithered to the floor. The commotion continued for several minutes. Once everything was back to normal, the captain addressed the passengers, explained about the turbulence, and requested them to stay seated with their seat belts fastened. Elínborg picked up her papers and rearranged them in the correct order in the file. She did not like these tinny propeller planes.

She returned to her reading. Konrád was questioned about various details and gave clear answers. But he could not answer the question that interested Elínborg most: what about the Rohypnol found in Runólfur's body? Konrád had not forced him to swallow it, and Nína had almost no memory of events.

The plane was making its descent towards the runway. A light layer of snow still lay on the ground, contrasting with the muted hues of the landscape. Elínborg knew that two police officers were waiting for her at the little airport as before, to take her to Runólfur's home village. She thought back to her kitchen at home, and Teddi's bewildered expression when she had been struggling to understand the connection between what Konrád had said and the oily odour in the hall from Teddi's jacket.

'What? What about paraffin?' Teddi had asked.

'Konrád said Runólfur had been burning something,' said Elínborg. 'But he hadn't burned anything. It wasn't paraffin that Konrád smelt.'

'What does that matter?' asked Teddi.

'Soon after we traced him, Konrád told me that he'd smelt paraffin in Runólfur's flat. We didn't find any paraffin – and Konrád's description was a bit vague. At least, I think it was. I believe he smelt something like this. Maybe that's enough – after all, if you leave your jacket in the hall the smell soon gets into everything.'

'And?' asked Teddi.

'It's an absolutely vital clue,' answered Elínborg, and fetched her mobile to ring Sigurdur Óli back.

'The confession's rubbish,' she said.

'Oh?'

'Konrád thinks he's doing the right thing, taking the fall for his daughter. But I don't believe they had anything to do with Runólfur's death.'

'What are you on about? If it wasn't them, who was it?'

'I've got to look into it a bit further,' said Elínborg. 'I'll have to see Konrád tomorrow. I'm sure he's lying.'

'Please don't start stirring things up,' pleaded Sigurdur Óli. 'I've just congratulated you on solving the case.'

'That was a bit premature. Sorry.' She switched her phone off, and turned to Teddi. 'Can I borrow your jacket tomorrow?'

Early the next morning she had sat down with Konrád in the interview room. He said he had not slept much.

He looked exhausted, dishevelled and nervous. He hardly answered Elínborg's greeting. As usual, he asked after Nína. Elínborg replied that she was much the same.

'I think you're lying to us,' said Elínborg. 'You were telling the truth all along and we didn't believe you. The same applies to your daughter. We didn't believe her, either. So you decided to take the blame. You'd rather go to prison than see her locked up. You're middle-aged but she's still young, with her life ahead of her. But there are two problems with your confession, which I don't think you've given enough thought to. She's never going to go along with your version of events. In addition, you're lying.'

'What would you know about it?'

'I know,' said Elínborg.

'You're determined not to believe a word I say.'

'Oh, I do – some of it. Most of it, actually, up to the point when you say you went for Runólfur.'

'Nína didn't do it.'

'I don't know if you remember, but you told me you'd smelt something like paraffin when you got to Runólfur's flat. You thought he'd been burning something. Was there a smell of burning as well?'

'No, there was no smell of burning.'

'So you just smelt the oily smell?'

'Yes.'

'Do you know what paraffin smells like?'

'Not particularly. It just seemed sort of oily.'

'Was it a strong odour?'

'No, it wasn't. More like a background scent in the air.'

Elínborg picked up a plastic bag and took out the jacket that Teddi had been wearing the day before. She placed it on the table.

'I've never seen that jacket before,' said Konrád, unprompted, as if to avoid any more trouble.

'I know,' said Elínborg. 'Please don't come any closer, and don't sniff it from close up. Can you smell it?'

'No.'

Elínborg took the jacket, shook it vigorously, then folded it back into the bag. She stood up and put the bag out in the corridor. She sat down facing Konrád. 'I know this isn't very scientific, but can you smell anything now?'

'Yes,' replied Konrád. 'I smell it now.'

'Is that what you thought was paraffin, in Runólfur's flat?'

Konrád took two deep breaths. 'Yes! That's just the same as in Runólfur's flat when I arrived,' he said. 'Perhaps a little bit fainter.'

'Are you sure?'

'Yes. That's it exactly. What jacket is that? Whose is it?'

'It's my husband's,' said Elínborg. 'He's a motor mechanic, and co-owner of a garage. His jacket hangs all day in his office at the garage, so it absorbs the smell of lubricants. Every car workshop in the country smells the same. It clings – and it's hard to get rid of.'

'Lubricants?'

'Yes. Lubricants.'

'So? What about it?'

'I don't know. I'm not sure what it means, but please don't go making any more confessions until we've spoken again.'

Elínborg was jolted abruptly back to the present as the plane made a jarring touchdown.

29

At the guest house in the village, Elínborg was given the same room. She took her time settling in. Night was falling and she was in no hurry. On the way from the airport she had rung Sigurdur Óli in Reykjavík and others involved in the investigation to try to gather more information on Runólfur's family: his mother; his father, who had gone smiling to his death; Runólfur's friends in the village, and their families. Her enquiries had not yielded much – not surprisingly, as it was all so last-minute. If her hunch was correct she would learn more in the next few days.

Her hostess recognised her at once. She was surprised

to see her back in the village and made no attempt to conceal her curiosity: 'Is there something special that's brought you back so soon?' she asked as she showed Elínborg to her room. 'I don't suppose this is just a social visit, is it?'

'I seem to remember someone said nothing ever happens here,' said Elínborg.

'Yes, that's true. Not much going on,' replied the woman.

'Don't worry about me,' said Elínborg. She went to the village's only restaurant, took a seat, and ordered the fish again. On this occasion she was the only customer. The ubiquitous Lauga took her order without a word and disappeared into the kitchen. Either she did not remember Elínborg or could not be bothered to make conversation. She had been more talkative on Elínborg's previous visit. Before long she reappeared and placed the plate of fish on the table.

'Thank you,' said Elínborg. 'I don't know if you remember me. I was here a few days ago. The fish was excellent.'

'I always use fresh fish,' said Lauga. She gave no indication of whether she remembered Elínborg. 'Thank you.' She was about to return to the kitchen, but Elínborg stopped her.

'Last time I was here I met a girl who was looking at

the videos over there in the window,' she said, pointing at the niche by the door. 'Where do you think I might find her?'

'There are still a few girls left in the village,' said Lauga. 'But I don't know who you mean.'

'She was about twenty, I should think, with blonde hair, and a narrow face – quite pretty, slender, wearing a blue down parka. I imagine she comes here now and then. This is the only place in the village to rent videos, isn't it?'

Lauga did not answer at once.

'I'd appreciate it if you could—' continued Elínborg.

But Lauga interrupted: 'Do you know her name?'

'No.'

'Don't know her,' said Lauga, shrugging. 'She may be from the next fjord.'

'I just hoped you might be able to help me. Never mind,' answered Elínborg, and started on her fish. It was every bit as delicious, fried exactly right, fresh, and perfectly seasoned. Lauga certainly knew how to cook. Elínborg thought that perhaps Lauga's talents were wasted here, in the back of beyond. Silently, she apologised to the place. She knew she had a tendency to be prejudiced against life outside the city. She ought to be thinking that the villagers were lucky to have such an outstanding cook among them.

334

Elínborg ate at her leisure. For dessert she chose freshly baked chocolate cake, with a cup of good coffee.

Three youngsters in their early teens – two boys and a girl – came in to look at the videos. One of them switched on a large television above the counter and selected a sports channel. He set the volume far too high and Lauga came out and politely asked him to turn it down. He did so at once.

'Tell your mum I can cut her hair tomorrow afternoon,' she said to the other boy, who nodded. He looked over at Elínborg, who smiled at him but received no response. The girl sat down to watch the game and before long all three were glued to the screen. Elínborg smiled to herself. She debated whether to have a liqueur with her coffee and decided to indulge herself. She suspected that tomorrow was going to be a rough day.

Eventually Elínborg stood up and settled her bill at the bar. Lauga took her payment without speaking. Elínborg sensed that the youngsters were observing her every move. She thanked Lauga and called out a friendly goodnight to the kids. They made no reply beyond a nod from the girl.

Deep in thought, Elínborg walked back towards the guest house. As she was considering how to pursue her enquiries the following day she caught a glimpse of a young blonde woman in a blue down parka, hurrying along the pavement on the other side of the main street. Elínborg halted, uncertain whether it was the same girl. Concluding that it was, she called out to her. The girl slowed down and looked in Elínborg's direction. 'Hey!' called Elínborg, and waved.

They stood on opposite sides of the road.

'Don't you remember me?' Elínborg called out.

The girl stared at her.

'I was just asking after you,' said Elínborg, and stepped into the road.

The girl backed away, then strode on. Elínborg started to cross the road towards her but the girl broke into a run. Elínborg ran after her, calling out to her to stop, but she just ran even faster.

Elínborg, who was wearing flat shoes, did her best to keep up, but she was not as fit as the young woman and soon fell behind. Finally Elínborg slowed to her normal walking speed and watched her quarry disappear between two houses.

Elínborg turned around and walked back towards the guest house. This was incomprehensible. Why wouldn't the girl speak to her now? She had wanted to help before. What was she running away from? And Elínborg was convinced that Lauga had known exactly who Elínborg had meant when she'd described her. There must be a reason why Lauga was unwilling to help. What were they concealing? Or was Elínborg being led astray by an over-active imagination? Perhaps the village itself was affecting her, dark and silent and isolated as it was.

She had her own keys to the front door of the guest house and to her room, so there was no need to disturb anyone there. She rang Teddi, who told her that all was quiet on the home front and asked, as usual, when she would be back. She told him she didn't know. They said goodnight, and Elínborg settled down with a book about oriental cuisine and its connections with eastern philosophy.

She was dozing off over her book when she heard a quiet tap at the window. When the knocking was repeated more insistently, she jumped out of bed and went over to the window, cautiously pulled back the curtains, and peered out into the dark. Her room was on the ground floor at the rear of the building. Initially she could see nothing, but then she discerned someone standing out in the darkness. She was looking into the eyes of the girl in the blue parka.

The girl beckoned, then vanished into the night. Elínborg stepped away from the window, dressed hurriedly, and went out, closing the door quietly behind her so as not to disturb her hosts who were asleep on the upper floor. She could see very little. She walked around to the back of the house where her bedroom window was but saw no sign of the blue parka. She dared not call out. The girl's behaviour seemed to indicate that she wanted to avoid being seen, at all costs. She was clearly nervous about having anything to do with Elínborg, the detective from the city.

Elínborg was about to abandon her search and return to her room when she noticed a movement on the road. The street lighting was sparse. She went closer and saw that the girl was waiting for her. Elínborg hurried towards her, only for her to take to her heels. The girl ran a short distance, then stopped again and looked back. Elínborg halted. She was not going to play chase a second time. The girl edged closer and Elínborg approached her, but the girl once again backed away and moved farther off. Finally Elínborg realised that she wanted her to follow, but at a discreet distance. She did as the girl wished, trailing her at a leisurely pace.

It was cold. A biting northerly wind cut sharply through her clothes, with ever-increasing force. The woman and the girl walked on with the wind in their faces. Elínborg grimaced and clutched her coat more tightly around her. They walked along by the sea, past the cluster of houses above the harbour which formed the centre of the village, and on northwards. Elínborg wondered how far they were going and where the girl was leading her.

They had moved away from the seashore now. Elínborg

strode along the road which ran out of the village, past a large building which she assumed must be the community centre. A single light bulb was burning over the entrance. She heard the roar of a nearby river in the dark and then they crossed a bridge. She kept losing sight of the girl. It was a moonlit night. Elínborg was so cold that she started to shiver: the wind had risen still more and it was now blowing a gale.

All at once she spotted a ray of light on the road ahead. The girl had stopped at the side of the road and switched on a torch.

'Is this really necessary?' said Elínborg breathlessly. 'Can't you just say what you want to say? It's the middle of the night, and I'm freezing.'

Without so much as looking at Elínborg, the girl hurried down off the road towards the sea. Elínborg followed. In the dark she reached a waist-high stone wall and followed it around to a gate, which the girl opened. It squeaked a little.

'Where are we?' asked Elínborg. 'Where are you taking me?'

She soon found out. They followed a narrow path past a large tree. In the glow of the torch Elínborg made out concrete steps leading up to a building – she could not tell what it was. The girl turned to the right and up a shallow slope. In the torchlight Elínborg saw a white cross, and in the next flash of light a slab of cut stone that had subsided into the ground. She could see an inscription.

'Is this a churchyard?' whispered Elínborg.

The girl made no answer but walked on until she came to a simple white wooden cross. In the centre was a plaque with an inscription in small letters, and on the grave itself lay a bunch of fresh-looking flowers.

'Whose grave is this?' asked Elínborg, trying to decipher the inscription in the wavering beam of the torch.

'It was her birthday the other day,' the girl murmured.

Elínborg gazed at the grave marker. The torch went out. She heard footsteps fading into the distance, and realised that she had been left alone in the churchyard.

30

It took Elínborg a long time to get to sleep, and after a few hours' rest she got up early. Overnight the wind had dropped, and a light snow was falling. She did not know whether she would see the girl again, nor why she had taken her down to the churchyard. Elínborg had managed to read the inscription on the grave marker: it was a woman's name. She thought about the woman who lay in the grave, the flowers someone had recently placed there, the story buried in the earth, an enigma.

She stayed in her room all morning, making phone calls to Reykjavík and preparing herself for the day. It was early afternoon when she strolled down to the restaurant.

Although the lunchtime rush was over, some customers still lingered. Lauga had someone helping her in the kitchen. Elínborg ordered bacon and egg and a coffee. She felt that the other diners were looking at her askance, as if she were an intruder, but she pretended not to notice. She took her time, lingered over her lunch, and had a second cup of coffee while she observed her surroundings.

Lauga took Elínborg's empty plate, and wiped the table top. 'When do you think you'll be going back to the city?' she asked.

'That depends,' said Elínborg. 'The village does have certain things to offer, even though nothing ever happens here.'

'No, I suppose not,' said Lauga. 'I hear you were out all night.'

'Really?'

'Rumour around the village,' explained Lauga. 'There are plenty of rumours here. You shouldn't believe everything you're told in a place like this. I hope you're not going to put your faith in rumour.'

'No, I have no intention of doing so,' said Elínborg. 'Is it likely to snow today, do you know?' she asked, glancing out of the window. She did not like the look of the overcast sky.

'That's what the forecast says,' replied Lauga. 'There's likely to be a storm this evening and tonight.'

Elínborg stood up. She was the only customer remaining.

'It does no one any good to go stirring up the past,' Lauga went on. 'It's all over and done with.'

'Speaking of the past,' said Elínborg, 'you must have known a girl called Adalheidur who lived in the village? She died two years ago.'

Lauga hesitated. 'I know who she was, yes,' she said at last.

'What did she die of?'

'What did she die of?' parroted Lauga. 'I'm not going to talk about that.'

'Why not?'

'I just don't want to.'

'Can you help me find any of her friends, or family? Someone I could talk to?'

'I can't help you with that. I run this restaurant. That's my job. It's not my job to tell stories to strangers.'

'Thank you,' said Elínborg. She walked to the door and opened it. Lauga was standing in the middle of the restaurant, watching her go, as if she had more to say.

'You would be doing us all a favour if you just went home to Reykjavík and never came back,' said Lauga.

'Who exactly would I be doing a favour by doing that?'

'All of us,' answered Lauga. 'There's nothing for you here.'

'We'll see,' said Elínborg. 'Thanks for the meal. You're an excellent cook.'

343

On her way back to the churchyard Elínborg decided to make one house call. She went up the steps of Runólfur's mother's home and rang the doorbell. She heard a faint ringing from indoors and the door opened. Kristjana remembered her at once and asked her in.

'Why are you back?' she asked, sitting in the same chair as before. 'What do you want here?'

'I'm looking for answers,' replied Elínborg.

'I don't know that you'll find any, not here,' commented Kristjana. 'This is a rotten place. Such a rotten place. I'd have left long ago if only I'd had the guts.'

'Isn't this a good place to live?'

'A good place to live?' asked Kristjana. She wiped her lips with a tissue, then set about twisting it in her fingers. 'Don't go listening to people's lies.'

'What would people be lying about?' Elínborg recalled what Lauga had said about listening to rumours.

'Everything,' replied Kristjana. 'There are a lot of scum living here, let me tell you. Scum who love to slander respectable people. Have you been hearing things about me? I'm sure they're drooling over the stories about my poor Runólfur. They enjoy that. But don't you go believing everything they say.'

'I've only just got here,' replied Elínborg. Kristjana's manner was different, more aggressive than at their first meeting. Elínborg did not intend to discuss Kristjana's

344

husband's death since she did not know whether the woman was aware of the true nature of the events.

There was, however, another matter that she wanted to ask her about. Elínborg considered her best approach, then plunged in: 'The only thing I've heard,' she said, 'is that he had a strict upbringing. That you were pretty strict with your son.'

'Strict? With Runólfur? Ha! What bloody nonsense. That lad needed a firm hand. Who told you that?'

'I don't remember,' said Elínborg.

'Strict with Runólfur! Of course they would say that – those scum, bringing up their brats to be hooligans. Hooligans! They broke one of my windows just the other day. No one will admit to it. I reckoned I knew who'd done it, and I got in touch with their parents but they wouldn't listen. People have got no respect for their elders these days.'

'So *were* you strict with him?' asked Elínborg.

Kristjana glanced sharply at her. 'Are you blaming me for what he was?'

'I don't know what he was,' replied Elínborg. 'Maybe you can tell me.'

Kristjana sat in silence, wiped her mouth with her tissue, and went on twisting it in her hands. 'Don't believe everything you're told in the village,' she said. 'Have you found his killer?'

'No, I'm afraid we haven't,' said Elínborg.

'Some people were arrested – I saw it on the news.'

'That's right.'

'Did you come here to tell me that?'

'No, actually I didn't. I want to ask you if you think anyone from around here might have hurt your son.'

'You asked me that last time – whether he had any enemies here. I don't think so. But if he really was the monster you seem to think, then I can't be sure.'

'I asked you about women in his life as well,' said Elínborg cautiously.

'Yes, well, I don't know anything about any women,' Kristjana replied.

'There's one woman I'd like to ask you about. She lived here. Her name was Adalheidur.'

'Adalheidur?'

'Yes.'

'I remember her, but I didn't know her personally. Her brother runs the garage.'

'The garage?'

'Yes.'

'You mean she was Valdimar's sister?'

'That's right. Or half-sister, really. Their mother was nothing but a tart – she used to go with all the seamen back in the old days. They had some name for her, I don't remember what it was. Something rude. She had

346

those two brats – out of wedlock, of course. Two little bastards. And she drank, too. Died young – relatively young, but burnt out. She was a good worker, though. I used to work with her in the fish factory – a hard-working lass.'

'Did your son know her? Did he know Adalheidur?'

'Runólfur? Well, they were about the same age – they were at school together. I only ever saw her when she came to the factory with her mum – always with a runny nose. She wasn't a healthy kid, rather weak and feeble.'

'Did Runólfur have a relationship with her?'

'What do you mean – a *relationship*?'

Elínborg hesitated. 'Were they more than just acquaintances? Was there . . . was there some other relationship between them?'

'No, nothing like that. Why do you ask? Runólfur never brought girls here.'

'Did he know any other girls in the village?'

'No, not really.'

'I gather that Adalheidur died a couple of years ago?'

'She topped herself,' said Kristjana blankly, running her fingers through her grey hair. Elínborg wondered if she had been dark-haired when she was young. With her brown eyes, it was not unlikely.

'Who? Adalheidur?'

'Yes. They found her on the shore, down below the

churchyard,' said Kristjana tonelessly. 'She'd drowned herself in the sea.'

'She killed herself?'

'Yes, certainly looked that way.'

'Do you know why?'

'Why? Why the girl did herself in? No idea. I suppose she was unhappy, poor thing. Must have been unhappy, since she did it.'

31

In daylight Elínborg was able to form a clearer sense of the location of the churchyard, which lay to the north of the village, next to the sea. It was enclosed by a low stone wall that was sorely in need of repair and had even collapsed in places, and was partially obscured by the tall, withered winter grass. A picturesque little wooden church, painted white and with a red roof, stood at the end of the churchyard.

The small gate was ajar.

Elínborg found the cross she was looking for easily. Around her were low, mossy gravestones, lying flat on the cold ground, their inscriptions worn and indecipherable, while other stones stood upright amidst the grass, resisting the elements. In among the old memorial stones were simple wooden crosses, like the one that marked Adalheidur's resting place.

The cross was quite without ornament, identified only with a plain black plaque bearing Adalheidur's name, the dates of her birth and death, and the inscription *Rest in Peace*. Elínborg noticed that Adalheidur's birthday was the date on which Runólfur had been killed.

She raised her eyes. The sky was overcast, but it was a windless day and the sea was mirror-smooth. She looked out along the fjord towards the ocean, to the distant horizon, and felt a sense of peace within herself. The spell was broken by the shrill call of a redwing, which perched briefly on the church tower before flying off into the mountains.

Elínborg realised that she was no longer alone. She glanced up towards the road, and saw the girl in the blue down parka standing there watching her. They stood there for some time without speaking, looking at each other, before the girl set off down towards the churchyard and clambered over the wall.

'It's pretty here,' said Elínborg.

'Yes,' the girl agreed. 'It's the prettiest place in the village.'

'They certainly knew what they were doing when they chose this spot for the churchyard,' said Elínborg. 'By the way, thanks very much for leaving me here alone last night,' she added.

'I'm sorry,' said the girl. 'I didn't know what to do. I still don't know what I'm doing. When you came back here . . .'

'Did you know I'd return?'

'I wasn't surprised. I expected you. And I've been waiting.'

'Please tell me what's worrying you. I can see there's something you want to tell me.'

'I saw that you called on Kristjana.'

'You villagers don't miss much.'

'I wasn't spying on you. I just noticed. She knows all about what happened. Did she tell you?'

'What *did* happen?'

'Everyone knows about it.'

'About what? And who are you? What's your name, for a start?'

'My name's Vala.'

'Why all this pussyfooting around, Vala?'

'I think most people here know what happened, but they'll never say. And I don't want to tell, either – I don't want to get him in trouble. So . . . I don't know whether I even ought to be talking to you at all. It's just that the silence is unbearable. I can't take it any more.'

'Why don't you tell me everything? Then we'll see. What are you scared of?'

'No one here talks about it,' said Vala, 'and I don't want to get anyone into trouble.'

'About what? Get who into trouble?'

'Everyone keeps their mouth shut and pretends nothing happened – that nothing ever happens here. That everything in the garden's rosy.'

'And isn't it?'

'No, it isn't.'

'So what is it like? Why did you bring me down here last night?'

The girl made no reply.

'What do you want me to do?' asked Elínborg.

'I'm no snitch. I don't want to tell tales about people. And I don't want to speak ill of the dead.'

'No one needs to know what we talk about,' Elínborg assured her.

Suddenly, Vala changed tack. 'Have you been in the police for long?'

'Yes, quite a long time.'

'It must be a horrible job.'

'No. Sometimes it is, like when you're sent to a secretive little place like this. But there are better days. For instance, when I meet a girl like you and I think I can do something for her. Who was it that died who you don't want to tell tales about?'

'I never finished secondary school,' the girl said, evading

352

the question. 'Maybe I'll go back and get my qualifications one day, and go to university. I'd like to study something.'

'Who was Adalheidur?' asked Elínborg, indicating the simple white cross on the grave.

'I was just a little girl when it happened.'

'When what happened?'

'I was probably about eight at the time, but I never heard anything about it until I was twelve or thirteen. There were all sorts of rumours floating around and I remember they seemed very sad but exciting too, in a weird way. They said she'd gone mad. She was supposed to have got some illness, some mental thing. She only worked part-time, and cooked and cleaned for her brother. She was mysterious, kept herself to herself. She didn't speak to people, cut herself off from what went on in the village, lost touch with everything and everyone. She had almost no contact with anyone but her brother. He took wonderful care of her after she got ill. Or I thought she was ill, anyway. That's what they said, when I was a little girl. They said poor Addý wasn't well. She seemed like a grown woman to me – she was twelve years older. Her birthday's nearly the same as mine – there's five days' difference. She was the same age I am now when it happened.'

'Did you know her at all?'

'Yes, we worked together at the fish factory. She was a

353

lot older, of course, like I said, and not easy to get to know – reserved. I was told she'd always been that way, slightly odd. She'd been a loner who kept out of other people's way, and they left her alone, too. They said she'd been fragile and sensitive. Not someone you would notice. That made her easy prey, I suppose.'

Vala took a deep breath. Elínborg sensed the girl's distress. 'Then, when I was older, I heard other things about Addý and what had been done to her. Some people found out about it but said nothing. Maybe they found it hard to believe. Or embarrassing. Or shameful. It took years before the whole village knew. I think everyone is aware of the truth now. I've no idea how the rumours started, because Addý herself never said a word. She never made any accusation. Maybe he boasted about it when he was drinking. Maybe he was proud of what he did. I doubt that he had any regrets, somehow.'

Vala fell silent. Elínborg waited patiently for her to continue.

'Addý never told anyone the truth. Except her brother, probably, in the end. I think he must have heard the rumours by then, too. She was living with a shame of her own making. I've read a lot about women like her. Most of them, if not all, need special therapy. Apparently they blame themselves. They live with their anger and cut themselves off.'

'What happened?'

'He raped Addý.' Vala gazed at the cross. 'The word spread gradually that she'd been raped, and who the man was, but she never said anything and no one was ever charged. No one was tried. And no one lifted a finger to help her,' said Vala.

'Who did it?' asked Elínborg. '*Who* raped her?'

'I'm sure Kristjana knows about it. Knows perfectly well what her son did. She lives in a state of denial. She has a rough time here. The kids make fun of her, break her windows.'

'You're talking about Runólfur?'

'Yes. He raped Addý – and she never got over it. They found her in the sea down here, just below the churchyard. She'd floated down here, to her place of rest.'

'What about Runólfur?'

'Everyone here knows who killed him.'

Elínborg gazed at Vala for a long time. In her mind she saw an elderly man swerve over calmly into the oncoming traffic – and smile at the heavy lorry bearing down on him.

32

Back at the guest house Elínborg did a few hours' work in her room, which she had converted into an ad hoc office. She made a number of phone calls to Reykjavík to gather more information. She spoke to Sigurdur Óli and they planned their next move. Police officers would be sent to the village but it would take time for them to reach her. Sigurdur Óli urged Elínborg to take no further action until backup was in place. She told him not to worry. Konrád and Nína were still in custody, and Elínborg was not surprised to learn that Konrád had changed his story once again: he now denied killing Runólfur and maintained that his daughter Nína was also innocent.

Darkness was falling when Elínborg left the guest house, crossed the main road and walked down towards the harbour – the same route she had taken on her first visit. The garage was at the northern end of the village and she headed in that direction. She thought about the snow that was forecast, and hoped she would not be snowed in here. She looked up at the sign over the door; now she knew for certain that a shotgun had once been fired at it. Vala had told her that years ago, when he was still drinking, Valdimar had taken a potshot at his own sign.

Elínborg stepped into the reception area. Everything was as before, and Elínborg reflected that it had probably not changed since the day when the garage had opened for business. On the wall behind the counter hung a pin-up calendar displaying a photo of a scantily clad girl. It showed the year 1998. Days, weeks, years had no meaning here. Time seemed to stand still. Everything in sight – the counter, the old leather armchair, the desktop calculator, the order book – was coated in a thin layer of sooty grime from engines, spares parts, lubricants and tyres.

Elínborg called into the garage, but received no answer. She advanced cautiously into the workshop, where the Ferguson tractor stood in exactly the same place. As on Elínborg's last visit, there were no other vehicles inside. Against the wall were two open tool lockers.

'I heard you were back,' said a voice.

357

Slowly, Elínborg turned around. 'You must have been expecting me,' she said.

Valdimar was standing behind her, wearing a checked shirt and ragged jeans. In his hand he held a set of overalls, which he started to put on. 'So you're on your own, are you?' he asked.

Valdimar must have been well aware that Elínborg was alone. Yet there was no veiled threat in his question, which seemed calculated to engender trust rather than fear.

'Yes,' replied Elínborg without hesitation. As he slipped the overalls over his shoulders and pushed his arms through the sleeves, Valdimar reminded her of her husband Teddi.

'I live up above,' explained Valdimar, pointing at the ceiling. 'I didn't have much work on, so I took a nap. What time is it?'

Elínborg told him the time. She did not feel at any risk. Valdimar was calm and polite.

'So you don't have far to go to work,' she said, smiling.

'It's convenient,' replied Valdimar.

'I've been down at the churchyard,' Elínborg told him. 'I saw your sister's grave. I gather she committed suicide two years ago?'

'Have you ever lived in a little place like this?' asked Valdimar. He moved closer to Elínborg, cornering her against one of the tool lockers.

'No, I never have.'

'They can be weird.'

'I imagine they can.'

'Outsiders like you can never really understand what
t's like.'

'No, I don't suppose we can.'

'I hardly understand some of it myself – and I live here.
Even if I explained it to you, it would only be a fraction
of the truth. And that fraction of the truth would be seen
as a lie by Haddi down at the filling station, for instance.
Even if you spoke to every single person – and spent
twenty years doing it – you'd never get more than a tiny
glimpse of what it's like to live in one of these villages.
How people think. The relationships within the community.
The ancient bonds that link people. And keep them apart.
I've lived here all my life, and there's still so much I don't
understand. But this is my home. Even though your friends
may suddenly turn into your worst enemies. And people
keep their secrets, to the grave and beyond.'

'I'm not sure . . .'

'You've no idea what I'm talking about, have you?'

'I believe I know some of what happened.'

'They know you're with me,' said Valdimar. 'They know
why you came back. They know you came here to talk to
me. They all know what I did, but they don't say anything.
No one says a word. Not bad, is it?'

Elínborg said nothing.

'Addý was my half-sister, four years older than me. We were close. I've never met my father – I don't know who he is, and I don't care to know. My sister's father was some Norwegian seaman who stopped here just long enough to knock our mum up. They didn't think much of my mum, here in the village. It took a long time before I realised that she was a pariah. You find out, bit by bit, because you get teased. Otherwise you'd never be any the wiser. She was a good mother to us, and we never had anything to complain about – even if we had the odd visit by a social worker, some strange caller carrying a briefcase, not like anyone else, who looked my sister and me over and asked stupid questions. They never found anything wrong – because, although she had her problems, my mother was a fine woman. She worked her fingers to the bone at the fish factory, and although we were poor we never went without. My mum, with her two little bastards – that was what we were called – was known by a certain name in the village. I shan't tell you what. I got into three bad fights about that – got my arm broken once. Then she died, and was at peace. She's lying in the churchyard, next to her daughter.'

'Your sister didn't go so peacefully,' said Elínborg.

'Who have you been talking to?'

'That's not important.'

360

'There are good people here, too. Don't get me wrong.'

'I know that,' said Elínborg.

'Addý didn't tell me anything. Not until it was too late,' said Valdimar, his features hardening. He grasped a large spanner that lay on the front tyre of the tractor and swung it in his hand. 'It's one of those things that happen. She closed up. She was alone when he attacked her. We were short of money, so I got work on a freezer-trawler, and I was out at sea for weeks at a time. I'd just gone when it happened.'

Valdimar fell silent. Hunched forward, he tapped the spanner gently against his other hand. 'She never told me anything. Never told anyone. But when I got back she was like a different person. She'd changed in some unfathomable way. She wouldn't let me near her. I didn't know what was happening – I was just a sixteen-year-old kid, after all. She hardly left the house, locked herself away, wouldn't meet her two best friends. I wanted her to go to the doctor, but she wouldn't. She asked me to leave her alone – said she'd get over it. She wouldn't say over what. And she did make a partial recovery. It took a year or two. But she was never the same again: she was always frightened. Sometimes she would fly into a rage for no apparent reason. Other times she just sat and cried. She was depressed and anxious. I've read about it since – she was a textbook case.'

'What happened?'

'She was raped by a man from the village, in a quite horrible way. She couldn't bring herself to tell me, or anyone else, exactly what he did to her.'

'Was it Runólfur?'

'Yes. There was a dance in the village. He tricked Addý into going with him down to the river near the community centre. She had no reason to suspect anything – she knew him well. They'd been classmates right through school. I'm sure he thought of her as easy meat. When he was done, he went back to the dance, carried on having a good time as if nothing had happened. But he dropped a hint of what he'd done to one of his friends, and that was how it spread gradually around the community. Except for me. I never heard a word.'

'So that's where it began,' Elínborg murmured, as if to herself.

'Have you found out about any other women he raped?' Valdimar asked.

'The woman we've got in custody. No one else has come forward.'

'Maybe there are more like Addý,' said Valdimar. 'He threatened to kill her if she spoke out.' Valdimar stopped knocking the spanner against his hand, looked up and met Elínborg's stare. 'All those years, she was a broken woman. However much time passed, it made no difference.'

'I believe that,' said Elínborg.

'And when she was finally able to confide in me it was too late for her.'

After Addý had finished speaking, brother and sister sat together for a long time in his flat over the garage. Valdimar held his sister's hand and stroked her hair. He had sat next to her as she told him her story, which grew more difficult and heartbreaking as it went along.

'It's been so horribly hard,' she whispered. 'I've often been on the point of simply giving up.'

'Why didn't you tell me?' asked Valdimar, dumbstruck with horror. 'Why have you never said anything before? I could have helped you.'

'What could you have done, Valdi? You were so young. I was hardly more than a child myself. What was I supposed to do? Who could have helped us against that animal? Would it have made any difference if he'd served a few months in jail? Rape isn't a serious offence, Valdi. Not to the men in charge. You know I'm right.'

'But how have you kept it bottled up all this time?'

'I've just done my best to live with it. Some days are better than others. You've been such a comfort to me, Valdi. I don't think there can be a better brother in the world.'

'Runólfur,' murmured Valdimar.

His sister turned towards him. 'Don't go doing anything foolish, Valdi. I don't want anything bad to happen to you. I'd never have told you otherwise.'

'She didn't tell me until the day before she gave up the fight,' said Valdimar, with a look at Elínborg. 'I let go of her for a minute – and that was enough. I didn't realise she was in such a bad way, how deeply he'd wounded her. They found her that evening on the seashore below the churchyard. Runólfur moved to Reykjavík soon after he raped my sister, and after that he only made brief visits here.'

'You need advice. You must talk to a lawyer,' said Elínborg. 'Please don't say any more.'

'I don't need a lawyer,' replied Valdimar. 'What I needed was justice. I went to see him, and I found he was still at it.'

33

The pill worked faster than Runólfur expected and Nína leaned heavily against him on the way up to Thingholt, towards his home. She seemed very susceptible to the drug. She clung on to him and he had to half-carry her the last few steps. They did not go in from the front of the house but through the back garden, so he did not expect anyone to notice them. He did not switch on any lights when they entered, and he laid her gently on the sofa in the living room.

He shut the door, went into the kitchen, lit candles, arranged them in the bedroom, and then lit two more in the living room. He took his jacket off. The candlelight cast an eerie glow over the flat. He was thirsty. He drank a large glass of water and put on some music from one of his favourite films. He bent over Nína, took the shawl, bundled it up and flung it into the bedroom before pulling off her San Francisco T-shirt. She was not wearing a bra.

Runólfur carried her into the bedroom, then removed the rest of her clothes and undressed himself. She was unconscious. He squeezed himself into her T-shirt and looked down at her naked motionless body. He smiled, and bit off the corner of a condom wrapper.

His whole mind was focused on the young woman.

He lay down on top of her unmoving body, stroked her breasts, and thrust his tongue into her unresponsive mouth.

About half an hour later he left the room and changed the music. Serenely, he picked out another film theme, and turned the volume up a little higher.

As Runólfur was returning to the bedroom there was a knock at the door. He looked towards it, not believing what he was hearing. On two occasions since he moved to Thingholt revellers had come to his door late at night, in search of a party on their way from the city centre after a night's drinking. They had either forgotten the address or were lost, and he had only been able to get rid of them by answering the door. He stood in the living room, glanced into the bedroom, then back at the door. The knocking was repeated, louder this time. His caller was persistent. One such night-time visitor had been calling out for someone named Sigga who he thought lived there.

Runólfur hurriedly put on his jeans, half-closed the bedroom door, then cautiously opened the front door and peered out. There was no porch light and he could only vaguely discern a figure standing on the doorstep.

'What—?' he began, but got no further. A man shoved hard against the door, burst into the flat, and swiftly shut the door behind him.

Runólfur was so astonished that he did not even try to resist the invasion.

'Are you alone?' asked Valdimar.

Runólfur recognised him at once. 'You?' he asked. 'How . . . ? What do you want?'

'Have you got someone with you?' asked Valdimar.

'Get the fuck out of here!' hissed Runólfur.

He saw the handle of a cut-throat razor in Valdimar's hand, and a split second later the flash of the blade. In a moment, Valdimar had clenched his hand around Runólfur's throat and thrust him hard against the wall, holding the razor to his skin. Valdimar was a much taller, stronger man. Runólfur was paralysed with terror. Valdimar scanned his surroundings and, through the half-open bedroom door, saw Nína's feet in the bed. 'Who's in there?' he asked.

'It's my girlfriend,' stammered Runólfur. Valdimar's steely grasp on his throat made it hard for him to get the words out. He felt as if his neck were in a vice. He could hardly breathe.

'Girlfriend? Tell her to get out!'

'She's asleep.'

'Wake her up, then!'

'I . . . I can't,' said Runólfur.

'Hey, you!' Valdimar shouted into the bedroom. 'Can you hear me?'

Nína did not move.

'Why doesn't she answer?'

'She's fast asleep,' said Runólfur.

'Asleep?'

Valdimar swivelled suddenly to stand behind him with the razor still at his throat, and grasped his hair in the other hand. Propelling Runólfur ahead of him, he kicked the door open fully.

'I can slit your throat whenever I want,' he whispered into Runólfur's ear. He nudged Nína with his foot, but she did not move. 'What's wrong with her? Why doesn't she wake up?'

'She's just asleep,' protested Runólfur.

Valdimar made a small cut in the skin of his throat, which stung painfully.

'Please don't hurt me,' begged Runólfur.

'No one sleeps that heavily. Is she drugged? Did you give her something?'

'Don't cut me,' whimpered Runólfur.

'Did you give her something?'

Runólfur made no answer.

'Did you drug her?'

'She . . .'

'Where is it?'

'Don't cut me again. It's in my jacket pocket, in the other room.'

'Hand it over.' Valdimar marched Runólfur ahead of him back into the living room.

'You're still at it,' he said.

'She likes it this way.'

'Like my sister did!' howled Valdimar. 'She asked for it, did she? Asked you to rape her, you filthy bastard?'

'I don't know what she told you . . .' gasped Runólfur. 'I didn't mean . . . I'm sorry, I . . .'

Runólfur took the pills from his jacket pocket and held them out to Valdimar.

'What are these?' asked Valdimar.

'I don't know,' said Runólfur, his voice faltering in terror.

'What are they?'

Valdimar sliced again at Runólfur's throat.

'Ro . . . Rohypnol,' groaned Runólfur. 'It's a sleeping pill.'

'You mean a date-rape drug?'

Runólfur said nothing.

'Swallow them,' Valdimar told him.

'Don't . . .'

'Swallow them!' bellowed Valdimar, making another cut. Blood flowed down Runólfur's neck. He placed a pill between his lips.

'And another one!' ordered Valdimar.

Runólfur was in tears. 'What . . . what are you going to do?' he asked, putting another pill in his mouth.

'And another.'

Runólfur had given up resisting and swallowed the next pill. 'Don't do anything to me,' he begged.

'Shut up!'

'I could die if I take too many.'

'Take your jeans off.'

'Valdi, please . . .'

'Get them off!' said Valdimar, making another small incision in Runólfur's neck. He whined in pain. He unbuttoned his jeans and dropped them to his ankles. 'How does it feel?' Valdimar asked.

'Feel?'

'How does it feel?'

'What . . . ?'

'How does it feel to be raped?'

'Don't . . .'

'Like it, do you?'

'Please don't,' sobbed Runólfur.

'How do you think my sister felt?'

'Don't . . .'

'Tell me! What do you suppose it's been like for her, all these years?'

'Don't . . .'

'Tell me! Do you think she felt the way you do now?'

'I'm sorry, I didn't know . . . I didn't mean . . .'

'You disgusting shit!' whispered Valdimar in Runólfur's ear, then slit his throat cleanly from left to right. He released his hold on Runólfur, who collapsed to the floor. Blood gushed from the wound. Valdimar stood by the dead man, then opened the front door and strode out into the night.

Elínborg listened to Valdimar's account in silence, watching his face and listening to the intonation of his voice. He showed no remorse for what he had done. It was more as if he had carried out a task that had to be completed if he were to regain his peace of mind. It had taken him two years but now it was over. If anything, Elínborg felt, he seemed relieved.

'You don't regret what you did?'

'Runólfur got what he deserved,' answered Valdimar.

'You appointed yourself judge, jury and executioner.'

'He was my sister's judge, jury and executioner,' retorted Valdimar. 'I see no difference between what I did to him and what he did to Addý. My only concern was that I might lose my nerve. I thought it would be more difficult. I didn't think I'd be able to do anything to him. I was expecting more resistance, but Runólfur was a pathetic, cowardly little shit. I should think most men like him are.'

'But there are other ways to achieve justice.'

'Like what? Addý was right. Men like Runólfur get put away for a year, or maybe two. If they are even prosecuted, that is. Addý . . . Addý said to me that Runólfur might as well have killed her. It made no difference. I don't see what I did as a serious crime. In the end, you do what you have to. Something must be done, to put things right. Should I just have stood aside and allowed him to carry on? I wrestled with that question until I couldn't take it any more. When the system takes the side of the filth like that, what are you supposed to do?'

Elínborg thought of Nína and Konrád and their family, and how their world had been ravaged. She remembered the sad little gathering at Runólfur's home – Unnur and her family, who had nothing but their silent pain.

For Valdimar, that was not enough.

'Had you been planning this for long?' asked Elínborg.

'Ever since Addý told me. She didn't want me to do

anything. Didn't want me to get into any trouble. She always worried about her little brother. I don't know whether you really understand. What she went through – both when he violated her and for the years afterwards. All those long years. Really, Addý no longer existed. She wasn't my sister any more, not the real Addý. She was just a shadow, a travesty of herself, who was withering away and dying.'

'An innocent man and his daughter are in custody because of you,' said Elínborg.

'I know, and I feel terrible about that,' replied Valdimar. 'I've been keeping up with the case and I intended to give myself up. I really don't want innocent people to suffer because of me. I would have given myself up. I was going to. There were some things I needed to sort out first, and I've been doing that for the past few days. I don't suppose I'll be coming back here.'

Valdimar put down the spanner. 'How did you work out it was me?' he asked her.

'My husband's a mechanic.'

Valdimar looked at her, at a loss.

'The father of the girl we've got in custody thought he smelt paraffin in Runólfur's flat. She must have woken up just after you left, because when her father arrived there was still a trace of the smell of your clothes in the air. He assumed that Runólfur must have been using paraffin to burn something. I was reminded of it by a smell in my own home, so I asked the father about it. It seemed to be an oily smell, a garage smell. I thought of you at once – the man who's always in his workshop. I thought about Runólfur's past, and this village, and made a few enquiries.'

'I went straight from here to Reykjavík, in my work clothes,' said Valdimar. 'It was Addý's birthday that Sunday, and it felt like an appropriate time to make it right. I don't think anyone noticed me go. I left in the early evening, and I was back by the next morning. I hadn't made any preparations or planned anything. I didn't really know what I intended to do. I just set off as I was, in my overalls. I took an old straight razor with me.'

'The pathologist said the cut was smooth, almost feminine.'

'I've slaughtered a few beasts in my time.'

'Oh?'

'There used to be an abattoir here. I often worked there during the autumn season, after the sheep round-up.'

'When people here heard that Runólfur was dead, they must have put two and two together?'

'That's quite possible, but no one ever mentioned it to me. Maybe they felt the score had been settled.'

'Do you think Runólfur's father knew what his son had done?'

'He knew. I'm sure of it.'

'You told me the other day that you once visited Runólfur in Reykjavík,' said Elínborg. 'That must have been before you knew about the rape?'

'Yes. I ran into him in the middle of town and he invited me over. We met quite by chance. I didn't stay long. We were from the same village, but I didn't know him particularly well and . . . I didn't like him, really.'

'Was he renting a place at that time?'

'He was staying with a friend. Some man named Edvard.'

'Edvard?'

'Yes. Edvard.'

'When was this?'

'Five or six years ago.'

'Can you remember precisely? How many years ago, exactly?'

Valdimar thought about it. 'It was six years ago, 1999. I was in Reykjavík buying a second-hand car.'

'So six years ago Runólfur was living in Edvard's home?' asked Elínborg. She recalled Edvard's neighbour mentioning a lodger.

'Yes, so he said.'

'Was it in the west of town?'

'Not far from the centre, near the dry dock. That's where Runólfur was working.'

'Runólfur worked at the dry dock?'

'Yes. He said he worked there part-time when he was at college.'

'Did you meet this Edvard at all?'

'No, Runólfur just told me about him. Made fun of him. That's why I can recall it so clearly – I remember being struck by how nasty Runólfur was about him. He called him a wimp, but of course Runólfur was . . .'

Valdimar did not complete the sentence. Elínborg had taken out her mobile phone and at that instant a police car drew up outside. Two uniformed officers got out. Elínborg looked at Valdimar.

He hesitated, looked around him, passed a callused hand over the tractor seat, and glanced at the half-open tool lockers.

'Will I get long?' he asked.

'I don't know,' answered Elínborg.

'I don't regret what I did,' said Valdimar. 'And I never will.'

'Come on,' said Elínborg. 'Let's get this over with.'

34

For seven hours Edvard sat in an interview room while his home was searched, without result. Elínborg questioned him repeatedly about the period when Runólfur had lodged with him, and before long Edvard admitted that he had rented a room to Runólfur temporarily while he was flat-hunting. That was around the time of Lilja's disappearance. Edvard also confirmed that Runólfur had been working at the dry dock, a short walk away, but he claimed to have no idea if Lilja had come to his home and met Runólfur. He maintained that he knew nothing of whether Runólfur might have harmed the girl – and that he himself had certainly not touched her.

'Did you give Lilja a lift to Reykjavík?'

'No.'

'Did you drop her off at the shopping centre?'

'No, I didn't.'

'What did you and Lilja talk about on the way to town?'

'I didn't drive her anywhere.'

'She was looking for a birthday present for her grandad – did she mention that at all?'

Edvard said nothing.

'What else did you discuss? Did she talk about visiting you?'

Edvard shook his head.

'Did you offer her a lift back to Akranes?'

'No.'

'Why did you offer girls from the college lifts into Reykjavík? What did you want from them?'

'I didn't.'

'We know you did – at least once.'

'That's not true. She's lying.'

'Did Runólfur get you to offer Lilja a lift?'

'No. I never gave her a lift.'

'Did you ever hear Runólfur talking about Lilja?'

'No. Never.'

'Did you talk to him about Lilja?'

'No.'

'Did you kill Lilja in your home?'

'No. She was never there.'

'Was there anything odd about Runólfur's behaviour around that time?'

'No. He was always exactly the same.'

'Did you suggest to Lilja that she might like to call round after she'd finished her shopping?'

Edvard did not answer.

'Did she have some reason to visit you?'

Edvard still did not speak.

'Did she know where you lived?'

'She could easily have looked me up in the phone book. I don't know.'

'Did Runólfur kill Lilja in your home?'

'No.'

'Did he dispose of her body at the dry dock?'

'The dry dock?'

'Well, that was where he was working.'

'I've no idea what you're on about.'

'Did you help him get rid of the body?'

'No.'

'Did you suspect that Runólfur was involved in her disappearance? Has it been preying on your mind ever since?'

Edvard hesitated.

'Did you suspect . . . ?'

'I don't know anything about what happened to Lilja. Nothing whatsoever.'

Elínborg went on questioning Edvard for hours but got no more out of him.

She had no hard evidence, nothing to support her theory that Lilja had been killed by Runólfur at Edvard's house six years before. And, even if she was right, Edvard might have remained ignorant of it. He could be lying, but it would be difficult to prove.

The previous day Elínborg had brought Valdimar to Reykjavík, where he had been remanded in custody. Konrád and Nína were released, and were reunited with the rest of the family in Elínborg's office at police headquarters. The eldest son had flown home from San Francisco. The reunion was not a joyful one: Nína was still traumatised by having believed that she had killed a man and although she and her father had now been exonerated, she would nonetheless have to confront her demons.

'There's someone I think you should meet,' said Elínborg. 'Her name's Unnur.'

'Who is she?'

'She knows what you've been through. I'm sure she'll want to meet you, too.'

They shook hands on parting. 'Just let me know, and I'll put you in touch with her,' said Elínborg.

She escorted Edvard off the premises, then went to her car. Instead of driving home she headed for Thingholt, to

Runólfur's flat. She had the keys with her. Before long the place would be handed back to the landlord and new tenants would move in. As she drove, Elínborg's mind went to Erlendur: that morning she had received a disquieting phone call.

'Is that Elínborg?' said a jaded male voice. 'I was told I should speak to you. It's about a rental car that's standing outside the churchyard here.'

'Where?'

'Here in Eskifjördur. It's parked by the churchyard. There's no one in it.'

'And what's that got to do with me?' asked Elínborg.

'I ran the number and found out it was a rental vehicle.'

'Yes, so you said. Are you with the police there?'

'Yes, sorry – didn't I say? It was hired to someone who I'm told works with you.'

'Who?'

'It's rented to someone called Erlendur Sveinsson.'

'Erlendur?'

'The rental company says he's with Reykjavík CID.'

'Yes, he is.'

'Do you know what he's doing over here?'

'No,' answered Elínborg. 'He went on leave a fortnight ago. He said he was going to the East Fjords, but that's all I know.'

'I see. The car's been here for a while. It was parked in

front of the church gate so we had to move it, but we haven't been able to trace the driver. I mean, it's all right, but I felt I should check, since it was left there – by the churchyard.'

'I'm sorry. I can't help you at all.'

'No, well, never mind. Thank you.'

'Goodbye.'

Elínborg switched on the lights in the kitchen, living room and bedroom of Runólfur's flat. She thought about the phone call from Eskifjördur but did not know what to make of it.

The crime scene had not been disturbed. Now Elínborg knew exactly what had taken place that night: how Nína had been brought there; how Valdimar, on his quest for revenge, had disturbed Runólfur during the rape; how Konrád had arrived on the scene to find his daughter in a state of confusion and despair. Elínborg could not make up her mind: had Runólfur got what he deserved? She did not really believe in poetic justice.

Elínborg had only a vague idea of what she was looking for; although she did not expect to find anything, she felt it was worth a try. Forensics had already combed through Runólfur's home but Elínborg was looking for evidence of a different nature.

Starting in the kitchen, she opened every drawer and cupboard, examining pots and pans, bowls and cutlery.

She searched the fridge and the freezer, stirred through an old tub of vanilla ice cream, went through the contents of a small wardrobe by the entrance, checked under the fuse-box cover and tapped at the parquet floor, looking for a secret hiding place. She ransacked the living room, turned an armchair upside down, removed all the cushions, took every item from the shelves. She examined the collectible superhero figures and gave them an experimental shake.

In the bedroom she lifted up the mattress, searched the two bedside tables, then opened the wardrobe and took out the clothes, examining each garment before laying it on the bed. She placed the shoes on the floor, stepped inside the wardrobe, and tapped at the sides and floor. She envisaged the dead man and the evil which flowed through him like a river of darkness – deep and cold and merciless.

Elínborg took her time, searching every inch of the flat. By the time she had finished it was the middle of the night.

She had not found what she was looking for.

No clue to the fate of the missing Akranes girl.

35

Elínborg lay down in bed next to Teddi and tried to sleep. Her mind craved peace but all she found was suffering and sadness.

'Can't sleep?' whispered Teddi beside her in the dark.

'Are you awake?' she asked in surprise.

'Good to have you home,' said Teddi.

Elínborg kissed him and curled up against him. She knew she had a short, restless night ahead of her.

She thought of Theodóra.

'What is your job, Mum?'

That innocent question entailed another, more important one: her little girl was gradually becoming aware of a world that was overwhelming and frightening. She might as well have asked her mother: 'What kind of a world am I living in?'

Elínborg closed her eyes.

She saw Addý stumbling up out of the hollow by the river, looking around in terror in case the rapist returned to attack her again. In the community centre the dance went on. All she could think of was getting home without meeting anyone. She didn't want to be seen, didn't want anyone to know. She couldn't tell anyone what he had done. When she reached home she locked all the doors and closed the windows, and in the kitchen she rocked back and forth, back and forth, trying to erase the horror from her mind. She wept and shook, and wept, and wept.

Elínborg buried her head in the pillow.

Far away, she heard a quiet knock at a door, saw a small fist raised to knock again, harder. She saw Lilja standing on Edvard's doorstep. Runólfur appeared in the doorway.

'Oh,' said Lilja. 'Isn't this Edvard's house?'

Runólfur smiled at her. He glanced around to check whether she was alone, whether there was anyone on the street to see them.

'Yes, he'll be home any time. Won't you come in and wait?'

She hesitated. 'I was going to . . .'

'I'm expecting him back any minute.'

Lilja looked out to sea. She could see Akranes across the bay. Lilja was in the habit of trusting people. She was a well-brought-up, polite girl.

'Do come in,' said Runólfur.

'All right. Thank you,' she said.

Elínborg watched the door close behind them, and fell asleep, certain in the knowledge that it would never open again.

Jar City

Winner of the Glass Key Award for Best Nordic Crime Novel

'Highly recommended . . . thoroughly gripping'
Time Out

A man is found murdered in his Reykjavík flat. The only
clues are a cryptic note left on the body and a photograph
of a young girl's grave. Delving into the dead man's life
Detective Erlendur discovers that forty years ago the victim
was accused of an appalling crime, but never convicted.
Had his past come back to haunt him?

As Erlendur struggles to build a relationship with his
unhappy daughter, his investigation takes him to Iceland's
Genetic Research Centre, where he uncovers disturbing
secrets that are even darker than the murder of an old man.

'A fascinating window on an unfamiliar world as well as
an original and puzzling mystery'
Val McDermid

'A chilling read'
The Times

'Plausible, well-constructed . . . poignant and clever'
Times Literary Supplement

VINTAGE BOOKS
London

Silence of the Grave

Winner of the CWA Gold Dagger

Winner of the Glass Key Award for Best Nordic Crime Novel

'Here is a new voice that demands to be listened to'
Reginald Hill

Building work in an expanding Reykjavík uncovers a
shallow grave. Years before, this part of the city was all
open hills, and Erlendur and his team hope this is a typical
Icelandic missing person scenario; perhaps someone once
lost in the snow, who has lain peacefully buried for decades.
Things are never that simple.

Whilst Erlendur struggles to hold together the crumbling
fragments of his own family, his case unearths many other
tales of family pain, anger, domestic violence and fear; of
family loyalty and family shame. Few people are still alive
who can tell the story, but even secrets taken to the grave
cannot remain hidden forever . . .

'A fascinating mystery . . . Indridason is a writer worth
seeking out'
Daily Telegraph

'A writer of astonishing gravitas and talent'
John Lescroart

VINTAGE BOOKS
London

Voices

'A slow-burner that draws you more and more deeply into the investigation and into the dark dilemmas of the principal characters'
Spectator

It is a few days before Christmas and Reykjavík doorman and occasional Santa Claus, Gudlauger, has been found stabbed to death. It soon becomes apparent that both staff and guests have something to hide, but it is the dead man who has the most shocking secret.

Detective Erlendur quickly discovers that the placidly affluent appearance of the hotel covers a multitude of sins.

'Indriđason reaches extraordinary psychological depths'
Mail on Sunday

'Once again Indriđason demonstrates that the best Scandinavian crime writers can hold their own against their British and American rivals'
Andrew Taylor, author of *The American Boy* and *Bleeding Heart Square*

VINTAGE BOOKS
London

The Draining Lake

'A beautiful, sad, haunting tale of lost love and lost illusion, regret and betrayal'
The Times

A skeleton is found half-buried in a dried out lake. The bones have been weighed down with an old Russian radio transmitter: is this a clue to the victim, and the killer's, identity?

Detective Erlendur is called in to investigate and discovers that there may be a connection with a group of students who were sent to study in East Germany during the Cold War, and with a young man who walked out of his family house one day, never to return. As the mystery deepens Erlendur and his team must unravel a story of international espionage, murder and betrayal.

'Beautifully written and translated, the novel has both a strong sense of place and themes that transcend it; it confirms Indridason as one of those crime writers who rises above genre, combining suspense with moving insights into the human condition'
Sunday Times

'A haunting, compassionate work'
Observer

'Indridason manages to keep the reader guessing . . . right to the last'
Sunday Express

VINTAGE BOOKS
London

Arctic Chill

'An international literary phenomenon – gripping, authentic,
haunting and lyrical'
Harlan Coben

A dark-skinned young boy is found dead, frozen to the
ground in a pool of his own blood. The boy's Thai half-
brother is missing; is he implicated, or simply afraid for his
own life? While fears increase that the murder could have
been racially motivated, the police receive reports that a
suspected paedophile has been spotted in the area.

Detective Erlendur's investigation soon unearths the tensions
simmering beneath the surface of Iceland's outwardly liberal,
multi-cultural society while the murder forces Erlendur to
confront the tragedy in his own past.

'An utterly absorbing detective story. In Erlendur – morose,
grouchy, but hugely likeable all the same – Indridason has
created a character in the Morse/Rebus mould who could
stand comparison with either'
Scotsman

'A highly believable mystery, seamlessly translated'
Independent

'This novel has great clarity, emotional depth and
resonance'
Sunday Telegraph

VINTAGE BOOKS
London

Hypothermia

'An intelligent, gripping and moody tale with superior
characterisation'
The Times

One cold autumn night, a woman is found hanging from
a beam at her holiday cottage. At first sight, it appears like
a straightforward case of suicide; María had never recovered
from the death of her mother two years previously and she
had a history of depression. But then the friend who found
her body approaches Detective Elendur with a tape of a
séance that María attended before her death and his curiosity
is aroused . . .

Driven by a need to find answers, Erlendur begins an
unofficial investigation into María's death. But he is also
haunted by another unsolved mystery – the disappearance
of two young people thirty years ago – and by his own
quest to find the body of his brother, who died in a blizzard
when he was a boy

'Chillingly creepy'
Guardian

'*Hypothermia* is one of the most haunting crime novels I've
read in a long time, unsentimental yet informed throughout
by Indridason's extraordinary empathy with human suffering'
Sunday Times

VINTAGE BOOKS
London

And coming in June from Harvill Secker,
Arnaldur Indridason's brand-new thriller . . .

Black Skies

A man is making a crude leather mask with an iron spike
fixed in the middle of the forehead. It is a 'death mask',
once used by Icelandic farmers to slaughter calves, and he
has revenge in mind.

Meanwhile, a school reunion has left Sigurdur Óli unhappy
with life in the police force. While Iceland is enjoying an
economic boom, his relationship is on the rocks and soon
even his position in the CID is compromised after he agrees
to visit a couple of blackmailers as a favour to a friend, and
walks in just as a woman is beaten unconscious. When she
dies, Sigurdur Óli has a murder investigation on his hands.

Moving from the villas of Reykjavík's banking elite to a
sordid basement flat, *Black Skies* is a superb story of greed,
pride and murder from one of Europe's most successful
crime writers.

VINTAGE BOOKS
London